Women, Islam and Globalization
in the Twenty-First Century

Women, Islam and Globalization
in the Twenty-First Century

Edited with an Introduction by

Nilgün Anadolu-Okur

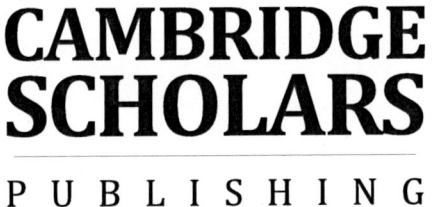

**CAMBRIDGE
SCHOLARS**

P U B L I S H I N G

Women, Islam and Globalization in the Twenty-First Century,
Edited with an Introduction by Nilgün Anadolu-Okur

This book first published 2009

Cambridge Scholars Publishing

12 Back Chapman Street, Newcastle upon Tyne, NE6 2XX, UK

British Library Cataloguing in Publication Data
A catalogue record for this book is available from the British Library

ISBN (10): 1-4438-1309-5, ISBN (13): 978-1-4438-1309-9

To My Anatolian Grandmothers

CONTENTS

PREFACE

In the post-9/11 world, one of the most intractable socio-political and cultural issues for the twenty-first century is the turbulent relationship between Muslims and non-Muslims. The reality which shaped the public opinion globally soon after the terrorists' attacks was a natural outburst of old, deep-seated feelings such as distrust and suspicion of Muslims in the Western world. With the attacks on the twin towers of the World Trade Center and the Pentagon, the world had witnessed the dawn of a new era in global terrorism whose main actors were Muslims. Thereafter, the hatred and stereotypical depictions targeted not only the Muslims as a homogeneous religious group, but the Islamic faith, its traditional values, and its Prophet. A war was in progress.

Muslims had to endure an offensive legacy for generations to come. One could only wish that such a terrifying polarization between the East and the West should never have taken place. Due to extraordinary circumstances there seems to be no human solution to the lack of trust between the two sides.

After almost a decade of prolonged religious and cultural stigmatization, the anti-Muslim sentiment still exists, accompanied with a blend of fear, conceit and crippling effects of miscommunication between the East and the West. Despite considerable international diplomacy the adverse effects of anti-Muslim propaganda persist. Meanwhile, new wars are waged in order to bring an end to anti-democratic governments and eradicate terrorist organizations which have nestled in some Muslim countries. As human casualties and material losses multiply on both sides, old hostilities are re-kindled and "democracy" waits yet to be delivered. In fact, restoring peace, building bridges and initiating harmony among disenchanted nations takes considerably longer than initiating long-distance wars.

Whereas Muslim tradition as a whole is not much different than Jewish or Christian faith—whose monotheistic roots and its systems of operations share more similarities than differences—Islam, in practice, does not have a homogenous character. Diversity among Muslim countries has always outweighed similarities in religious practice as it has been in structuring of governmental systems. Moreover, Islamic tradition and teachings of the Qur'an had already been subject of inquiry by Muslim scholars, from within, particularly with regard to women's rights and roles in Islam.

Since each Muslim country had developed its own set of values determined by a particular perspective on life and culture—through its legislative and executive systems which organized its rules of conduct and operation—women's rights issue remained a highly-debated argument. Additionally, international campaigns targeting human rights issues in Muslim countries initiated numerous studies in a legitimate effort to bring clarification to misunderstandings, or help resolve social conflicts in a particular society. In this respect family systems, education, women's roles and rights were examined widely in a deliberate effort to clarify the confusion and myths commonly held in the West about Islam. The counter-argument holds a multitude of axiological and etymological negations about Muslim identity which need to be further investigated.

Our research would not have come about without the multi-disciplinary reaction developed in response to stereotypical depictions about Muslim women both in the Muslim world and in the West. Through an interdisciplinary approach this study aims to serve a dual purpose. First, it aspires to capture the individual character of a group of Muslim countries with eight representative essays. Secondly, it intends to rescue Muslim women from stereotypical and reductionist depictions initiated by Muslim men with reference to their association with and understanding of women's rights issues in a global arena.

In this respect, the study seeks to be an original work, whose ultimate goal is to see Muslim women freed from dogmatic demarcations. In our respective conclusions, we propose to provide a constructive meaning to Muslim identity, but essentially to Muslim womanhood. The focus is on assessment of civil and political rights, family laws, educational opportunities, participation in civil life, historical struggles for emancipation and suffrage, opportunities of representation, property ownership, religious traditions and professional lives of Muslim women in a wide range of countries where Islam is not only the established faith of the land but a principal way of life either governing or balancing additional spheres of an individual's life. In an assemblage of eight interdisciplinary essays, a social drama, and an interview conducted with the dramatist, this study reveals varying aspects of Muslim womanhood in Pakistan, Iran, Saudi Arabia, Turkey, Lebanon and Morocco. It also provides a much-needed understanding of a crucial contemporary dilemma faced by Muslims who live in European countries such as France, Germany and in the United States. The contributing authors hope to improve understanding, foster dialogue and breed tolerance among the readers.

The time seems particularly ripe for renewed interest in Muslim women's issues. By illustrating the boundaries that circumvent the female

Muslim identity under mounting scrutiny of globalism we hope to illuminate the ramifications of a future quandary that will be charting its course throughout the next decades of the twenty-first century.

As the editor of the volume, I want to assert that the views reflected by the authors of the following chapters are not necessarily mine. Neither the CSP, nor I concede any responsibility (legal or ideological) about their content. Original in perspective, they represent individual reviews and should be treated as such. However the binding factor for the contributing scholars, besides tackling a contentious subject with insight and clarity remains the same: Muslim women's rights and roles need to be re-evaluated concerning their relationship to Muslims and non-Muslims alike as they stand susceptible in the cross hairs of culture, upbringing and politics in a new century.

ACKNOWLEDGMENTS

I want to thank the contributing scholars who have been unvaryingly patient in responding to my numerous appeals for assistance during the editing process.

I am most grateful to Professor Michael McGaha for his thorough review and valuable input. Dr. Heon C.Kim took time from his own research to read this manuscript. I have profited throughout by their incisive and stimulating criticisms.

I thank my students at Temple University's College of Liberal Arts. Through our dialogues we were able to comprehend the pressing issues about women's rights, equality and justice. During our stirring class discussions on global matters, including prejudice, racism, discrimination and stereotypes we were educated collectively. Brent Olson, of Columbia University, provided assistance at different stages of my research.

I would like to thank our editors at Cambridge Scholars Publishing, particularly Amanda Millar, Carol Koulikourdi and Soucin Yip-Sou for their genuine support and understanding throughout the project.

I am indebted to my son, Ali Murat Okur, for his encouragement and meticulous technical assistance which expedited the completion of the index and formatting. I want to acknowledge my brother, Professor Dr. Yücel Anadolu, of Ankara University, who generously devoted his time during an extensive search for cover images around the historic Kale and Çıkrıkçılar district in Ankara.

Above all, I owe a very special debt of gratitude to my Anatolian grandmothers—women of grace, patience and peace—whose formative influences I want to acknowledge and to whom I dedicate this book.

Philadelphia, Pennsylvania
November 10, 2009

INTRODUCTION

Islam is the fastest growing religion in the world with an estimated 1.5 billion followers. In the aftermath of the 9/11 attacks, reactions to discriminatory practices in non-Muslim countries have led to further reinforcement among Muslims and even non-Muslim sympathizers, globally. Nevertheless among Muslim nations men embrace varied perspectives about the status of women and generally undermine their roles. This is more prevalent in countries which are governed by clergy who receive their support directly from the state. In such societies women's liberties, dress styles, veiling, *hijab* and *tesettur* are dictated and controlled by men, rather than by women. As Muslim states' rules and regulations are fostered by governmental policies which range from religious theocracy to rigid fundamentalism, the precincts differ far and wide among Muslim countries.

Restraints on women's liberties have been usually introduced and fortified by men. In relatively secular societies, where women's rights are governed and protected by *constitutional* decrees, debates on women's liberties still exist, though on a different plane. In such societies insular administrations occasionally attempt to override women's rights by bringing alterations to the constitutional system. Even worse, in a gesture to *please, obey or defend* men, specific groups among women may choose to forfeit their rights and change their images from secular to conservative in accordance with policies advocated by men in power. In some cases women even go further to support and adopt ideologies contrary to their upbringing. Certainly, with regard to emancipation and civil liberties, women's perspectives vary; there is no one singular form or a standard *modus operandi* that can summarize or categorize women's choices and desires.

Our volume purports to articulate, through interdisciplinary essays, Muslim women's struggles, challenges, preferences and needs as they practice their rights of womanhood and motherhood at the dawn of the twenty-first century. Through a contemporary analysis of Muslim women's lives in Pakistan, Iran, Lebanon, Turkey, Saudi Arabia and Morocco we aim to provide a positive subtext to Muslim identity, essentially to Muslim womanhood. Whether Islam or the Islamic law, as a set of established guidelines, is utilized to govern a Muslim society's operational modes—including societies where interpretation of the Islamic law is currently going through a *transition*—Islam is *the* established faith throughout the entire Muslim world. It is adopted and practiced as a principal way of life governing numerous spheres in a devout Muslim's life. This fact is unanimously held by the authors who contributed to this volume.

In a case-study developed through interviews conducted in the Southern province of Sindh, Aslam focuses on male-instigated suppression against women in Pakistan. She outlines the present status of women according to "Pakistani-Islam", which is akin to "a force that 'legalizes' submission of women by granting divine legitimacy" to constraints, abuse and violence committed against them. Aslam also evaluates the standard of "morality" and its "evolution" through Darwin, Spencer, Stephen, Kant and Durkheim's views on moral consciousness in a society. She compares and investigates the background to specific ideologies which have led to concepts such as *moral* or *immoral* as these value systems actually influenced and determined the status of women in Pakistan. She also documents the rationale behind what is called the "*morality-construct*" on the lives of Pakistani women. Consequently, as she warns, women are categorized as "evil, unchaste or immoral," which justifies any degree of collective violence, including "honor-related" crimes committed against them. Her findings imply that there is much to be improved about Pakistani women's status, especially in rural areas where honor killings are a threat for those people who do not comply with the dictates of the Shari'a doctrines.

Anadolu-Okur's discussion of the beginnings of the Turkish women's movement illustrates the significance of Ataturk's reforms for the advancement and longevity of women's emancipation in Turkey. Without the state-sponsored constitutional reforms and the Turkish Constitution, women would not have achieved legal rights, nor could they have been able to keep the freedoms that they had been exercising since the 1930s. One of the greatest ideals of Mustafa Kemal was to advance Turkey "to the level of contemporary civilizations", and he saw no end to advancement.[1] In February 1937 he had six principles written into Article 2 of the Turkish Constitution, which included: *Republicanism, Nationalism, Populism, Revolutionism, Secularism, Etatism* (also *Statism*). Currently secularism is challenged by skeptics in Turkey who attempt to portray it as "anti-Islam." They dismiss the fact that Mustafa Kemal **did** include Islam in the reform ideology as he remarked: "Islam sanctions freedom of religious opinion."[2] Furthermore he asserted:

The government is obliged to respect freedom of thought and freedom of conscience. So long as mankind's thinking with regard to religious questions is not freed from myths and is not illuminated by the light of knowledge there will be historians everywhere who act out religious comedies.[3]

Additionally, Mustafa Kemal stated that sovereignty was indivisible for a nation whose very existence depended on its people's past sacrifices and heroism. Modern statesmen are expected to acknowledge these facts and remain truthful to the makers of that history. In this respect individuals who risked their own lives in order to revive an "ailing nation" (a eurocentric term which refers to the collapse of the Ottoman Empire) under Western occupation deserve recognition. Any historian who understands and appreciates the formidable history and the founding principles of the Turkish Republic, from a Turko-centered perspective, unmistakably comprehend that the Turkish women's movement owes its birthright to the abolition of the old order of Shari'a and the caliphate system. Democracy and citizenship are crucially connected to past and current debates about identity, nationalism, sovereignty and women's rights.

Reza focuses, from a critic's perspective, on Iran's strict allegiance to Shari'a law in interpreting women's rights. As power and public discourse in Iran are dominated by men, who are mostly ayatollahs, women have no say in the affairs of the state. Moreover, those who attempt to express their opinions are viciously silenced. Addressing a major controversy in the Iranian legal system, Reza asserts that Shari'a laws on the rights of women were codified solely through the legal verses of the Qur'an, rather than through verses which recognized and fostered equality of men and women in dignity and honor. However, the old values lost their validity over time and clashed with the new circumstances: "The laws pioneered by the Qur'an and considered appropriate then have had a negative impact on women's rights today." Moreover, as Reza remarks, Muslim women's status suffered largely due to "male-oriented discriminatory laws and rules in almost every public and private domain of human life." The Cairo Declaration (1990), which was fashioned after international human rights documents, and bore a resemblance in format and terminology, actually restricted women's freedom and afforded no liberties other than what is already contained in traditional decrees of Shari'a. Furthermore, in Iran's legal system, which appears to be equally accommodating (for example Article 19 addresses the principle of equality for all people regardless of their *color, race, and language*), there is no provision to include "gender". Additionally the constitutional articles have been formulated in specific ways which abide by Shari'a laws' limitations imposed upon women. Thus any article needs to be interpreted according to these standards which are profoundly discouraging for women's rights activists.

While this volume was being prepared for publication, news about Iran's flawed elections erupted violently. In the aftermath of the June 2009 elections the power remained unchanged in the hands of President Mahmoud Ahmadinejad despite allegations of fraud. Protests were immediately curbed by a state-sponsored massacre targeting demonstrators on the streets of Tehran. As videos which secretly captured Neda Al Soltan's murder were being circulated on the world-wide web, the face of Muslim women's collective struggle for freedom, democracy and hopes for emancipation was altered globally. Neda, the young activist, was simply *"calling for"* a secular democracy to be instituted in Iran.

Although French President Nicolas Sarkozy denounced the "burka" and called it a "prison" for Muslim women living in France, certainly women are not going to shed their shrouds overnight. Moreover some may find religious subservience convenient. However it would have been a major accomplishment if Muslim women were able to speak up and do as they want without facing opposition by men. Apparently limitations to women's freedom loom larger than life itself even in France.

It should be clear in Jallad's argument that Muslim women's rights and choices throughout the world do not necessarily yield to simplistic interpretations and assumptions. As Deniz Kandiyoti remarked, "Women are full-fledged social actors, bearing the full set of contradictions implied by their class, racial and ethnic locations as well as their gender."[4] Jallad asserts that Muslims, particularly modern Muslim women, are caught between two different worlds that are simultaneously superimposed upon one another. Women who live in gated communities in Lebanon, Saudi Arabia and Egypt are faced with constantly having to reconcile their situation as women who actually *belong* to a traditional Muslim environment but *carve out* and *shape* their own private spaces *from* the context of living in a modern, inevitably Western world.

One could argue that these women are—and have to be—simultaneously Muslim and Western, one identity not excluding the other. Naturally their identities are carefully wrought by the entities that they live in, placing their actual world at a peculiar intersection which consists of freedom and modernism enjoyed within a limited perimeter. As gated communities grow in popularity, they provide a contented duality for women who choose to remain Muslim and *western* simultaneously. A Harvard-trained architect, Jallad points out that "overlapping" of identities is closely connected with physical characteristics of space in these gated enclaves.

The traditional "inward looking" characteristics of Islamic architecture are compromised with the "transparent", and outward-looking architectural styles introduced by western architectural concepts. Jallad's focus lies on cases where the overlap emphasizes the divergence between the Muslim and the Western worlds as women's status and their relationship to the outer world is formed by the physical environment they live in.

In her essay about the headscarf controversy Tuzun speculates that Turkey might become "another Malaysia" in future. With the Islamic headscarf widely considered a threat to secularism and gender equality, Turkey's republican modernism resorted to legal action first in 1982 when the Council of Higher Education banned the wearing of the headscarf in universities. However, the ban was gradually "softened" in 1984 and 1987 during the administration of the centre-right Motherland Party (MP) in which the Islamists "constituted the single most powerful faction in the party organization." 1989 marked the beginning of a long debate on the constitutional ban of headscarves and the counter-attacks carried out by Islamists.

Tuzun illustrates the history of the headscarf debate in Turkey according to a detailed timeline. The Constitutional Court's decision which argued that religion is a matter of private conscience and should not be politicized was followed in 1997 with a stricter ban which forced young women with headscarves either to quit their education or remove the headscarf outside the university gates. The grievances of headscarf wearing students added fuel to the political campaigns of right-wing and Islamist parties, further politicizing a religious symbol closely connected with personal civil rights and liberties. Unlike Iran, Turkey's secular constitution clearly indicated that headscarves or turbans are not compatible with the foundational principles of the Republic. As the rift deepens, Tuzun asserts, Turks are less certain what the future will bring, since Islamist tendencies are on the rise globally. She evaluates the Turkish case within the larger international context and elaborates how the current revivalism of religion as a global phenomenon is assisted by a host of particular theoretical positions, such as cultural relativism, identity politics, and postmodernism.

Swick explains how Muslim women's seclusion from public life led to the entrenchment of various patriarchal and un-Islamic traditions. She asserts that during this period of entrenchment initiated by men, women suffered the greatest loss in terms of preserving their rights. In her view, a divide between Islamic Law and International Human Rights Law is superficial, contrary to former claims of some academicians, activists and politicians. Instead, merging the two systems in a compatible method might help improve the daily lives of Muslim women. Swick notes that despite the centuries which separate them, the two systems can work jointly and combine the *synergy* that emanates in order to create justice and produce healthy dialogue about eliminating dogma as it conveys empowerment to women. Swick argues that the two systems are embraced by the Moroccan government and their simultaneous effects help Moroccan families function more effectively under the Family Law embraced by the King Muhammad VI.

The final section in the volume is dedicated to a play by Bina Sharif, preceded by an interview she gave to Mera Moore about the interrelatedness of an author's identity and her art. The play was included in order to reveal the origins of the current global predicament between the East and the West from the perspective of a Muslim dramatist. Drama *represents*, in its varied forms, what life presents to us as "facts", which may sometimes be hard to bear or live with. Sharif's play provides an alternative look to Muslim women's lives in the twenty-first century. Within the context of globalization, some Muslim women might hope to integrate with, or assimilate their cultural values with those of the Western world. Nevertheless it is a tragicomic endeavor—a basis for deep-seated antagonism and alienation—which often proves futile, because the West might not accept the terms of their existence. In *Fire* Bina Sharif examines the existentialist pursuit of an immigrant Iraqi woman whose life experiences *resemble* those of Muslim women, leading ephemeral lives stuck between two cultures. Their frustrations generate—symbolically— further tension between the East and the West. Bina Sharif brings to her works unique perspectives about multiple identities of Muslim immigrant women who often struggle financially, spiritually and culturally facing internal and external conflicts as a result of the war. The interview by Mera Moore provides further insight into how Sharif's Muslim heritage has influenced her career as a dramatist, as she discusses a number of her plays including *Afghan Woman* and *Democracy in Islam*.

The authors in this volume are critically aware of the negative effects of the divide between the East and the West, Muslims and non-Muslims. However in the post-9/11 world, despite the crippling effects of Eurocentric negations on race, ethnicity, religion and culture, they want to renew their faith in peace and remain *centered* in their warm embrace of truth, justice and righteousness. "Dawn invites prayers for the lost relatives in Muslim faith," remarks Moore in her Afterword. When the faithful unite, in the East as well as in the West, hopes for women who live in *war- zones* can be raised and restored to their original dignity. Only then, in Afghanistan, Iraq, Iran, Lebanon, Malaysia, Morocco, Pakistan, Saudi

Arabia, and in Turkey, can women's voices be heard clear and loud, as that of Neda, in order to address the complex set of issues that confront Muslim women—in the vortex of defeat or hope, surrender or survival.

Notes

[1] Onder Renkliyildirim, trans. *The Speech: Mustafa Kemal Ataturk,* (Istanbul: Metro Kitap Yayinlari, 1982), 21-22.
[2] Ibid., 113.
[3] Ibid.
[4] Deniz Kandiyoti and Ayse Saktanber, eds. *Fragments of Culture: The Everyday of Modern Turkey.* (London: IB Tauris, 2002). 8.

ISLAM IN PATRIARCHAL CULTURES:
MORALS, HONOR AND GENDER ISSUES
IN PAKISTAN

MALEEHA ASLAM

The present face of Pakistani-Islam resembles a force that "legalizes" submission of women by granting divine legitimacy to several forms of constraints, abuse and violence against them. It is quite common to raise issues of morality, in the name of custom, tradition and most importantly religion, so that women's rights can be compromised. This essay attempts to understand what it means to be moral or immoral in a local context. Secondly, it seeks to document the impact of a peculiar morality-construct, quite similar to any power-construct, on the lives of Pakistani women. People perceive and categorize women as evil, unchaste or immoral-justifying against them collective violence, including honor-related crime. The research brings forth the existence of other non-Islamic and un-Islamic local practices, for instance, marriage with the Qur'ān that is masqueraded as Islamic. The Qur'ān and Hādith are read like menu cards and randomly selected references, usable for creating gender biases which are promoted by local religious authorities. Finally, this essay establishes Islam as a religion that has been shamelessly exploited by its followers for serving their cultural, economic and political interests.

In an effort to explain moral behaviour through classical and contemporary social theories, I will address the factors involved in the human choice for being moral and describe the function that morality performs within a power construct, serving political and economic interests of a society.

Charles Darwin, Herbert Spencer and Leslie Stephen among evolutionists argued that morality, like nature, has evolved. Darwin placed the origin of moral sense in the social impulse. He believed that those communities that included the greatest number of the most sympathetic members would flourish best and rear the greatest number of off-springs.[1] Darwin believed this is because man is a "reflective being" fully aware that his impulse is "temporary" but the "social factor is permanent, ever present and persistent." This constitutes the difference between the "actual strength" and the "legitimate strength" of an impulse. Eventually, man realises to attach importance to persistent impulses. Stephen, however, argued that during evolution humans generate not Darwin's altruistic conduct but a type of "character", an internationalization of an external morality leading from a law of "Do this", to "Be this." Spencer also theorised that the "coercion" factor of society diminishes after some time and moral consciousness becomes a natural and smooth process.

For Kant, "will is not moved to act solely by desire or inclination, but rather by reverence for the moral law, which in turn is derived from reason alone." He characterized "duty" as opposed to "self interest", unlike Hume and Hobbes who attempted to reconcile the two. Kant made an effort to prove that "pure reverence for the practical law" provides "a *motive* which far outweighs all the worth of what is commended by inclination."[2] The rationality argument was maintained for quite some time with Kemp endorsing the same in 1957. According to him, we try to find logical, impeccable proof of the advantages of adhering to moral principles. Living in cooperation with the society is a practical principle as well as a moral principle. It reduces choice, but ensures preservation. To promote one's self-interest against a particular social interest can also be rational, but not moral.

Among classical thinkers, Durkheim while presenting his *homo duplex*,[3] argued that to him "moral" is synonymous with "social" and "individual" stands opposed to "moral" because Durkheim's "individual" denotes the body's egoistic passions and sensualities. He concluded that "moral" is a source of solidarity, forcing man to regulate his actions by something other than his own egoism. There is an emotional structuring of an individual's sensory and sensual being through this collective effervescence that captures the "force" of the "social". This force binds people to the ideals valued by their social group.[4]

Like Durkheim, Bauman from amongst the contemporary thinkers is critical of Kantian law of duty that gives rationality an importance that undermines the significance of "spontaneous sentiment". Bauman focuses on the immoral, rationalising impulses of "totalising" social orders. He presents the modern world as a rationalizing world implicated in dehumanizing acts of violence. He argues that people are not made cruel by modernity but modernity invents a way in which cruel acts can be done by non-cruel people—removing them from facing the consequences of their actions. He believes that modernity led to a "forced categorization" of the people, and individuals perceive each other as "the dangerous other in need of elimination".[5]

Foucault's work is significant in understanding human morality within a power construct. He explains the function moral norms are expected to perform. Both individual and collective potential of human beings is utilized to serve economy in the most cost-effective fashion making society a political target. In other words, the social moral norms are formed to serve political and economic interests of a society. In this set-up, power is not precisely thriving on splendor, but on regulatory and corrective mechanisms. The human body becomes a site of servitude, a system that faces constraints, obligations and prohibitions.[6] Grouping human beings for being moral or immoral is a dividing practice. Bourdieu, like Foucault, argued that classification and categorization schemes, defining human behavior and interaction, create limitations.[7]

Geographical Area of Research

The research was conducted in Khairpur Mir's, in the southern province of Sindh in Pakistan. Geographically, Sindh stretches between the Punjab plain and the Arabian Sea. The province, along with its district of Khairpur, is an ideal sample to explore issues regarding women, local culture and Islam. Rural Sindh's reputation for having low social development indicators such as grave poverty conditions, established feudal base, powerful religious authorities like *pīrs* and *śūfīs*[8], severe gender inequalities and a large female population that is powerless and disadvantaged is well-known. Khairpur is in the Upper belt of Sindh, an area considered to be more conservative and unfriendly towards women than Lower Sindh. For generations, a specific cultural trend in Khairpur has allowed denial and violations of women's rights, supported and promoted by the local religious authorities in the region. It is common in Pakistan to hold its colonial legacy responsible for all transgressions within the present day society. In order to avoid the colonial argument, Khairpur as an area that remained independent of British Raj,[9] suggested an ideal selection. It allowed the researcher to focus on the local hierarchical structure and its role in the creation of a peculiar power culture that is defined through divine sanctions.

For administrative purposes, Sindh is divided into 22 districts. Each district is headed by an elected government representative known as a *nazim*. District Khairpur has six sub-districts, called *ta'luqas* and 76 union councils.

Study Sample and Methodology

The findings are based on a qualitative research that was conducted as a multi-method, single-embedded case study having a flexible design. Case study here implies a methodological design of research and not a case in point. The field work in Pakistan spanned over a period of eight months. Data was collected through multiple sources of evidence based on archival and historical documents, interviews, community meetings, direct and participant observations, and focus group discussions.

The research was conducted in the villages of Rażlmeman (union council Mudd), Visṛīvāhān (union council Ṭheṛī), 'Umarkāṇhar (union council Nurpur), Laṛhī (union council Kahūṛah) and Gaṇvarjonejo (union council Darāzā-Gaṇmbaṭ). The sample communities were finalized with the help of a local NGO acting as a support-base organization during this research. Some of these communities have a reputation for having a strong culture of *pīrī-murīdī* (master-disciple), whilst others are highly Shari'a-inspired, forming an interesting environment to undertake a study of morality related issues. The area had a high crime rate against women and the local police advised the researcher against taking risks.

The study had two units of analysis: generation and gender. Both were believed to lend different meanings to the concept of morality and therefore they were considered vital for this type of research. Generation groups were formed on the basis of those born before the partition of India in 1947 and those who were born during the post-partition time period. The logic was to study a group of Muslim respondents who had lived and responded to the local culture of a multi-faith Sindh as it was before 1947; a group of Muslim respondents from the first generation of Pakistanis for whom Islam had become an identity issue; and a group of younger generation respondents who were exposed to the forces of modernity. For the pre-partition generation, the sample consisted of men who were thirteen and women who were eight at the time of partition. The post-partition sample was further divided into two groups with the first consisting of middle-aged respondents and the second representing the younger generation. Therefore, the sample constituted of the following:

Table 2-1

| | PRE-PARTITION GENERATION PPG | POST-PARTITION GENERATION (I) | POST-PARTITION GENERATION (II) |
		PPG (I)	PPG (II)
Age Group (Men)	70 and above	40-69	18-39
Age Group (Women)	65 and above	35-64	15-34

In the beginning, for the purpose of developing a feel for the local moral norms and for forming generational groups, a "morality questionnaire" was introduced in the communities. Low literacy level, especially among women, created difficulty in getting the forms completed. However it did not affect their participation in the community meetings. Though the statistical data of the questionnaire is shared throughout the essay, it must be noted that it is based on a small number of respondents (85 males and 45 females) due to the limitations already explained. Moreover, the research was essentially qualitative and quantitative data is used only to assist the reader in visualizing the local context. Having stated this, as a qualitative researcher, I can confidently state that despite the small number of respondents who filled out the forms, the results have a certain *transferability value*, keeping in mind the closely-knit village communities where people influence each others' thoughts and are inheritors of a common social history.

Initially in all the five sample communities two formal meetings—each with male and female communities—were planned. Eventually only fifteen such meetings were carried out after considering several factors. In each meeting the turnover among men was 80 to 100, and among women it fluctuated from 35 to 50. Women mostly remained occupied in domestic chores and in attending to children that hindered their participation in formal meetings. Methodologically this was adjusted by increasing the number of informal routine conversations and participant observations. It also proved to be beneficial for establishing a rapport with the respondents for focus groups that were scheduled for the advanced stage of research.

Through the application of quota sampling, informal detailed interviews were conducted with people attending the shrines and mosques. The details are stated below:

Table 2-2

SITE	MALE RESPONDENTS	FEMALE RESPONDENTS	TOTAL RESPONDENTS
Shrine of Dastagīr-Rānīpūr	18	10	28
Shrine of Rożá Dahnnī	8	3	11
Shrine Sachal Sarmast	24	15	39
Mosque Jām'īá Therī	16	Nil	16
Total			94

Other than collecting police records on recent honor crimes, five complainants and the families of victims of *kāro kārī*[10] were interviewed with the help of the district police. The data was documented in a way so as to incorporate "verbatim" to the maximum. Each utterance holds significance as it involves not just a meaning but also an emotion or an attitude and in some cases even a pre-determined judgment. For example, locally there is no word reserved for fornication or adultery. People refer to it as "*na jāizi*"[11] that literally means *unjustified*—a harsh verdict!

Research Findings:
Women's *"Morality-Construct"* in the Local Sphere

The Pakistani idea of an ideal woman is that of one who is: *gūngī, behrī, andhī* (deaf, dumb, blind).[12]

The results of the questionnaire[13] used for determining social attitudes and opinions reveal that among men, 5 out of 6 (83%) from PPG; 23 out of 26 (88%) from PPG (I); and 32 out of 53 (60%) from PPG (II) believe that in a moral society, women *must* stay indoors. Among women, 1 out of 1 (100%) from PPG; 15 out of 18 (83%) from PPG (I) and 11 out of 26 (42%) from PPG (II), hold similar opinions. It is worth-noting that the younger generation of both men and women has begun to question domestication of women. There are 21 out of 53, i.e., 40% of men and 8 out of 26, i.e., 31% of women within PPG (II) who disagree with the notion that women ought to stay indoors.

Similarly, the disagreement of 5 out of 6 PPG men over the proposition: *"unrelated men and women must not talk to each other under any circumstances"* to ensure a moral society, is an interesting finding. The PPG men are less conservative than PPG (I) that had 16 out of 26 (62%) individuals in favor of such an attitude. The women from PPG (I) turned out to be more flexible, with only 6 out of 18 (33%) agreeing to the norm and 14 out of 26 (61 %) disagreeing with it. Please refer to Table 3 and 4 below:

Table 2-3

PROMPT: WOMEN MUST STAY INDOORS							
Categories	Total		Agree		Disagree		Unsure	
	Male	Female	Male	Female	Male	Female	Male	Female
Pre-partition Generation	6	1	5	1	0	0	1	0
Post-partition Generation I	26	18	23	15	3	2	0	1
Post-partition Generation II	53	26	32	11	21	8	0	7
Source: Author's Field Data								

Table 2-4

PROMPT: UNRELATED MEN AND WOMEN MUST NOT TALK TO ONE ANOTHER UNDER ANY CIRCUMSTANCES								
Categories	Total		Agree		Disagree		Unsure	
	Male	Female	Male	Female	Male	Female	Male	Female
Pre-partition Generation	6	1	1	1	5	0	0	0
Post-partition Generation I	26	18	16	6	10	11	0	1
Post-partition Generation II	53	26	24	8	28	14	1	4
Source: Author's Field Data								

This also establishes gender and generation as the two major levels of analysis in any social inquiry.

During community meetings, the respondents were asked to share the norms of their community and to inform about the attributes that they considered a man and a woman of "good" character, i.e., *bā ikhlāq,* should possess. The highlights of the data thus collected are stated below:

Pre-partition Male and Female Generation

Mostly, men believed that anyone prioritizing family ties and relations is essentially of high morals and virtue. In Laṛhī, the men condemned Shaista Almani stating that she was "characterless" on grounds that she by-passed the boundaries of her cultural traditions, i.e., *rīt-ravāj* and caused feud among blood relatives.

The moral code of conduct for women is often translated as modesty, i.e., *shar'm hai ā.* A Visṭīvāhān woman from PPG defined the concept:

> *Bāikhlāq* woman is the one who talks less. The *shar'm vālī mā'ī* was the one who cried on her wedding day […] otherwise people thought her as an immodest and an indecent girl. By being happy, a bride only shows her interest to be with a man–and that is highly immodest. Also, she must not be joyous on leaving her home […] this is very disrespectful towards her

parents. In our days, women used to *advise* the bride to cry to avoid rumors and the label of being *bai-shar'm*."

Social environment and social group decide the level of latitude that is to be granted to women. If the social group consists of the same tribe, caste, class or clan, women may enjoy freedom in dress code and movement. However, there is no general principle as regards to who is perceived to be a stranger. There was a time when Muslim women did not limit their freedom of movement even in the presence of Hindu men. At present, in Pakistan as a predominantly Muslim country, the Muslim women of one village are possessively shielded and guarded from men of nearby villages. Women moving freely are labeled immoral. An old woman of Ganvarjonejo confided that the notion of "the other" was non-existent in the pre-partition days. She reflected upon her experience as follows:

> I was thirteen at the time of partition. A Hindu man owned a bangle kiosk in the corner of Sachal's shrine. The shop-keeper himself adjusted bangles on our wrists. Those days were nice […]. When business was owned by Hindus—our men allowed us everywhere. Once Muslims took over business, our men barred us and imposed *pardah.*

Conversely, the older women in Visṛīvāhān, rejected the conclusion that it was the men who had imposed *pardah* on women. Instead, they defended it by stating:

> This is part of our body now. Often the young girls make fun that *mā'ī*, you have grown old and ugly […] now you don't need to cover […] but even then we do, because this has become part of our body.

Post-partition Male and Female Generation I

Morals are based on the principle of observing *hadūd.* This group shared the view that a husband is a woman's *majāzī-khudā* whom she must listen to and obey. A respondent substantiated his argument by stating:

> The Prophet said that if Allah had allowed prostrating to a mortal, I would have asked a wife to prostrate to her husband.

After listening to a vignette that suggested Islam grants permission to husbands to beat their wives, they said:

A woman becomes *malkieyyat* of her husband when she is married to him. She is required, and *must* do whatever she is told by him.

Women must be beaten if they become *bāghī* against the norms and mores of the society.

The men believe that doubting women, perceiving them as morally weak, and undertaking disciplinary action to keep them on a straight path is directed by the Qur'ān and Hadīth. A respondent from 'Umarkā*n*har confidently voiced his opinion:

> The number of women in hell will be more than that of men. This is written in the Qur'ān and also that the religious power of woman is half to that of man—you can ask any *maulvī*. The Prophet said she is an evil.

In this regard, the closest reference that I have come across is that of Jabir who reports: "Allah's Messenger said, *the woman advances and retires in the shape of a devil, so when one of you see a woman, he should go to his wife, for that will repel what he feels in his heart (for the other woman)"*. (Sahih Muslim Book 008; No. 3240). In this context, the community respondent's quote is an obvious example of sacred narratives being "selectively reduced," and quoted free of context.

In La*ṛ*hī, a respondent echoed these words:

> Women are bound to err. They are *jāhil* and they remain locked at home [...], therefore, it is the man's duty to keep her on the straight path.

A worshipper in the mosque of Ṭheṛī suggested:

> "A good husband [...] must teach *sharīāh* to his wife and ask her to adopt *pardah*. He must do so strictly. She must be conveyed assertively that she cannot appear in front of *nā-mahram*, (men who are not related to her). [...] She must be a good mother to his children."

In Ra*ż*lmeman, a male respondent argued against *pardah*:

> *Sharīāt* is quite confusing in the Pakistani context. For example in real *sharīāt* a man's head should be covered as that of the Prophet's. In Pakistan [...] our *sharīāt* is that only women will cover head. That's why I am not very keen on *sharīāt.*"

By and large, *pardah* is upheld as a primary manifestation of a woman's sound character—an authentication of her virtuousness.

Additionally, men possessing high morals are also expected to cover themselves properly. The attitude is that of asserting Muslim identity through observing a particular dress code. This is substantiated by the following excerpts based on interviews with the worshippers in Ṭheṛī mosque:

> Muslim men and women must wear loose clothes. Prophet Muhammad (Pbuh) said it is indecent to dress up in a provocative way.

> Both men and women must keep their *shar'm gāh* covered. […] body parts (must) not be prominent. Their bodies are not for public but for themselves or their *mahram*. (Allah) has imposed *limits* so that human beings behave and society remains on the right path.

> Dress is the basic thing that determines human behavior. Women must be in *pardah* and must not talk to *nā-mahram* men. Women's private parts include her voice, because even that has an attraction for men. Western dresses are indecent. Our men do wear trousers, but it is not good. Trouser is *firangī kā libās* (dress of the British), not ours.

Women associate *pardah* with an invisibility that is liberating for them, as well as with security, modesty, decency, nobility and higher social status. Their responses are stated below. Although they denied that it is their men who enforce *pardah* on them, their whole logic behind observing *pardah* is based on their perception of men as intimidators and offenders. This "geography of fear" under which the women are aware of being "watched" and "followed" by men was originally used by Schepple & Bart in 1983 and quoted by Kelly in 1996 (Jackson and Scott 1996: 192). Therefore, on the basis of my data, I interpret that *pardah* is not a moral issue for women, but a practical choice.

> While in *pardah,* women stay away from people's gaze […] they can hide themselves from men.

> A woman in *burqā'* is considered to be respectful. Such a woman is not expected to go around in public areas and if she does, the others give her a preferential treatment saying 'attend to the *burqā'-vālī* first.'

During the research, one particular case was closely observed. A seventeen year old girl from Mirpur-Maki'ālo was brought to the shrine of Rānīpūr by her husband and mother-in-law who believed that a spell had caused infertility in the young girl. Without a *cā dar*, or *burqā,'* she was pushed by her family into the open courtyard where the *pīr* was treating his clients. There were other young women with unkempt hair and uncovered bosoms who were dancing in a state of trance among male visitors. *Pardah* was not an issue in this sphere, thus raising questions about the "moral construct" that idealizes it within the same society.

Media and entertainment industry is blamed for spoiling the younger generation. The post-partition middle-aged group has a reason to doubt and criticize the youngsters because they believe:

> We live in the age of *fiḥāshī* (vulgarity) [...] how can *sharīāh* be implemented?

A female respondent of Laṛhī echoed similar views by condemning the media:

> A good Muslim woman worships Allah and does not waste time in watching films and other *ghalt* (wrong) excursion and entertainment.

Religious education is considered to be in consonance with the practices of high morals whereas worldly education is condemned. In this realm, the *sharīāh*-oriented community of Visṛīvāhān is more conservative in comparison to Raẓlmeman that is influenced by *ṣūfism*. Women are generally conscious of their roles. They emphasize the need for following tradition, culture and religion in order to eliminate vice from the society. For them, the concept of good morals largely hinges on observing *pardah*, and being *khidmatguzār*. This is contrary to the perception of men who believe women are the causes of evil and are vulnerable to becoming possessed by demons.

Post-partition Male and Female Generation II

The Laṛhī community was given a reference of Khadija sending a marriage proposal to Prophet Muhammad (Pbuh). The men were questioned as to why her action is considered non-controversial whilst a similar action if undertaken by a girl today, will be admonished. The following responses were gathered:

> Khadija did not watch films and did not have dirty ideas in her mind like the girls of the present generation.[14]

> Khadija had *kirdār* and she was not *kanvārī*. One has to keep women away from dirty exposure so that they behave. Presently, sending marriage proposals to men is against *sharīāt*.

The men believe that it is their prerogative to doubt women and undertake corrective action against them for the sake of society. A social obsession with female sexuality also emerges, only to suggest that a virgin is not to have the same level of freedom enjoyed by other women. In Visṛīvāhān an interesting discussion raised some dissenting voices. Largely, young women prefer owning *pardah* and feel secure in it as they stated:

> A *pardah* is the *zevar* and *zīnat* of a woman. The concept is to cover the *sattr*. A woman's whole body is a *sattr* because she is *muqaddas* (sacred). She is not a thing in the bazaar that everyone passing by can stop, look, accept or reject.

> A very beautiful woman in *pardah* will invite no onlookers but an ugly woman without *pardah* will invite all.

Ahmed (2006: 99-100) notes that *hijāb* is increasingly being worn by younger Pu*kh*tūn women in Pakistan as it elevates their status among other members of a group, even if the latter are higher in familial hierarchy and older in age. One of the advantages of wearing a *hijāb* is that such a woman earns the reputation of having high morals that allows her to influence the main events in a community. Another dimension is that most women are questioning the stereotypical explanations surrounding *pardah* and are faced with opposition from all ranks of society, even from within:

> We are only observing *pardah* because our men have asked us to do so.

> Our mothers, grandmothers think that an educated girl will write (love) letters. When we give an opinion they order us to seal our lips. They intimidate us by saying: 'your feathers need a trim.' They think that by learning, we will become bad-girls.

A girl added that the society defines moral norms for women in order to serve the economic and social needs of men:

> Nowadays boys are demanding educated wives. Therefore, the communities have no choice but to educate the girls [...] for the boys, as this is their demand. The men twist and turn religion at their whim.

Through another vignette, it was suggested that Islam allows men to beat their wives. The argument that followed is mentioned below and reveals the level of awakening in the younger women, i.e., PPG (II), something lacking in the PPG (I). Only to reiterate, they have opposition from within.

> Yes. She should be beaten for disobeying her husband. After *nikah* beating one's wife is *jāi'z.*

> Violence is cruelty and why couldn't he have taken a glass of water himself. Are his hands and legs broken?

> Whatever men believe in, they say [...] this is it, this is Islam. Had we been true Muslims we could have changed our society for better. All these dirty things that we see [...] this crime, is that supported by Islam? All we can think about is that beating women *is* Islam.[15] This is violence and is nothing but cruelty.

> If a woman is nice, what can a man do? He will never beat her [...] she must behave, respect and obey him.

During community meetings, fertility of women remained a significant topic of discussion. A young girl from this group contributed to the discussion as follows:

> A woman's greatest contribution to this society is children. A woman becomes superior to a man only when she becomes a mother.[16]

Here, gender roles are accepted and rationalized as warranty of an elevated status to otherwise disempowered women. Islam reiterates that paradise is under the feet of mothers; motherhood makes a woman feel "empowered" and "moral" at the same time.

Religious authorities known as the *maulvīs,* play an important role in maintaining the local construct of women's morality. During sermons, the men are constantly reminded about the desired gender roles. Some of the excerpts from one such sermon are mentioned below.[17] Conforming to socially defined gender roles and expectations is regarded as moral behavior. Modernization is condemned as something that leads to immorality. Maximum effort is directed in ensuring the maintenance of status quo. The keen audience includes post-generation II males, who can then be expected to create difficulties for post-generation II females, some of whom are beginning to question the stereotypes.

A "good" woman is expected to be obedient, as is reflected in the following teaching of the *maulvī:*

The Prophet said: 'the woman who declares faith in her husband [...] in Allah [...] in *rasūl* [...] is pious and (if she) serves her husband [...] even if she gives one glass of water to her husband with a smile [...] she will enter paradise from the same door from which I will enter.

On a similar note he said:

God sent woman on earth to be obedient. The Prophet said 'tell them (women) about the things in Qur'ān and bring them into obedience.

During an interview with the researcher, the Qazi of Madrasa Dār-ul-Hudá Ṭheṛī expressed doubt on a woman's level of religiosity and hence her morality in the following words:

The Prophet himself said that the religious power of a woman is half to that of a man.

Both statements remind us of the male voices of post-partition generation I, and indicate that religious authorities do influence people's mindset. The *maulvī* continued:

Hadīth directs that you must have *nikah* with a woman who gives birth to a lot of children. This proves that Islam forbids family planning. We have to make the prophet proud of his *ummah* (nation).[18]

In Allah's Qur'ān, it is of utmost importance for women to stay in *pardah*[...] Women are responsible for all domestic chores. Those who read for a Masters degree or do jobs [...] let it be known that these things are not permitted in our religion.

The Qazi of Madrasa Dār-ul-Hudá Ṭheṛī expressed similar views in the following words:

The education for girls is *jā'iz* (justified) till the time it is within *cār dīvārī*(four walls).. Outside the walls, it is illegal. Women can be allowed worldly education depending on the circumstances. Nonetheless under normal circumstances this should not be considered as a preferred or available option.

Such dimensions of female morality in Sindh, as evidenced by the data, have existed for centuries with Sadiq Ali mentioning similar patterns in 1901, especially amongst *Saiyids*.[19] He identified *Balouch* as being a tribe that was harsh in implementing standards of morality for women, leading to killings. This aspect is covered later in a section reserved for honor-related crimes.

Morality and Constraints:
Cultural Practices Masquerading as Religion

Leila Ahmad argues that Islamic institutions only brought an endorsement and a license to the anti-female mores and prejudices that in reality had pre-existed in those very societies. In other words, Islam *lent* itself to being interpreted as a religion that supported a deeply negative and debased conception of women. Henceforth a number of abusive practices towards women became legally and religiously sanctioned Muslim practices.[20]

Stated below are some similar cultural practices through which Pakistani women are routinely abused in the name of Islam. Under the pretext of Islam, women are denied even the rights that are clearly theirs. Here, it is argued that there is no way that Allah's Islam can be equated to the Islam that is practiced by the people in a given Muslim society. The female "morality-construct", as explained in this essay, after decades of practice has come to allocate an extremely disadvantaged and powerless position to the women in Pakistan. There is a need to understand the abusive practices unleashed against Pakistani women as only a by-product of the lowly status they have been allocated in the society.

Bibiān of Pakistan

Bibi'ism has never been used as an acronym before. I use it to explain a distinct form of female subjugation, as institutionalized by few among the high, and mostly Saiyyid class of Pakistani society. At times, it is practiced ritualistically in the form of "Marriage to the Qur'ān," and at other times simply through *haq bakhshnā*, i.e., waiving or relinquishing a right. In traditional societies mostly fathers are obligated to arrange marriage for their daughters. *Bibiān* is a term used for those women of marriageable ages who are forced by their fathers to waive their rights of marriage formally, and at times secretly. A few *bibiān* are made to solemnize marriage vows with the Holy Qur'ān, eliminating chances of marriage to a mortal. Such an imposition may or may not accompany physical violence. A *bibi* is proudly projected as a woman of high virtue, and morality and is *reserved* for the service of Islam. She becomes inaccessible to outsiders and spends time worshipping quietly, confined in her isolated quarter. Food and basic necessities are provided to her within these four walls. Sometimes, these *bibis* receive requests from the poor to write amulets for small ailments.

The *pīrs* build matrimonial alliances themselves, but do not allow their women to marry (Ansari 1992: 28). *Bibi'ism* is practiced to serve the economic interests of the father of a woman. A *bibi* married to the Qur'ān is considered a woman of high morals, and is *reserved* for the service of Islam. Notwithstanding, on occasions, as mentioned before, they have challenged the system.

It is difficult to acquire data on this practice, as the *bibiān* are mostly from influential families. Despite this, their existence is an open secret. A local informant mentioned the seven unmarried daughters of Pīr Abdul Qādir Shah Mamoon, a cousin of Pīrs of Rānīpūr, Nūr-ul-Hudá Shah. Novelists such as Manik Sindhi, Ahmed Salim and Qaisra Shahraz have written extensively about the practice. During my stay in Ṭheṛī and Rānīpūr the locals showed *havelīs* of *bibiān* from the street. Similarly, some female devotees at various shrines also mentioned their consultation sessions with the *bibiān* of Pīr Pagāṛo's family. Most interestingly, Pīr Pagāṛo has given public statements, condemning this practice. The *bibiān* are of varied age groups. Some old *bibiān* were asked to surrender their rights of marriage at a very young age, whilst the male members of the same family conveniently practiced polygamy. Although it is against the teachings of Islam, by using religious symbols like the Qur'ān, the practice of polygamy is justified on the pretext of Islam.

A man, PPG (I), from Muhallá Par'evān, Ṭheṛī, said:

As children, we used to hear the word *bibi*. We used to think that it is a "thing" —some interesting thing. I remember, climbing the walls of these *havelīs* to see inside. The *bibiān* were women, young and old, clad in *cā dars* behind these huge walls—isolated from the whole world. They were given food inside their rooms. No *nā-mahram* was allowed near them. They would grow old and die.

The male community of Laṛhī confirmed the existence of this practice. A respondent from PPG (I) explained the reasons in the following words:

Property is the key issue. Such things are done to save material loss to any group. There is no such thing as 'Marriage to the Qur'ān' in the Qur'ān itself. They bring the Qur'ān along so that they can defend their injustices later. Mostly, the powerful *jāgīrdārs* and the *pīrs* indulge in such things. *Ẓulam* takes place in the name of Qur'ān.

These *bibiān* are quite different from the *bibiāne* about whom Ahmed (2006) writes. Whilst her research focuses on the *bibiāne* of NWFP who remain actively engaged in socially meaningful work, the *bibiān* of Sindh, which constitutes my sample community, remain isolated and participates merely in writing amulets from behind their closed quarters. Most surprisingly, Nūr-ul-Hudá Shah, who placed the foundation stone of bringing this practice into media attention in form of a drama series entitled *Jungle* on Pakistan Television (PTV), argued against the acquired information during an interview with her:

> (*Jungle*) was the creativity of my mind. [...]. The fact is that no ceremony takes place. It is just that when a father does not marry away his daughter, something that is his religious duty, he requests the daughter to pardon him to make things easy on the Day of Judgment. This is *haq bakhshnā*—a request.

I interpret *haq bakhshnā* as a practice through which the feudal class misuses religion to meet their economic interests. The practice continues due to fear of publicity in the media. Whilst the ritualistic elements, like observing a *mehindi*[21] have been eliminated; "declared or undeclared, the practice continues."[22]

Non-consensual Contracting of Marriage

The sample communities were told a vignette based on a routine social practice of equating a bride's silence at the time of vows with that of her consent to marry (See Annex 6, Para-I). This is in contradiction to the Islamic teachings, according to which a bride must audibly give her consent three times.[23] A male respondent from PPG (II), Laṛhī, reflected on the vignette:

> Women are denied things because of the culture, but society uses the *ṭhappá* of Islam. A woman married without consent is appreciated as a Muslim woman with high morals and ethics, having the decency to remain quiet and accepting her parent's decision. This is something that appeals to [...] and is a requirement of both Islam and our culture. It is not this or that [...], it is both.

Therefore, one can conclude that if Islam gives her the *right* to declare her decision, it simultaneously imposes a *duty* on her to be respectful towards her parents. Her decision to waive her right in order to perform her duty is like a litmus test that authenticates her credentials of being "a good Muslim" woman. However, it is important to note that it is largely her *cultural* training that makes her happy even if she settles for less.

Denying Access to Worldly Education

During his stay in Sindh from 1848 to 1849, and again in 1878, Bourdieu argued that Muslims were particularly resistant to any idea of educating their women (Ali, 1987). Women are generally perceived as being evil. Modern education is taken as a harbinger of moral decline. The only improvement is that today it is possible to generate a debate on the issue among PPG (II). Those who deny worldly education to Muslim women base their arguments on religious references on *pardah*. The following dialogue between two women of Visṛīvāhān belonging to PPG (II) reveals the scope of the debate:

Researcher: "Does Islam allow education to women?"
Respondent-1: "Religion allows education, but the culture does not."
Respondent-2: "No. Religion allows only Qur'ānic education."
Respondent-1: "Islam says go for education, even if you have to go to China."
Respondent-2: "That is only for men [...] women cannot leave their houses."
Researcher: The Prophet told Muslims to go to China. Did they teach Qur'ān in China? Or were the Chinese Muslims?
Respondent-1: This is what I am saying [...] Prophet Muhammad (Pbuh) did not say: 'Seek knowledge in China provided they are Muslims and will teach you Qur'ān, and provided you are yourself a man.'
Respondent-2: Islam says that women must stay indoors. It is better for them. The Qur'ān guides man to offer prayers in a mosque but to a woman, it says, 'stay in your own room.'

Morality and Violence: Price of Being or Being Perceived as 'Bad'

Concept of *kārī*) [...] although it doesn't appear in the Qur'ān, the view survives in Pakistan and some other Muslim countries that a man has the right to kill a female relative if she violates certain rules and norms. The violation could be a woman's refusal to an arranged marriage, flirtation with a man, or even having the misfortune of being raped. All these situations bring discredit upon the family, and hence 'justify' an honor-killing. These murders are officially classified as criminal offences in Pakistan, but in practice the authorities allow them to go unpunished.[24]

Simply stated, honor killing is carried out in the name of honor. If the offender claims that he killed the other to save his honor, he is not indicted. In recent years people kill in any dispute and subsequently state that the action was invoked to save family honor.

Shirkat Gah, one of the most prominent Pakistani national NGOs working on women's rights issues and producing valid data, published a report on honor killings[25] in November, 2001. According to it, throughout the 1999, Sindhi newspapers revealed 353 incidents of honor related issues, 446 honor-killings, out of which 271 were women. In July 2004 official statistics presented to Senate of Pakistan disclosed that 4,000 people were killed in the name of honor in a period of six years. Among a total of 2,774 female victims, 1,578 were killed in Punjab; 751 in Sindh; 260 in the NWFP and 185 in Balochistan. The corresponding figures for males reveal that 675 were killed in Punjab; 348 in Sindh; 188 in the NWFP and 116 in Balochistan.[26] These statistics, taken at face value, clearly indicate that women are more vulnerable than men.

According to the statistics maintained by the office of the Inspector General Police (IGP) in Islamabad, Interior Division, Government of Pakistan, it can be stated that most of the murders that take place in Sindh are in the name of honor.[27]

Table 2-5

	Violence Against Women From 1993-2002
Murder	73 *(51 cases belong to honor-killing)*
Beating	5
Other	9
Total	87

Other important statistics on Sindh during the same time period reveal eight cases of acid throwing by relatives, 772 rapes, in which all accused are relatives and about 25 gang rapes, once again, by relatives.

In another set of archival data that was acquired from the District Police in Khairpur, the following figures are worth noting:[28]

Table 2-6

CATEGORY	1972-1977	1978-1988	2000 – APRIL 2004
Murder of women on morality charges	41	91	99
Siyah (Black) *kārī*	57	157	46

Regarding the evolution of the practice of honor killing in Sindh, there are two prominent opinions. Mostly, it is believed to be a trend introduced by the Balouch (Jhal Magsi and Khuzdar) and the Arab tribes during their visits to the area for purposes of trade. In Khairpur, people mostly link *kāro kārī* to their own landed aristocracy. Some hold the opinion that the incidents increased with industrialization, and people indulged in honor crimes as a means to meet their economic interests. It became common for people to kill their women as a *kārī* (*immoral*, referring to "color black" literally) and then allege a man as an offender in the case, pressuring his family to offer money to settle the dispute or otherwise threaten him to be prepared to serve a sentence. For few men, the reasoning behind honor-killing is the woman herself. A man, from Laṛhī, PPG (I) explained:

> A woman is the root cause of *kāro kārī*. Men lose their mind over women, and commit a crime. If a woman is young, she entices him to be sinful—through her beauty. If she is old, she rules her son […]. Apparently, men are the boss but it is the women who control them—in subtle, clever way.

There is a miniscule chance that a woman may successfully escape an attempted honor-killing. If she manages to seek refuge in a *va ḍero's* house and is spared her life, she is kept as a *bāndi* to her family's disappointment. A man from Laṛhī, PPG (I) narrated an incident from village of Goṭh Sagū:[29]

> There was a *mu'āmlá* between a girl and a village boy. The *jirga* decided for *kāro kārī* […]. In this case, the *sardārs* were telling one another that you take her, no, no, you take her […] she is *kārī*. In the end they did not kill her, but took her for themselves and the villagers were quiet. To the

community, the feudals said: 'we have made her our *bāndi*.' They put up a nice pretence for everyone to prove their kindness by providing abode to a *kārī*. But, we know, they will do everything (alluding to sexual assault) with her. She is young and [...], now tell us [...] is killing better or is this better? Think from the parents' point of view. Is it better to live with the feeling that she is [...] you know [...] and [...] or better to have her finished in one blow.

This passage also indicates that once a woman is "categorized" as immoral or *kārī*, such social conditions are created that she becomes a site of never-ending servitude and slavery, dominated by the landed aristocracy. The social environment is so harsh that dying once is regarded better than dying every day by leading a stigmatized life. This reminds one of both Foucault and Bourdieu and their theories regarding the categorization and classification of human beings to serve the power constructs of a society.

Culture or Shari'a

Literature informs us that there is no proper burial afforded to a *kāro* and *kārī*. Their deaths are referred to as *harām* (Shirkat Gah 2001). The male communities largely suggested that honor-killing is a cultural practice. A PPG (II) respondent from Laṛhī expressed:

A girl submits under the pressure of *rīt-ravāj*. *Kāro kārī* is not supported by *sharīāt*. Benazir's family was angry when she preferred the Zardari clan over the Bhuttos for marriage. The Prime Minister of this society cannot transcend the boundaries. Even **she** is expected to preserve the family honor.

When he was asked whether the girl *cannot* or *should not* transcend boundaries, he responded that it was both. He continued that the primary responsibility of preserving family honor falls on women. When probed as to why, he remarked:

She is our daughter, our wife our sister, our mother. She has to live a life to fit in all of these roles.

Another man added:

This is all very confusing. Honor-killing is *bāsharīāt* [...] *rajm* is allowed in Islam. The act of *zāni* and *zānia* is considered *harām* in Islam and therefore Islam allows us to kill them.

He was countered:

> No. It (Islam) does not. In Islam, *killing*[30] is *harām*. We all know that the powerful people kill for *sayyāsat* and *mufād* [...] they do not have a proof of anything before declaring people as *kāro and kārī* [...] just because they are strong they get away with it.

It is difficult to ascertain whether social pressure forces families to kill in the name of honor. The male group of PPG (I) in Laṛhī supported the practice of *kāro kārī*, believing that it facilitated the disciplining of younger generations. However, they were countered by two other respondents from the same group:

> People support *kāro kārī* to satisfy the society they live in. It's a shame that we submit to social pressure.

Sometimes the family itself pressures a *jirga* to practice *kāro kārī*, and the *jirga* resists them. He quoted the example of a Shahānī community in Rānīpūrī:

> In October 2004, Samar *sā'en* had to judge a woman brought by her husband who had accused her of adultery. *Sā'en* judged that there will be no punishment and that the husband, if he still holds a grievance against his wife, must divorce her. The parents and siblings of the girl appealed to *sā'en* that she be declared a *kārī* and immediately killed. He [...] dismissed the case.

People sometimes commit crimes to serve their economic interests. In Khairpur two children aged five were stigmatized as *kāro kārī*. The actual dispute between the families was over land distribution.[31] In Visṛīvāhān, a young girl from PPG (II) condemned the practice of *kāro kārī*, however, she supported the idea of other kinds of severe punishment as a substitute to honor-killing. Her response evidences the prevailing mindset:

> The act is wrong. She should not cheat on her parents and family, and must not go against the *bunīād* of Islam. But still, *killing* is equally wrong. The accused must be locked in the house, beaten, forbidden to go out of the house, but not killed. If *voh* (that)[32] is *harām* in Islam [...] so is killing another human being.

Muslim men and women take the denunciation of sexual relations outside wedlock as their social and moral duty. When her opinion on *rajm* was sought, a young woman challenged the validity of a death sentence by arguing that in most cases, the decision makers were of doubtful character:

> It is all politics. Who are the people who will establish the *zānī* and *zānia*? [...]. They are themselves corrupt and they only play politics. Death sentence is wrong because the judges are corrupt.

The following data provided in Table 18 reflect that among men, 4 out of 6 (66%) from PPG; 18 out of 26 (69%) from PPG (I) and 29 out of 53 (55%) from PPG (II) condemned *kāro kārī*. In comparison, from PPG (II) 19 out of 26 (73%) among women—a much higher proportion in comparison to men—forcefully rejected the practice and called for its end. Note that the segregated result for each community is likely to change the trend.

Table 2-7

<table>
<tr><td colspan="9" align="center">PROMPT:
KĀRO KĀRĪ IS IMPORTANT TO KEEP SOCIAL DISCIPLINE</td></tr>
<tr><td>Categories</td><td colspan="2">Total</td><td colspan="2">Agree</td><td colspan="2">Disagree</td><td colspan="2">Unsure</td></tr>
<tr><td></td><td>M</td><td>F</td><td>M</td><td>F</td><td>M</td><td>F</td><td>M</td><td>F</td></tr>
<tr><td>Pre-partition Generation</td><td>6</td><td>1</td><td>2</td><td>0</td><td>4</td><td>1</td><td>0</td><td>0</td></tr>
<tr><td>Post-partition Generation I</td><td>26</td><td>18</td><td>8</td><td>5</td><td>18</td><td>12</td><td>0</td><td>1</td></tr>
<tr><td>Post-partition Generation II</td><td>53</td><td>26</td><td>15</td><td>4</td><td>29</td><td>19</td><td>9</td><td>3</td></tr>
<tr><td colspan="9" align="center">Source: Author's Field Data</td></tr>
</table>

Many respondents felt more comfortable supporting a severe punishment over a death penalty for those who are alleged to have *transgressed*. Among men 5 out of 6 (83%) from PPG; 22 out of 26 (84%) from PPG (I) and 40 out of 53 (75%) from PPG (II) agreed with the prompt. Among women, the opinion was widely divided in PPG (II), with 8 out of 26 (31%) agreeing; 10 out of 26 (38%) disagreeing and 8 out of 26 (31%) remaining unsure on the issue.

Table 2-8

PROMPT: TRANSGRESSORS MUST BE SEVERELY PUNISHED								
Categories	Total		Agree		Disagree		Unsure	
	M	F	M	F	M	F	M	F
Pre-partition Generation	6	1	5	1	1	0	0	0
Post-partition Generation I	26	18	22	13	3	4	1	1
Post-partition Generation II	53	26	40	8	10	10	3	8
Source: Author's Field Data								

I would like to document a few excerpts from two tragic case-studies that I collected during my field work. These excerpts were prepared subsequent to conducting interviews with the families of those killed in the name of honor. The cases were under investigation by the police stationed in Khairpur. The family members, rather than feeling guilty, argued in favor of the justification of their actions.

Case-study 1
Victim: Tehmīza Khatoon (15/16yrs)
Complainant: Zubair Ahmed Chandio (Brother of Victim)
Date of Crime: 3-4-2003
Crime No: 12/03 u/s 302-PPC

Police Station: Ahmedpur –Khairpur

Interviewees: Mother of the victim and Zubair Ahmed
Zubair: We woke up at the time of *Fajr* prayer. My father noticed that Tehmīza was not in bed. We looked for her. Rafiq's house was opposite ours […] we have a common courtyard […] my father went there and saw them, *ghalt kām karte huve* (doing a wrongful act), so he shot her. On hearing the noise, Rafiq's family came over and started beating my father and, in the meantime, he (Rafiq) escaped.
Zubair: We woke up at the time of *Faj'r* prayer. My father noticed that Tehmīza was not in her bed. We looked for her. My father went to the neighbour's (Rafiq's) house and saw them, *ghalat kām kartay huay* (doing something wrong)[33] so he shot her. Rafiq escaped.
Mother: My husband killed my daughter because she committed *nājā'īzī* (an illicit act.)
Zubair: She was a *woman*.[34] When a woman is born, she is a blessing. Prophet Muhammad (Pbuh) also said: woman is a blessing. I agree. But, when she becomes a *zehmat*, then she should be killed.

Researcher: On finding them together, was there a chance to just simply scold them and then [...] maybe, arrange a marriage for them?

Zubair: No, that was not possible. The first time my father looked at them [...] he was overwhelmed by *gherat*. Therefore he had to act.

Researcher: In Islam there are four witnesses required to confirm an illicit act. What are the names of witnesses in this case?

Zubair: There are witnesses for the murder [...] Rafiq's family.

Researcher: And the witnesses for the act that led to the murder?

Zubair: It was just my father. There are no witnesses.

Researcher: Don't you think that the murder is therefore Un-Islamic?

Zubair: This can't be Un-Islamic, because it was done in the name of honor. Had he (father) told anyone, he could not have killed her. Had he not killed her, it would have created hindrances for us for life. We would have ended up [...] hiding our face from everyone [...] our village is a small one.

Researcher: What is honor?

Zubair: It is an emotion. When a human being looks at something as *this*, he gets impulsive and instinctively gets ready to do such a thing. Any father or brother who will look at his sister like this...would not be able to tolerate.

Researcher: How will you justify that she was "immoral" [...] as you are suggesting?

Zubair: I was her elder brother. She did not show respect towards us. Our respect, honor, was rolled over in mud. Had she shown respect, this would not have happened. She did not respect us; this is why we declare her as "immoral." This all led to bad things. She [did not give] gave a damn to the honor and respect of her father and brother. What kind of a sister was she?

Mother: I have no respect for her. She left her house in the middle of the night to commit *nājā'īzī*.

Zubair: We have told Rafiq's father: Listen, we have killed our daughter [...] now you kill your son too so that we get "saitel".[35] But he is not doing so.

Researcher: Why?

Zubair: They are holding their son dear.

Researcher: Did you not hold your daughter/sister, dear?

Zubair: No—because she was at fault.

Researcher (to the Mother): Instead of Tehmīza, if Zubair had done a similar deed [...] would you or your husband have killed him?

Researcher: How will you justify that Tehmīza was "immoral"...as you are suggesting?

Mother: If *kārī's* family would have killed him [...] they would have [...] but we would not kill our own son.

Researcher: But the deed is the same, isn't it? It is forbidden in Islam to have sex outside marriage, right? So, why Tehmīza and why not Zubair?

Researcher: Was she properly buried? Was she buried in a public graveyard?

Zubair: Yes. But as the time passes, there won't be any mark left. Then no one will recognize whose grave it is. It does not have a stone.

Researcher: Funeral?

> Zubair: I was in the police station so I don't know [...] though it is not correct to (offer prayers) in such cases.
> Researcher: Why?
> Zubair: Because this is *nājā 'īzī*. When a human being commits bad deeds, it is not right to offer the funeral prayers.
> **Source: Author's Field Data**

In connection to the victim's brother's assumption that her funeral should not have taken place, I would like to mention that Ahmed (2006) also mentions that for some types of deaths, including suicide, Islam forbids attendance over funeral (93). However, she does not provide the source of her information. Muslim scholars have argued that Islam does not forbid funeral of a fellow Muslim.[36]

> Case-study 2
> Victim: Bilqees (22 yrs)
> Complainant: Allah Dād (Husband of the victim)
> Date of Crime: 17-4-2004
> Crime No: 23/04 u/s 302-PPC
> Police Station: Pīrjogoṭh–Khairpur
>
> *Interviewee:* Allah Dād
> Allah Dād: That day I was in the village and a man came running and said that your brother has *kārī* Bilqees. I went home and saw that she was lying dead in a pool of blood. Later on, the man who was declared *kāro* said to me that: "I have committed *nājā 'īzī* (injustice) with you." He apologized and I pardoned him.
> Researcher: Why did you pardon him?
> Allah Dād: He had brought the Qur'ān along.
> Researcher: Please continue.
> Allah Dād: How it happened? Why it happened? I don't know. But I think it is something like what is very common and generally happens in villages [...] the problem of *kāro kārī*—you know![37] I agree with my brother. She should have been killed. In the name of *gherat*, Sindhis do commit murders [...] we know it [...] we see it around us.
> [...]
> Researcher: Had you seen her, would you have murdered her?
> Allah Dād: I myself cannot guess how I would have behaved in *jazbāt* (high emotions).
> **Source: Author's Field Data**

A detailed analysis of these two cases and the other collected cases revealed that older women plot against young girls, in certain cases, even more so than men. Sometimes, family members murder the target, subsequently justifying the killing to the male guardian by maligning the victim on moral grounds. The police seek a complainant who is usually a supporter of the offender. Soon, the complainant reaches an agreement by pardoning the offender and the case is withdrawn. It reminds us of Bauman's argument that the social system itself provides a conduit for non-cruel people to indulge in cruel acts as they are removed from a face-to-face confrontation with the consequences of their actions. Killing is mostly taken as a routine happening.

Socially, honor killing is largely an approved practice. It was found that people condemn it due to their suspicion of the intention of the judges *(jirga)* and also that of the family members of the victim. But, generally, honor killing is regarded to have a support base in Islam. Some people believe that those who are "immoral" enough to indulge in what is believed to be an illicit relationship deserve to get killed. There are others who believe that murder is an unforgivable sin and is not justified or legal in any sense. However, the gender of the offender determines the gravity and consequences of the same deed. This presents an interesting interface between Islamic teachings and people's patriarchal preferences. Zubair's mother was not willing to kill him for the same deed, but upheld Tehmīza's murder as a righteous act; Allah Dād forgave the man who committed the offence, but supported Bilqees's murder. Does this mean that impulsive attitude and *jazbāt*, be it of killing or of sex outside the context of marriage, are somewhat *expected* and hence acceptable from men, but not from women? Such a biased attitude does not have a foundation in the Holy text, but certainly in the local culture that rejoices the birth of a son and mourns that of a daughter. This asymmetrical construction of male and female morality in the Muslim societies, and the practice of honor-killing is not the gift of The Divine, but a misdemeanour of the obscurantist people who granted a divine legitimacy to various forms of crimes committed against women to serve men's patriarchal and economic interests, including possible misogynistic inclinations.

Sex remains a taboo in a society where a girl child passes through stages of puberty, unnervingly stepping into adolescence as illiterate, domesticated, frightened, cloistered by the weight of morality and family honor that she cannot comprehend or articulate. Failing to be "morally" sound according to her family members, at the age of 16, Tehmīza,— still a child according to the UN Charter,— was brutally murdered and buried in a grave that has no epitaph.

Conclusion

The issue today is not to define Islam, but estimate the various forms that it has come to adopt. It is important to realize how Islam, the religion, manifests itself as a social, cultural, psychological and power phenomenon. We need to acknowledge how human morality, instead of producing desired results of social welfare, becomes a source and cause of human constraint, abuse, and crime—especially for women. It is not incorrect to claim that many "illegitimate" actions of the contemporary Muslim societies are considered "legitimate" simply because the logic for such actions is housed within the sacred institution of Islam. It is also true that people interact with religion according to their political and economic needs and interests. The women interviewed for this study verbalized their concerns over male monopolization of Islam and the consequential distortion of the religion—so that it can be tailored to serve patriarchal interests.

The exclusive "construct" of female morality, as shared extensively throughout this essay, proved that cloistering, chaperoning and limiting access to public places wins a "good" name and life to a woman. She must remain chaste, obedient and patient to attest her moral "goodness" to the society. If she deviates from the path assigned to her by the society, there is a likelihood that she will be asked to pay a hefty price—even with her own life. Durkheim's "force of the social," is experienced differently by men and women. Society does not expect the same level of submission to this "force" from men, as it does from women, who are routinely regulated and monitored and for whom corrective and punitive measures are also undertaken so that the power interests of the community could be served. The female body may not always be a site of torture, but according to the changing patterns of local power dynamics, even in the twenty-first century it bears the potential for enslavement and confinement. Ironically women were debased and transformed into a disadvantaged and dispossessed group, in the name of Islam—the religion that bestowed them the private and public *rights* centuries ago—which provided a share for them in their parental and spousal property, and a right of/to divorce among other benefits. Within this setting, when it is currently claimed that Islam, as a religion, emancipated women, there is not much to provide corroborative evidence. Cases of honor killings, forced marriages and imposed domestication, even enslavement, prove the contrary. The deplorable status allocated to women in specific Muslim countries has ultimately brought global humiliation to Islam and should therefore constitute a serious concern for the rest of the Muslim world.

Author's Note on Language, Transliteration and Spellings

The field notes were taken in Urdu, and therefore I have used the Urdu transliteration table instead of Sindhi. The table provided by the Library of Congress (LOC) has been followed. Seven roman letters out of a total of forty-three are not available in MS Word (Times New Roman) and are as under:

ṭ ḍ r̤ ṣ ẓ ṯ ẕ

These have been substituted with the following:

ṭ ḍ r̤ ŝ ż t ž

Glossary

(The glossary has been prepared by the author. In this regard the glossaries provided by Werbner (2003:314-333); Schimmel (1975: xxi) along with the 'Practical Dictionary-Urdu to English,' Naveed-Al-Shaikh: Rabia Book House, Lahore, were consulted.)

Bā	with
Bāghī	rebellious
Bāndī	Servant girl
Bāshariát	According to Shariát
Bibi	(Salutation used for women in Pakistan/ India)
Baikhlāq	one with good character
Bud'kirdār	one of bad character
Budm'uāsh	vagabond
Budnām	defamed
Burā'ī	evilness
Bunī ād	foundation
Burqá	a form of veil
Buzurg	venerable, old and respected
Cā dar	large scarf that covers the head and upper part of the body
Cār dīvārī	within four walls
Faj'r	Morning prayer; first among the five prayers in a day
Hadūd	limits
Harām	forbidden
Havelī	royal abode of the nobles of an area
Hijāb	form of a veil

Jām 'īá	all or whole; collectivity
Jirgá	a local consultative assembly of tribal influentials
Kanvār	virgin
Kāro kārī	boy-girl (local name for honor-killing)
Khidmatguzār	one who serves
Kirdār	character
Mahram	one who is related by blood or a vow
Mā 'ī	woman
Majāzī Khudā	metaphorical or an illusionary God
Malkieyyat	property
Mu 'āmlá	matter
Mufād	self-interest
Murīd/Murīdnī	lover, desirer of (God); disciple of a Ŝūfī saint
Muqaddas	sacred
Nā	not or no
Nājā 'īzī	unjustified; implicates sexual intercourse outside wedlock
Nikah	marriage vow
Pakhtūn	inhabitants of NWFP and Afghanistan
Rajm	stoning
Rīt-Ravāj	custom and traditions
Sā 'en	Sindhi salutation; see *Ŝāhib*
Sardār	a chief
Sattr	private parts of human body on which no one except the individual or his or her spousal relatives have the right; For Muslim men *sattr* begins from below the navel to the knee. Some debate exists with regard to defining privates for Muslim women.
Sayyāsat	politics
Shar'm	shyness; shame
Shar'm gāh	see *sattr*
Ṭhappá	stamp
Va ḍero	landed aristocracy
Vālī/vālā/vāle	feminine/masculine/plural of 'one with'; such as 'taxi-vālā:' a (man), who owns a cab
Zānī	*(m)* one who has pre-marital or extra-marital sex
Zāniā	*(f)* see zānī
Zehmat	trouble
Zevar	ornaments
Zīnat	*(f)* beauty that has an element of dignity
Žulam/žulm	cruelty

Notes

[1] J. Seth, "The Evolution of Morality," *Mind: Vol. 14, No 53* (Jan 1989): 27-49.

[2] R. Galvin, "Does Kant's Psychology of Morality Need Basic Revision?" *Mind, New Series, Vol. 100, No 2* (April 1991), 221-236.

[3] A basic reading of "Durkheim, Morality and Modernity: Collective Effervescence, Homo Duplex and Sources of Moral Action" by Shilling & Mellor (1998) presents that embodied individuals are internally divided between their egoistic impulses and their capacities for reaching beyond these asocial passions to the realm of conceptual thought and moral activity held in common by the society.

[4] C. Shilling and Philip A. Mellor, "Durkheim, Morality and Modernity: Collective Effervescence, Homo Duplex and the Sources of Moral Action", *The British Journal of Sociology, Vol. 49, No 2* (June 1998): 193-209.

[5] Ibid.

[6] Paul Robinow, *"The Foucault Reader: An Introduction to Foucault's Thoughts"* (United Kingdom: Penguin Books, 1984).

[7] For a better understanding of Pierre Bourdieu's philosophy in this context, consult *In Other Words: Essays towards a Reflexive Sociology,* trans. (in association with) Basil Blackwell, (Cambridge-Oxford: Polity Press, 1990) and *Logic of Practice,* trans. Richard Nice (Cambridge-Oxford: Polity Press, 1990).

[8] For both academics and devotees, the difference between *pīr* and *ŝūfī* is difficult to articulate. The terms are applied interchangeably at the grass roots level. For some, *pīr* is an advanced state—*māqām* (level) of a *ŝūfī*, in the realm of *tasawaf.* For others, a *pīr* is the direct descendent of Prophet Muhammad (Pbuh) and therefore different from a *ŝūfī.*

[9] Khairpur was allowed to maintain its status of an Independent Princely State even after the annexation of Sindh to the British Empire in 1843. A small enclave of Pīrjogoṭh was under the British rule for a certain time in order to counter the *Hur movement* (Ansari, 1992).

[10] "Honor killing", *Kāro* and *kārī* means 'boy' and 'girl', respectively. *Kārā* has another literal meaning, i.e., "black".

[11] This word has multiple uses in the local sphere. Therefore, each time it appears in the text, the interpreted sense is given along with it.

[12] Nūr-ul-Hudá Shah, during the interview.

[13] For methodological issues consult section 3.6.1 (1).

[14] During visits it was discovered that the girls had no access to films and in fact it was the favorite pastime for men.

[15] Original emphasis.

[16] She is superior only to one man, her son.

[17] Sermon delivered by Maulvī Fazalulah in Mosque Visṭīvāhān, Ṭheṭī.

[18] Prophet Muhammad (Pbuh) never condemned a girl child's education, and neither did he forbid birth control measures. The Mullah's reference to Prophet Muhammad's sayings is selective, incorrect, random and utterly out of context. At

best it is an attempt to grant a divine legitimacy to a cultural preference of having more children.

[19] Direct descendants of Prophet Muhammad (Pbuh) from Fati'mah—his youngest daughter—and Ali.

[20] Leila Ahmed, *Women and Gender in Islam: Historical Roots of a Modern Debate* (New Haven and London: Yale University Press, 1992).

[21] A marriage ceremony.

[22] Attia Daoud, during her interview with the author in Karachi, March 2004.

[23] Ā'ishá reports: "I asked Allah's Messenger […] whether it was necessary or not to consult a woman before her marriage. He said: "Yes, she must be consulted." Source: Sahih Muslim: Book 008: No: 3305.

[24] Asma Jahangir during her interview with the author (Cambridge: March 2003).

[25] Also known as *gherat ka qatal, kāro kārī, siyah kārī* and by other local names.

[26] The Dawn: 10th July 2004.

[27] Archival data consulted: (a) Cases of Violence Against Women in Province of Sindh for the Period of 1.1.1993-31.05.2003, Office of Inspector General (IG) Pakistan Police, Interior Division, Islamabad; (b)Cases of Violence Against Women in Province of Balouchistan for the Period of 1.1.1993-31.06.2003, Office of Inspector General (IG) Pakistan Police, Interior Division, Islamabad; (c) Domestic Violence against Women in Punjab for the Period of 1.1.1993-31.05.2003, Office of Inspector General (IG) Pakistan Police, Interior Division, Islamabad; (d) Cases of Violence Against Women in Province of NWFP for the Period of 1.1.1993-31.05.2003, Office of Inspector General (IG) Pakistan Police, Interior Division, Islamabad.

[28] Archival data consulted: (a) Cases of *Kāro kārī*: from 1.1.2003 to 15.12.2003; District Khairpur, Department of Pakistan Police, Khairpur, Sindh; (b) Cases of *Kāro kārī* from 1.1.1998 to 31.08.2002; District Khairpur, Department of Pakistan Police, Khairpur, Sindh; (c) Untitled Statistical Data on Murders, Honor killings between 1972-1977; 1978-1988 and from 2000 to April 15, 2004. (FOR) Office of the District Police Officer Khairpur, Sindh.

[29] The distance is one kilometer from Laṛhī.

[30] Original emphasis.

[31] Crime No: 79/03 u/s 324,504-PPC; Khairpur Police Station.

[32] Referring to fornication and/or adultery.

[33] The police record notes: "Chandio saw his daughter in an objectionable position."

[34] Original emphasis.

[35] A local casualism for "settled".

[36] Islamic scholars agree that funeral prayer is to be offered for all those who testify that "There is no god but Allah," regardless of their sins or transgressions. Source: Islam Online Fatwa Editing Desk: www.islamonline.net.

[37] The tone was very casual, as if referring to a routine, daily occasion.

ANATOLIAN WOMEN FACE EAST AND WEST: TRANSFORMING MODERNISM, IDENTIFYING SECULARISM AND RE-DEFINING ISLAMISM

NILGÜN ANADOLU-OKUR

Greek islanders called Asia Minor 'Anatolia', which meant, 'the light /or land of the Sun that rises from the East'. Since this part of the world lay to the east of the Westerners, who claimed to have written the history of world civilizations, Anatolia or Asia Minor, came to represent the geographical and conceptual divide between the East and the West. For travelers who arrive from the East, Anatolia seems to be situated in the West; for those who arrive from the West it seems to be situated in the East. In the past, it was even suspected that here lies a longitudinal vortex which facilitates "time travel" between Asia and Europe.[1]

On December 17, 2004 when the European Union formally agreed to start negotiations with Turkey, forty-five years had already passed since the country's initial application (July 31, 1959) for associate membership in the European Economic Community. However as the first Muslim nation which had shown the longest and the most dedicated interest in accession to the circle of European nations, Turkish domestic policy in 2004 was manifesting early signs of a major controversy. The difficulty was associated with the inevitable rise of Islamism and its bitter clash with the democratic and secular foundations of the Turkish Republic as they were structuralized in 1923 under the leadership of its first President Mustafa Kemal Ataturk.

Since 2004 the divide and the social rift has triggered a further breadth of disagreement both in Turkey and in the region. Turks in general want to be identified as a *characteristically* Islamic nation yet maintain close ties with the Western nations, particularly with their European neighbors. On the other hand Turkey stands alone in the midst of a volatile region semi-circled in the east and the south by Muslim states whose interactions with each other and particularly with Turkey can be equally problematic due to historical animosities. As to the status of Turkish women, they are caught amid a heated discussion because wearing a headscarf or turban at government offices or at educational institutions clearly contradicts Turkish constitutional law. However, recent administrations in Turkey have been positively in favor of women's headscarves in sharp contrast with the former republican ideals. Whereas Islamists have been fondly *politicizing* the headscarf issue as a public and political act of defiance, secularists are increasingly fortifying their ranks in order to reclaim and revive the Kemalist ideology, its reforms and secular politics, particularly in issues that are pertinent to women's rights, such as social status, civil liberties and healthcare. Consequently, in exploration of Turkey's historically unique position and atypical identity among Muslim nations, no single paradigm is as fitting and is as translucently apposite as the one suggested in the title of this chapter, "*Anatolian Women Face East and West.*"

Historically, Turkey's true experimentation with westernization and modernization had begun in the early decades of the nineteenth century during the *Tanzimat* era. The modernization initiative, launched in 1839, was intensified by additional reforms and continued until 1876 as an organized movement undertaken by reformist rulers such as Mahmud II and Abdulmecid I. It was also supported by Western-educated intellectuals such as Ali Pasha, Fuad Pasha, Ahmet Cevdet Pasha and Mithat Pasha. The Tanzimat goals included, among others, modernization of the Ottoman Empire, re-organizing its social and political institutions, building legislative bodies, restructuring the financial system and streamlining the Civil and Criminal Code according to the French model. Besides initiating a restructuring and modernization within the army, *Tanzimat* reforms also reflected a genuine interest in integrating non-Muslims and non-Turks into Ottoman society by improving their status and granting them civil liberties and equal rights throughout the entire Ottoman Empire. The centuries old *millet* policy was abandoned in order to formulate a more inclusive definition of "national identity" which would embrace all ethnic minorities that had engaged in political campaigns, even armed resistance, since the early 1800s in order to attain independence from the Ottoman Empire. By the end of the nineteenth century Greek, Armenian and Kurdish minorities were systematically involved in anti-Ottoman resistance movements in their quest for sovereignty.

If Tanzimat era reforms can be considered a precedent for Turkey's desire to project a new identity to the world, then its application to the European Union in 1959 was not a novelty at all. It clearly reflected and shared a resemblance—except in religious matters—to the structural re-organization goals of the *Tanzimat* reforms, particularly addressing economic and civil rights issues. However, since Turkey is largely a Muslim nation (99%), its immediate prospect of EU membership simply proliferates further tribulations and speculations about Turks' allegiance to orthodox Islam. As there emerges a serious *tête-à-tête* about Turkey's strategic, economic and political identity in the world, the debate continues within the country itself, though on a different level. There are no expedient answers to questions such as the following: Who can be considered a *"true Muslim?"* How far can modernism go? Is *secularism* under attack? By whose standards is Turkey considered *"secular"*? What does the international *Islamist* agenda actually entail for Turkey? In Turkey the debate continues on a daily basis as European Union nations meet behind closed doors in order to evaluate and re-evaluate Turkey's half-a-century old application for inclusion into their ranks.

In recent years Turkey's domestic politics have stirred much curiosity in the West. Consequently a dynamic discourse has ensued about the change in perceptions of the role of women who work in different sectors of industry, at government offices, in the court system and at educational institutions. As the concepts change, so do the images and reflections. Clearly Turkey has come quite a long way since the antiquated *mecelle* (Ottoman Civil Code, 1877) was used to determine and interpret civil liberties which concern women and their status within the society. Additionally even the first Turkish Civil Code, which was fashioned after the Swiss legal code and its Eurocentric terminology have gone through adjustments and transformations during the second half of the twentieth century. Moreover, in the light of political developments followed by a massive victory won in the 2007 elections by the Islamist AK party in power, it is unrealistic not to expect further volatility. The new developments might adjoin serious amendments to the present status of women once defined by the Turkish constitution named *Anayasa,* (*"Ana"* mother, *"yasa"*, "the law", in Turkish).

Meanwhile, an equally disturbing development is taking place on the opposite end of the scale. As Islamist politics advance, so do the ultra-modernist trends with their myriad forms and consequences which impact Turkish women's choices for image and identity in general. These trends clearly influence women's decisions in adopting unusual life styles or seeking employment opportunities in alternative fields of occupation, eventually compromising the once exemplary *Turkish family structure* of the olden times. Marital infidelity, divorce, separation, domestic partnership is on the rise. Women who cannot find legitimate employment seek financial gain in prostitution. Ethical, moral and legal controversies arise too often in matters which directly impact women's health, income and employment decisions. In vital issues and decisions such as abortion, domestic violence; in obtaining legal representation for inheritance rights and property ownership women do not have support. As the republican structure and its established system of values represented by objective legislators who safeguarded the constitutional rights of women face coercion, new articles are added to the Turkish Constitution. Moreover conservative women who favor the headscarf seem to be willing to forfeit their grandmothers' hard-earned rights of emancipation as they prefer to be swayed by slogans chanted by the political Islam. Tremors caused by such a major transformation are likely to determine Turkish women's present and future status in the world, particularly throughout the twenty-first century's Islamic globalization crusade.

On the home front, as Turkish woman's once reputable "homemaker" role is rapidly eroding, the society she operates in is also going through an unprecedented state of transition. Yet much of the discussion revolves around her external appearance rather than the disappearance of her once-celebrated rights and elevated social status. The nature of the present moral and social conflict in Turkish society—with its hybrid forms and manifestations in politics, economy, education, the job-market, marital status—can be attributed to the polarization created in the society around the heated *turban* discussions.

The course of the dialogue between the two warring parties,—namely the Islamists and the secularists,—or rather, the *lack of it,* constitute one of the arguments presented in this essay. Secondly, it provides an essential review of the historical facts which shaped the roles and duties of Anatolian women since the early days of the Turkish Republic, including their courageous struggle to attain specific rights as they waged a battle against certain limitations, dogmas and stereotypes imposed by the Muslim-Ottoman culture. Thirdly, in a comparative analysis of secular and non-secular ideology, two Turkish women and their specific roles are evaluated as they have defined modernism and re-interpreted Islamism throughout their respective careers.

Politics, Religion and the European Union

Essentially due to imminent changes and continuous re-alignments in its political climate, which are presently shaping Turkey's socio-political landscape at the state and society level, this analysis also seeks to address the controversy instigated by political parties upon religion. Although the clash of political Islam with the principles of *secularism* and *laicism* was never a rare occurrence in Turkish political history—as in the events which led to murder of Mustafa Fehmi Kubilay in Menemen, (December 23, 1930) by religious fanatics—the developments since the 2007 elections which ushered in the conservative AK party's victory, deeply affected the Turkish society and introduced resolute modifications to its once homogeneous social fabric. Women, for instance, increasingly began to adopt and wear the headscarf as a manifestation of their personal interpretation of the Turkish civil code and constitutional articles under the Erdogan administration. At present headscarves and loosely fitting long coats are generally interpreted by secular Turks as symbols of political choices and are less likely to be viewed as symbols of religious devotion in future decades.

In today's Turkey religio-political mobilization which led to social polarization continue to bring about further axiological developments which can be identified with the emergence of new ideologies and novel terms on a daily basis. Engaging in politicized religion is a new phenomenon for Turks; it is also perceived as a course of safe landing and a definite shot toward the green. Such a rudimentary analysis may be helpful in explaining the state's policy toward women's rights as they are transfigured by currents of domestic politics followed by the prime minister. However, among numerous paradigms one seems to be more fitting in illuminating the nature and centrifugal force of such a dramatic transformation in Turkey. "Vernacular politics", remarks Jenny White, "is a new term, which makes an argument for looking at political process as a hybrid form."[2] According to White it offers "a new conceptualization to grasp the multiple levels and unexpected convergences of what otherwise would be artificially distinguished as civic, political, and cultural/religious phenomena." She asserts:

> [it is through the merging of] discrete and even contradictory forms of organization and bases for solidarity with conventional scholarly differentiations–religious, and political ideologies embedded in local culture, civil society and political party organization based on local solidarities and interpersonal relations–…one finds the basis for Islamist success in mobilizing a varied population.[3]

A perpendicular jolt, similar to White's theoretically upward projection, is shaping Turkey's future at present. Consequently the generative nature of a dynamic thrust has given rise to an overflow of creativity in print literature, discourse terminology and etymology as Turkey struggles to adopt a social "reform" and adapt itself to political "change." The parameters of this development will be outlined in subsequent sections of the analysis. On the other hand traditional meanings conferred upon *secularism, laicism, modernism, Kemalism, fundamentalism* and *Islamism* throughout Turkish history will be elucidated as they occur within the text. In order to access the strictures of the current debate over "*Islam versus secularism*" and inspire a rather informed dialogue, one may begin with a current overview of definitions utilized by scholars whose studies relate to Turkey's present status and its application for full membership in the EU. The following section delves into an analysis of Turkey's current political climate, its status and assessment within the EU, as such topics contribute to basic human rights, specifically to women's rights debates, which constitute one of the most frequently tackled issues against Turkey in international courts.

According to Graham E. Fuller the Western world has not "correctly understood the Turkish '*secular*' experience in its totality, assuming that the Kemalist approach to the total suppression of Islam in the public space and complete state domination over religion is the model for the whole Muslim world."[4] A former high-ranking CIA official and political scientist, Graham Fuller compiled two consecutive essays in 2005 and assessed the AK party's early role in Turkey's political life. He stated that long-time suppression of Islamic political and social forces "led to schizophrenia" which was finally being resolved as the process of democratization helped the broad spectrum of political and ideological ideas to be fully expressed. Fuller predicted that such improvement, or "normalization" as he called it, would gradually lead to a social reconciliation, "as well as the organic integration of Turkey's Islamists into the political order and governance."[5] He maintained that through such growth Islamists gain an understanding of the diverse characteristics of political life in Turkey, which manifests a deeply rooted concentration on *secular* tendencies, particularly among the elite.

Fuller further remarked that Prime Minister Tayyip Erdogan's Justice and Progress Party (JP or "AK" Party, "*ak*"—a Turkish word meaning "*white*" *or* "*pure*"—whereas "AK" stands for the initials A and K, as in the "<u>A</u>dalet ve <u>K</u>alkinma Partisi"*)* is *not* an *Islamist* party despite its origins in *Islamism*. According to him JP identifies itself as a "conservative democratic party" and through JP Turkey is "coming of age politically", moving farther away from its original "Eurocentric" advocacy of American interests towards acquiring a separate and independent policy. Fuller stated that such a transformation is already proving beneficial for Turkey as its Arab, Turkic and Mediterranean neighbors are hoping to establish productive relations with Turkey. Through its "newly acquired independence", as he claimed, Turkey might be able to "play an independent role in bringing evolution and moderation to the Islamist politics of the Arab and Muslim worlds."[6]

In another article titled "The Erdogan Experiment" Fuller elucidated his own understanding of Turkey's *secularism*: "Actually it has been the antithesis of any American understanding of the term. Turkey's (traditional) secularism has meant total state domination of religion and the exclusion of religion by law from much of the public sphere." Meanwhile he claimed that the *"newfound secularism"* has changed the general outlook of the Turkish society remarkably:

> The AK (Adalet ve Kalkinma–Justice and Progress) Party seeks to permit freedom to wear hijab, currently forbidden in any state institution, including universities, not to impose it; the party seeks to permit graduates of religious schools to be allowed entry to universities, which is currently legally denied, rather than to seek special privileges for them. The AK party is still learning from its mistakes.[7]

In actuality Turkey's socio-political atmosphere is in flux as inquiries and extensive discussions regarding women's headscarves, the "Kurdish Opening", the pending EU membership, along with questions raised against certain articles of the Turkish Constitution for modifications takes place on a daily basis.

In March 2008, a closure case was brought against Mr. Erdogan's party with charges that "the party has been the axis for anti-secularist activities in violation of the Constitution." On July 30, 2008 the Constitutional Court fined the AK Party but did not disband it. Six out of eleven judges were in favor of banning the Party, but a total of seven votes were required. The 160-page document which summarized the charges of "anti-secular activities" brought against the AK Party was considered a major triumph by the secularists until the explosion of a major clamor referred to as *"Ergenekon"*—a pre-Ottoman creation narrative with origins in Central Asia—cast a shadow on their short-lived happiness. Accompanied with widespread anxiety, reminiscent of the Salem (1692) and McCarthy era events (1950-1954), *Ergenekon* led to a series of arrests. Former military generals, retired university professors, doctors, one former mayor, media editors, journalists, and a group of secular elites were accused of "allegedly conspiring in a series of anti-nationalist schemes in order to overthrow the Turkish state and planning an armed *coup d'état* against the government." During the turmoil which led to daily arrests throughout the 2008 and 2009, not only the secularist opposition was dismissed but the headscarf controversy and the previous charges brought against the AK Party were basically forgotten. At the same time, despite widespread fear for retaliation, pro-Kemalist sentiments continued to surge, especially among the youth. On a positive note, not banning the AK Party contributed to advance the democratization process and enhanced Turkey's image in the West, particularly on its way to the EU membership.

Meanwhile, AK government was harshly criticized by the opposition parties and the non-Kurdish public upon disclosing its plans for a general amnesty of PKK members and reconciliation with the Kurds through implementation of a series of socio-political reforms which might end the Turkish military's continued struggle with the separatist PKK (Kurdistan Workers' Party) attacks since 1984. The leader of Kurdish rebels Abdullah Ocalan has been in jail since 1999. The government's enthusiasm and ability to deliver on its promise of leniency for those willing to give up the armed struggle was tested on October 19, 2009 when 34 rebels surrendered to the authorities in Silopi amidst a cheering crowd of Kurdish men and women who welcomed their arrival. This scene, which might have pleased the EU commissioners, infuriated the general Turkish public, particularly the families of the fallen Turkish soldiers during the 25 year history of the conflict. The PKK has been engaged in a persistent war with hit-and-run attacks on Turkish territory along its southeast border which resulted in an estimated 40,000 deaths.

Despite domestic turmoil, in international meetings Mr. Erdogan and his government officials project an influential image and represent Turkey's independent agency over expanding democratic initiatives such as eradication of the "deep state", addressing freedom of speech and human rights, as well as maintaining its resolution on the "Kurdish Opening." The government also declares that it stands in defense of *moderation* in Islam, as well as in preservation of the republican principles. Additionally, it seems willing to advocate, in practicality, a participatory policy seeking input from all segments of the society for the sake of continuing "vernacular" dialogues. In Fuller's opinion through numerous transformations, re-alignments and trials Turkish society finally appears to have reached a new-found consensus concerning "what real 'secularism' should mean, and have carried the torch for not just proposing but for actually implementing reform while building respect for the Islamic past and tradition."[8]

Yet not many modern scholars share Graham Fuller's optimism on Turkey's achievements in providing a widely-accepted model for harnessing Islamic fundamentalism and *practicing* a new version of secularism. Taha Jabir al-Alwani, an Islamic scholar, believes Turkey proposes a unique case and the "model" it purports to be can neither be applied nor accepted by the rest of the Islamic countries. In an essay entitled, "Reflections on the 'Moderate Muslims' Debate," al-Alwani claims:

> Ever since it [Turkey] abolished the *khalifah* in March 1924, it has continued to swing between Kemalist secularism, which is openly hostile to religion, and Islam, which has sought to protect itself and keep what it can of Islamic identity alive. Turkish secularists moved away from Islam because they thought that Islam had, for many centuries, made Muslim rulers responsible for protecting the Ottoman people, whose only relation to the "family of Osman" was Islam. Therefore, they sought to put a complete divider between these secularists and Islam so that they could take Turkey back to its pre-Islamic paganism (*wathaniyah)* and realize their dream of joining Europe. Non-secular Turks, however, consider belonging to Islam and Turkey's leadership of the Muslims to be important elements of their nation's glory…[the] train of thought for both parties in Turkey is the glory of Turkey and how to revive it. The Turkish mind cannot rid itself of the pressure of Islamic memories. [9]

Whereas Turks take pride in the past, al-Alwani might be misleading in his analysis regarding his assertion that Turkey wants to revive its Islamic past. On the contrary, in Turkey the desire to join the Western world is so prevalent that, it manifests its stronghold among average citizens' daily conversations. Turks are weary of the prolonged wait, and frequent roadblocks which signal rejection and coercion. They are equally disappointed upon European nations' reluctance regarding their bid to join the EU. Anyone can cite at least two good reasons for Turks' growing impatience: delay tactics and counter-resistance by the Europeans. The facts surrounding the issue are twofold: Turks were told to "wait" before they were even allowed to start the application procedure; secondly, they met resistance from their European neighbors during each individual phase of their application. When the EU granted Greece—Turkey's old-time foe and current friend—acceptance, the Turkish public sentiment reflected ultimate distrust and desire to quit the EU race. Furthermore, when the Greek Cypriot Administration gained admission into the EU as the sole representative of the Republic of Cyprus on May 1, 2004, the Turkish Cypriots who own equal rights of representation in the affairs of the island, were not represented at all. Such developments led to an additional "crisis of trust" between Turks and the EU nations.

Despite severe opposition from countries such as Austria and even Germany, its long-time ally, Turkey held tight to its plan of joining the EU and continued to move along that path. On July 30, 2008 the EU welcomed a decision by Turkey's highest court not to ban the ruling AK Party on charges of Islamist activities. On November 5, 2008, the

European Commission declared Turkey a "functioning market economy," which marked a crucial gain towards acceptance into membership. On December 18, 2008 the EU agreed to initiate talks with Turkey on two additional policy areas, basically on 10 out of the 35 chapters. By then, Turkey had provisionally completed talks on just one of the areas.[10]

"Still, joining the EU is almost a national goal," remarked a young Turkish student. Then, is it feasible to conclude that rather than leading the Muslims with the antiquated *khalifah* system (as al-Alwani suggested), Turkey is actually mobilizing to lead the Muslim world in its ability to transform Islamism, re-interpret secularism and define modernism in its *own* terms, *by its own means*? On the other hand, discussions centered on the women's rights issue portray a blurred image.

With reference to terms such as *Kemalist* and *Islamist*, which are frequently utilized in this analysis, Jenny B. White asserts that both are "self-ascriptive terms referring to groups of people reactively polarized around certain issues."[11]

> The iconic Kemalist position combines a kind of authoritarian democracy with a Westernized secular lifestyle. Kemalists are concerned to safeguard laicism and its guarantees of free choice of lifestyle, particularly for women, but limited choice in the realms of religion and ethnicity....Self-defined Kemalists imagine themselves to be 'modern,' liberal, secular, and individualistic. They imagine Islamists to be 'traditional,' authoritarian, patriarchal, religiously fanatic and collectivist....Each side imagines itself to be free of the characteristics of the other...Kemalists and Islamists have a complicated relationship to Islam; this complexity is reflected in the varieties of political expression in Islam (29-31).

Having spent some time in Turkey during her graduate studies, White has achieved what most foreign observers tend to miss about Turkey: the ability to operate through the center of the cultural milieu which she conducts her research on. Centering herself in the historical consciousness and discourse of the Turkish people,[12] White successfully delineates and differentiates common errors typically unbeknownst to foreign scholars— such as the difference between the two related set of terms, i.e. "*secular*" and "*secularism*" versus "*laic*" and "*laicism*". These terms, as White asserts, require special attention as they carry separate meanings for each group that they represent. In her interpretation of the differences between such terms within the Turkish cultural context White asserts:

> '*Secular*' refers to people who present themselves as being nonreligious or who believe their religious beliefs to be a private, rather than public affair. "*Secularism*" is the separation of state and religion; *laicism* is the

subordination of religion to the state. The state controls the education of religious professionals and their assignment to mosques and approves the content of their sermons. It also controls religious schools and the content of religious education and enforces laws about the wearing of religious symbols and clothing in public spaces and institutions. Islamists have demanded an end to state control of public religious expression.[13]

For purposes of clarity it is important to elucidate the circumstances which originally led to the adoption of reforms including "separation of state and religion,"—which dismantled the Ottoman allegiance to the Islamic belief in *"din wa dawla"* (unity of religion and state)—with the foundation of the Republic of Turkey on October 29, 1923. After the abolition of the *khalifa* (the caliphate) system on March 3, 1924, the monopoly of the religious orders, brotherhoods, *dervish* and *tekke* lodges in the Ottoman society were outlawed. Evidently the ambitious members of the clergy were quite incensed about these unprecedented measures which ended their reign of supremacy and high regard among the faithful. They could not possibly agree to lose their grip and influence over the masses who had abided by the strict authority of religious leaders for centuries. Basically, through planned provocation instigated by the clergy, the republican reforms were met with brutal protest, causing large-scale unrest, violence and public anarchy. Consequently, the Republican regime hardened its policy on control of religion, risking further antagonism from disconcerted religious leaders and their supporters. Gradually, through the measures adopted by the administration, as White remarked "religious authority was replaced by secular law and religious affairs came under state bureaucratic control. Instead of religion, nationalism was taught as the new unifying principle."[14]

However, since the termination of religious authority over state affairs, followers of secularism have also experienced resistance. Often they feel threatened with the idea of "religious authority" eventually winning over secularism. Secular Turks avoid the thought of an "Islamic revolution" which might replace the republican ideals of the 1920s and 1930s. Therefore, Mustafa Kemal's ideals and reforms are firmly identified with secularism as they are endorsed exclusively by the followers of the same group rather than the right-wing, the conservative and fundamentalist Turks.

Interestingly, the AK (JP) Party administrators have publicly announced that they endorse not only the secularist but the republican aspects of Mustafa Kemal's ideals as well as the Republic's constitution. Yet the party politics and its wide base of followers project an incongruent image and less enthusiasm for the ideals sanctioned during the structuring of the Kemalist principles. On the other hand, in metropolitan areas and large cities, many college students cover their hair with scarves despite wearing tight fitting designer jeans with American brand names. In order to attend classes or take exams they wear wigs.

Besides being part of an obvious cultural confusion in their adoption of Western images, average income groups are also nostalgic about the Ottoman past. They show a renewed interest in Ottoman material culture, music, arts and literary achievements. Never had Turkish society manifested such a profound admiration and indulgence in Ottoman calligraphy, Iznik tiles, Sufi music and poetry, not since the end of the Ottoman era. Small shops in the archaic Covered Bazaar of Istanbul are booming with business as they cater to more local consumers than foreign tourists. Among the most sought-after relics of the Ottoman past are traditional textiles, silk cloth, antique Ottoman coins, old books, water-pipes—the *hokkah*— quill pens, Ottoman musical instruments, old manuscripts and photographs, silver and brass household utensils. In such a revivalist environment *Ottomanesque* themes and motifs grow in popularity as most Turks begin to praise and collect the cultural remnants of their Ottoman ancestors without fear of criticism from otherwise secular Turks. It is likely that at the dawn of the twenty-first century Turkey stands at the threshold of an "enlightened Ottoman renaissance," a unique phenomenon which can be analyzed through a new set of exegeses. For instance in his 2009 novel entitled *Masumiyet Müzesi (Museum of Innocence)* the Nobel-winning author Orhan Pamuk assigns his narrator/protagonist the task of establishing a "virtual museum" in order to capture the diminishing memory and accurate spirit of the past.

By reviving the Ottoman past are Turks seeking "wholeness" and continuity within their history? Are they looking for the "missing link"? Or, is Turkey still enduring the pains of growth as it tries to achieve its long-established goal of attaining "democratic freedoms"? Turks have been criticized by the members of the European Union who rejected Turkey's application based on allegations of laxity on issues such as "freedom of speech" and "human rights." The fact that Turkish democratic process had been interrupted more than once by military interventions, have taught them substantial lessons. To this effect, unlike previous decades, in present-day Turkey discussions about "politically charged" matters are now considered a natural outcome of democracy. However do all dare express their opinions openly? *Tesettur*, (not only as *veiling* but as a life-style)[15] among other popular issues, has been one of the most frequently discussed topics in Turkish media since the early 1980s as it circumvents and alters the image of the "modern" Turkish woman and stands as one of the most documented and ostracized symbols of Islamic revivalism, no matter how deceptive such a classification might be.

Despite the brief shadow of fear cast by the Ergenekon controversy, Turkish society is certainly struggling to transcend its archaic ideals through a vigorous social transformation. The state order is transfigured; the original Constitution (1924) has been revised and amended twice, respectively in 1961 and 1982. As a direct outcome of the 1980 military rule, the 1982 constitution has been criticized by many. Further amendments are likely to be added to its legislative, executive and judiciary organs as time goes by. Meanwhile, the election system is renewed as the roles of the political parties are continuously being re-evaluated. These historical developments indicate that Turkey has committed itself to a profound act of revitalization whose ramifications for Turks, but for women in particular, portend deeper inferences than what were originally predicted.

In general, women do not want to give up their hard-won rights; with or without the headscarf, Anatolian women are determined to safeguard their equal standing with men. Women on both ends of the scale seem to have a stake in learning lessons from the past. Most Turkish women are following in their grandmothers' footsteps as they actively strive to attain professional positions with graduate and advanced degrees. On the other hand, a great majority of educated women in *tesettur* choose not to work, particularly after marriage. Some of these women like being controlled by men and accept a secondary position. In this respect, men exert their dominance and superiority over women's affairs and choices. Gradually, submission leads to spiritual surrender, isolation and psychological submission of women. Another group of *tesettur* women carry their headscarves merely as political badges, or to rally the crowds as they receive substantial benefits from the power structure in return. Whatever the cause might be, women clad in *tesettur* clothing are consciously projecting an image different from the republican legacy and the Turkish Constitution in its present (2009) form. Clearly there is still work to be accomplished in this field. The following section provides a constructive analysis with regard to Turkish women's historical struggles and modern challenges which they might face at the turn of the twenty-first century.

Historical Inferences

Since the 1980s Islamic trends have begun to rise rapidly among Turkish women. Their earliest attributes were novel fashion styles in clothing which seemed, at least in the beginning, as usual tendencies entertaining women's legitimate desire to express freedom of choice in their dress codes. On the other hand, with the spread of global Islamic resurgence, which claimed to bring freedom of choice to women's lives, there came severe restrictions and liabilities which re-organized women's public roles and places within an individual society. These advances trailed alongside numerous legal issues which conflicted with the Turkish Constitution and its legal codes which paraphrase women's dress codes, as well as their religious, educational and political involvement in the society.

Concerning legal issues, significant controversies arise within the family system when men, women and children find themselves caught in bitter struggle with impending legal troubles, such as denial of inheritance rights or divorce to women. These problems usually originate from practices of polygamy, adultery, or domestic abuse directed towards women and children. Gradually women's legal rights in marriage—an innovation once introduced by the Republican reforms—are either dismissed or annulled in revisionist practices fostered by Shar'ia-style tendencies popularly held among men.

Today a group of Turkish women live muted and secluded lives, facing oppression at home or in the work place, depending where their priorities are positioned. Despite serious efforts which generated a substantial interest in women's rights in the late 1980s, there is still a wide gap between the "public" and the "private" spheres for women in Turkey. Most women who endure abuse at home, or in the work place do not press charges; if they do, they are not taken seriously. Legislative measures prove ineffective when it comes to bringing charges against family members. Children, parents and ailing relatives are usually taken care of by women under "unpaid work." Subordination grows as women suffer silently.

Nonetheless, as Islamic revivalism makes inroads and pierces through traditional Turkish values and reforms, many conservative women express satisfaction and pleasure in hopes of attaining "greater liberties" under the auspices of an Islamic mobilization. Meanwhile, prominent women such as Prime Minister Mr. Erdogan's wife and Mrs. Gul, the Turkish first-lady, wear *tesettur-style* long coats and head-scarves in strict alliance with their husbands' religio-political policies, dismissing extensive criticism from secular Turks. Those who oppose *tesettur* accuse others of "exploiting *tesettur*" and using the "religious freedom argument as a legitimate excuse in order to conceal their actual motives." Secularists perceive "*tesettur*" as the product of an antagonistic, "anti-secularist ideology" which might foreshadow a radical change, such as "instituting an Islamic theocracy in Turkey." On the other hand, *tesettur*-fans insist that their headscarves and long coats are not necessarily attached to a political agenda; their "pious appearance" and *tesettur* life-styles should not be perceived as an indicator of a "political crusade." Phases of women's occasional conversion from secularism to fundamentalism, from fundamentalism to modernism,—to ultra-modernism—as well as challenges and consequences involved in adapting to new life-styles, will be discussed in the following review of the Turkish women's long struggle of emancipation.

The Long and Winding Road

From a historical perspective, since the beginning of the twentieth century Islamic revivalism in Turkey has surfaced on a rising scale during times of political instability and social unrest, mainly during the past fifty years. Following each upheaval, constitutional principles and republican reforms have gone through various alterations and received "tailored looks" as they were eventually "fitted" to the taste of the specific political party in power. Henceforth, any study of the Turkish state from a socio-political perspective entails a basic understanding of not only the republican reforms and civil liberties but their basic components such as the rights of women, within the general milieu of mobilization which ushered in the reforms. Clearly, a brief look at the state's willingness to enhance women's causes, the amendments and policies which were introduced by the first Republican Constitution, as well as the force of opposition against proposed reforms during the early days of the Republican regime might be helpful.

Towards the end of the nineteenth century the Ottoman Empire was crumbling under the heavy weight of capitulations. The economic decline which had started almost a century before was hastened by the partition of its lands by European nations. The 1900s were troublesome years for Turks marked with threat of foreign occupation, domestic strife, poverty and hunger. As their resilience was being harshly tested, Turks did not have many choices. Surrender would only accelerate their devastation under the rule of an incompetent Sultan who had been cooperating with the British in order to secure a safe passage for himself.

Turks declared a national war of independence in order to regain their sovereignty by establishing a major defense line around their ancestral homeland known as Anatolia. To the astonishment of their enemies, in less than four years they emerged victorious—militarily rather than economically—from formidable circumstances, in defense of their motherland. With the organization of the Turkish Grand National Assembly on November 1, 1922, an independent Turkish state was officially formed.

In the aftermath of the Lausanne Peace Treaty signed on July 24, 1923, the Republican People's Party was established (September 9, 1923), electing Mustafa Kemal as its first chairman. The party leaders immediately adopted reforms in order to "modernize" the political, judicial and educational affairs of the state. Meanwhile, their efforts were frequently hampered by the hardliners within the National Assembly who objected to the abolition of the Sultanate, the eradication of the caliphate and the newly established Parliament itself.

As Turks gradually recovered from the losses of the war and moved towards establishing a democratic system, the newly elected members of the Parliament had already voted to abolish the Sultanate which meant a major blow for the supporters of the Sultanate and the Caliphate. Having failed to obstruct the Kemalist mobilization spearheaded by the young Parliament, the last Ottoman Sultan, Mehmet Vahdettin VI escaped to Malta on November 17, 1922, with the aid of the British who had been conspiring with Vahdettin in building a powerful front against the spread of Kemalist ideology. Yet their subsequent efforts to re-establish the Caliphate and re-appoint the Sultan as "the caliph of Muslims," first in Malta, and later in Mecca proved ineffective. His final residence became San Remo, Italy where he died in 1926. Later he was buried in Aleppo, Syria. The last Caliph Abdul Mejid II (1922-1924) was the cousin of Mehmet Vahdettin VI. The caliphate system was officially abolished on March 3, 1924, proclaiming an end to the leadership role of Ottomans within the long history of Islam. The last successor of the Ottoman dynasty Osman Ertugrul Osman died in Istanbul on September 23, 2009. Born in Yildiz Palace in 1912, he was only twelve years old when he was sent to exile with his family in 1924. However since 1991 he had been living in Istanbul due to an amnesty granted to his family.

As the new government eradicated the caliphate and the sultanate, the centuries-old Ottoman imperial systems were eventually deemed dysfunctional. Religion and religious affairs were no longer connected to the affairs of the state. However in the newly established civil order people were ought to maintain their freedom in order to conduct religious rituals and follow their habits of worship. In other words, there would be no separation or discrimination among Turkish citizens who are Muslims, Christians, Armenians and Jews. People would be able to follow their faith and perform their religious duties as freely as they used to during the days of the Empire.

On the other hand, the old order of state-sponsored Muslim institutions, schools, foundations and their employees had already lost their privileges. Without doubt, such a dramatic alteration of the established order sent tremors to the governmental structure and shook the administrative hierarchy of the world's leading Muslim state. It also marked a radical break from the Empire's imperialistic aspirations. From the perspective of the newly established state, the transformation undertaken by the parliament was not only a matter of vital interest for every Turkish citizen but of dire necessity as well. Nevertheless, for the conservative and the fundamentalist right-wing hardliners, the Kemalist reforms brought significant changes which disturbed the established order of the Ottoman society. The mullahs, sheiks and tribal leaders quickly expressed their resentment against the centralization of the state; they wanted to preserve their old privileges and expand their authority over the regions they represented. Their clandestine efforts to revive the old order through violence were restrained by government forces. Sheihk Said led a major Kurdish insurrection in eastern Turkey, on February 13, 1925. On December 13, 1930 a group of men among the Nakshibandi order organized a bloody attack in Menemen, near Izmir, killing three unarmed officials. The young lieutenant named Mustafa Fehmi Kubilay (age 24) approached the rebels and attempted to speak with the leader of the insurgency. Instead, he was shot and decapitated by the man who reportedly drank the young man's blood as the crowd clapped and cheered in approval.

Thus, like an ominous curse, the separationist and fundamentalist ideologies set off an inevitable polarization among Turks for decades to come. Despite a few attempts for reconciliation, Turkey's seculars, fundamentalists and Kurds still remain adversaries with irreconcilable set of issues and goals.

Separation of State and Religion:
Mustafa Kemal's Reforms

Why did Mustafa Kemal's reform ideology generate so much love and hatred at the same time? In order to assess the general framework of his plans for the newly established Turkish nationhood, one needs to analyze Kemal's position on the duty of the state. Actually the novelty of the plan rested in separation of religion and state affairs while granting numerous provisions on freedom of religious worship and individual conscience. The democratic ideals which he envisioned to summon included certain prerequisites centered on the principle of *secularism*.[16] Naturally the reforms would take considerable time to be rooted but the nation was young; the Turkish people had already demonstrated enormous patience, devotion and determination to replace an antiquated system of governance. The new democracy was going to give *agency* to the people rather than the Sultan.

Turks had discovered a national hero, a liberator, in Mustafa Kemal, who had rescued his country not only from foreign invasion but from the autocratic, imperialist rule of the Ottoman Sultan. His goals included eradicating poverty, illiteracy and class differences within the Turkish society. His credo was based on an altruistic policy; the majority of the people were ready to follow him. The dynamic and self-proclaimed leader of a tired nation asserted that he is ready to make the ultimate sacrifice in defense of the Republic: "Give me liberty or give me death!" or *"Ya Istiklal, Ya Olum!"*

Indeed, the republican reforms brought radical changes soon after the caliphate was abolished. In addition to introducing a coordinated series of improvements in governmental organization, implementing a sense of continuity in state affairs was equally important to preserve the Turkish identity. By establishing a *"renaissance frame of mind,"* the judicial, legislative and executive branches of the state would be modernized. Eliminating bribery, favoritism, coercion and corruption; replacing old-fashioned mental attitudes and the sluggishness of the Ottoman state with new ideas and establishing dynamic educational institutions were listed among the prerequisites of the reform ideology. Mustafa Kemal referred to Ottoman statesmen as "the gendarmes of the foreign capital" and criticized their admiration for "Westernism" as pitiful idolatry of colonialism. Some aspects of the Ottoman past were "decadent"; therefore he recommended adopting "a new sense of enlightened nationhood" and taking pride in the Turkish national identity.[17]

The Ministry of Shari'a and Foundations was replaced by the Chairmanship of Religious Affairs and the Directorate of Foundations under the supervision of the Prime Minister's office. Religious schools were closed on March 3, 1924 with the enforcement of the Unification of Education Law. Schools and educational matters were combined under the Ministry of National Education. Turban and fez were banned as hats became the official headgear for men. The provisions about headgear came to be known as the "Hat Law" and it was promulgated on November 25, 1925. Mustafa Kemal took the lead in introducing the new law and set the fashion in trend as he began wearing handsome hats during each public appearance. In his opinion a ban on traditional Muslim garbs and associative symbols in attire would erase differences in class, rank and religious order which constituted one of the major obstacles to elimination of stratification in Ottoman society for centuries.

Meanwhile, the new reforms which were taking effect gradually transcended traditional assumptions. The abolition of dervish lodges and the titles of *tarigahs* (religious sects or orders) took place in November 1925. Despite the hardships and numerous setbacks, the Turkish nation was clearly being re-invented by state-sponsored reforms.

The Turkish Civil Code, which was accepted on February 17, 1926, replaced the Ottoman Civil Code and the Shari'a law. Once the news about termination of these old laws reached the masses, large scale public protests, demonstrations and rioting ensued. Despite considerable resistance staged by the fundamentalists, the legislation was secularized; the Code of Obligations, the Criminal Code and the Commercial Code were both re-written and re-interpreted according to the new ideals adopted by the secular Republic.

Introducing a new Turkish alphabet was believed to improve the literacy level specifically among women. On November 1, 1928, following lengthy discussions with linguists and academicians, Mustafa Kemal's reform-minded team decided to replace the Arabic alphabet with the Latin alphabet. Kemal personally conducted public tutorial sessions introducing the new letters and their phonetic representations at town-hall meetings. In order to facilitate compatibility and ease in commerce and trade with the Western world, the antiquated systems of measurement and weight were replaced with the metric and cubic systems in 1931.

In 1917 due consideration was given to introduce a new "Family Law" which would end the widespread influence and monopoly of religion and the authority of Muslim clergy in this matter. Originally, among numerous Tanzimat era reforms (1839-1876), the most significant one was implemented by the Ottoman state itself and it involved the "codification" of the Shari'a law (compiling and restating the law of jurisdiction in certain areas, such as in women's rights), in order to establish a legal code which will address any problems women might experience, whether they were married or not. Initially this measure helped resolve conflicts and hastened delivery of justice however it antagonized the clergy who would later disapprove many republican reforms probably for the same reason. As a matter of fact, Noah Feldman claims that the state's interference led to the elimination of Islamic scholars' authority over matters that concerned people's personal lives. The state-induced law governed not only the state itself but the entire Ottoman livelihood:

How the scholars lost their exalted status as keepers of the law is a complex story, but it can be summed up in the adage that partial reforms are sometimes worse than none at all. In the early 19th century, the Ottoman Empire responded to military setbacks with an internal reform movement. The most important reform was the attempt to codify Shariah. This Westernizing process, foreign to the Islamic legal tradition, sought to transform Shariah from a body of doctrines and principles to be discovered by the human efforts of the scholars into a set of rules that could be looked up in a book. Once the law existed in codified form, however, the law itself was able to replace the scholars as the source of authority. Codification took from the scholars their all-important claim to have the final say over the content of the law and transferred that power to the state.[18]

The Education Reform: A Renaissance

As to women's education and rights, particularly in the area of suffrage (L. *enfranchisement*) extraordinary steps were taken. In order to preserve the family unit and protect the rights of married women, polygamy was forbidden. Marriages were required to be performed in accordance with the Civil Code, as opposed to the then popular semi-formal or custom-mandated religious ceremonies. Divorces were ordered to take place after a court decree. However the decree was not legally recognized until after the abolition of the Shari'a law in 1926.

Meanwhile educated women were involved in enlightenment of the society. They were asking their support of the emancipation movement basically through widely-circulated essays and editorials published in journals intended for female readership. For instance, an article authored by Perihan Arif Sariguzel was published in a women's journal entitled *Kadinlar Dunyasi* (Women's World), (1913-1921). The author criticized the subordinate roles attributed to women:

> Today women are created solely for the purpose of men and dedicate all their strength and sacrifice themselves and their lives to their husband's needs. To this slavery, is added ignorance.[19]

Her views were shared by another female author, Feride Izzet Selim Gedikpasa who emphasized the importance of education for women in her article entitled, "Kadinlarimizda Luzum-i Tahsil," (The Necessity of Education for Our Women). She remarked: "Ignorance, bigotry and captivity…these are oppressing our very souls and killing us."[20] At the same time an anonymous author justly indicated that Islam mandates women's education and shuns ignorance: "Prophet Muhammad required education and science for every believer, both male and female. Clearly humanity will prosper through knowledge and the Prophet ordered us to be educated; then why dwell in ignorance?"[21] Essentially during the second half of the nineteenth-century further steps were taken to educate women. For instance, in response to

Darulmuallim (Teachers Training School for Boys) which was opened in 1840, the first *Darulmuallimat* (Teachers Training School for Girls) was started in 1870. Additionally, in 1842, during the reign of the reformist Sultan Abdulaziz (1830-1876), a number of schools for girls—ranging from elementary to high school—were being operated in Istanbul. During the modernist era which launched a new set of reforms known as the *Islahat Reformlari* (1856), not only girls' future education was guaranteed but the centralization of educational system was implemented as a state policy. One of the decrees stated: "Schools have a duty to educate everyone, regardless of gender or politics. However their curriculum and teachers will be appointed and supervised by the Meclis-i Maarif (the Ministry of Education)." [22]

In spite of these minor developments not all women were able to attain equal opportunity in education. Income levels and class differences played a significant role. Education remained a privilege for the elite until certain measures were taken to eliminate the educational divide between men and women, the rich and the poor. In 1868 the Regulation for Public Education (*Maarif-i Umumiye Nizamnamesi*) guaranteed elementary education for all female children between the ages of 6 and 11.[23] However the most outstanding reform, initiated by the 1876 Constitution (*Kanun-i Esasi*), comprised a large-scale mobilization which finally instituted the nationalized public education and mandated elementary education for all school-age children throughout the Ottoman lands.[24] By 1886, several middle schools were opened for girls.

During the later decades of the Ottoman rule another system gained popularity among well-to-do Turkish families. Since girls were not allowed to attend the same school with boys, parents who were able to afford private tutors at home started *konak* education for their daughters. Most of these families lived in large "mansions"; therefore *"konak"* education referred to private tutors involved in homeschooling of girls. The teachers were usually female and western-educated Turks or foreigners, who taught a variety of subjects from math, literature and languages to music and painting for young and aspiring heiresses of affluent Ottoman families.

One of the most gifted graduates of *konak* education was Fatma Aliye Hanim (1864-1924) who later became an accomplished author, translator and pioneer warrior for women's rights. She owed part of her success to her father's distinguished status and learned the merits of scholarship from him at a young age. Cevdet Pasha was a highly educated Ottoman intellectual, a member of the *ulema* who authored *Mecelle* (the Ottoman Civil Code), based on the principles of the Hanefi school of Islamic Law or *fiq'h*. Fatma Aliye's advocacy for the improvement of women's status bothered the fundamentalist media; she was scorned by opponents of women's education. Despite the rigid cultural norms of the era, which limited women's freedom to a large extent, she continued calling attention to women's inferior status. *Nisvan-i Islam* (Muslim Women), which she wrote in 1891, focuses on inspiring women for better roles. Her editorials were continuously published in women's magazines and newspapers, such as in *Hanimlara Mahsus Gazete* (The Ladies' Own Gazette) which was published from 1895 throughout the 1920s. She persistently emphasized the importance of education and called it a "God-given right" of women:

> Since Cenab-Allah (the Almighty), who is the possessor of the virtue of knowledge bestowed it on all of his subjects, male and female, [then] is it the right of man to deny it to women? [25]

Women's enfranchisement was at the forefront of the women's reform movement even during the late Ottoman period when the society and the political institutions were going through radical changes. Between 1868 and 1908 numerous journals and newspapers with liberal tendencies emerged. These publications maintained a keen interest in women's issues by publicizing women's struggles and their demands through editorial columns. In 1868 an anonymous article appeared in the first Ottoman newspaper entitled *Terakki* (Progress), which was owned by two men, Ali Rasit Bey and Filip Efendi. In an article written by three women who asked to remain anonymous segregation in local transportation vehicles, restaurants and theaters was protested. The authors questioned "the logic of discrimination between men and women as to the seating." Similarly, both Ida B. Wells (May 4, 1884) and Homer Plessy (June 7, 1892) had initiated courageous crusades against segregation on trains which led to historic U.S. Supreme Court decisions and amendments. Turkish women had put "separate but equal" on trial at an earlier date than their African American counterparts. The authors of the article asserted that although they paid the same fare, the train cars reserved for women were unclean and dilapidated compared to those reserved for men, which were remarkably cleaner and modern. Women also protested the rules which forced them to take the dimly-lit side streets and dark alleys, rather than following the main road, as they were ordered to avoid any encounter with men according to the norms of the Ottoman culture.[26] On a different note, in 1869 an illiterate Muslim woman questioned the practice of polygamy and its negative effects on family life in a bitter letter she managed to have published in *Terakki-i Muhadderat*, with the assistance of a mediator. [27]

With regard to women who lived outside Istanbul and who were not as educated as the women in urban areas,—the "Anatolian women"—they emerged from seclusion initially during the National War of Independence while they volunteered their services in support of men. Whereas women became the new face of hope and liberation for a struggling nation, the rising tide of Turkish patriotism was reinforced with female labor force at the battlefront. In resistance to occupation forces, women ran to the aid of men and demonstrated their commitment as nurses, carriers, laborers, volunteer soldiers and guides. Women in villages and rural areas labored at ammunition factories, carried heavy weaponry to the front lines, cooked, cleaned and attended the wounded soldiers at decrepit army hospitals.

The sacrifices endured by the first generation of pioneer women did not go unnoticed. Emancipation and equality for Turkish women came in the mid-twenties in the form of rights and privileges they gained directly through state-sponsored policies and amendments to the Constitution. However their emancipation did not guarantee rights and privileges of future generations unless younger women stepped up to protect, defend and maintain the continued existence of reforms vigilantly. As a matter of fact political developments of the 1990s verified the urgency of this matter.

In the aftermath of WWI and the National War of Independence, it became clearly evident that women's nationalistic efforts and patriotism had already embarked a popular movement, legitimizing women's aspirations for emancipation. Nonetheless, some women still favored the continuity of Ottoman cultural norms over the reforms. They seemed complacent and satisfied with the dominance of patriarchal values in their personal lives. Women feared that by seeking equality they would lose respect within the family structure. Women's submissiveness benefited men immensely. Husbands in general were satisfied to see their wives acquiescent; so were the mullahs who still hoped to re-gain their past privileges in order to control the society, and define women's roles by dismissing their aspirations for education and emancipation. On the other hand, modern and reform-minded men sided with women's movement in order to voice their opposition against the influence of mullahs and the clergy upon the society. It would be many years before Turkish women could fully establish themselves with regard to civil liberties. On the other hand, in Western countries, particularly in the United States, the road to women's emancipation had also followed a complicated route. [28]

Turkish women obtained the right to vote and be elected first in municipal elections (1930), and later in village councils (1933). In 1934 following a victory in obtaining voting rights, they were also eligible to be elected into the Turkish Grand National Assembly. By 1937, 18 female deputies were elected, making up 4.5 % of the National Assembly, an all-time high, and a record which has not been matched since then.[29] However, despite ideological advancements which paved the way for further reforms, women were not allowed to establish autonomous political initiatives. For instance, the administration's refusal to authorize the Women's People's Party, which was established in June 1923, clashed with the principle of equality and freedom cited among the liberal parameters of the new state.[30]

Despite controversy and various challenges, throughout the first quarter of the twentieth century women's status gradually improved. "Women's movement" gained prominence within the mobilization efforts which launched the "Ataturk reforms." Among these grassroots reforms the most far-reaching was definitely the emancipation of women. Women achieved remarkable progress in joining the labor force and attaining political emancipation which were soon followed with pursuits of goals in educational, political and legislative arenas. Prior to these reforms, as W.E.B. DuBois once remarked, "women existed not for themselves, but for men; they were called after the men whom they were related to and "not after the fashion of their own souls."[31]

Without doubt Turkish women's emancipation signaled a landmark development on the route to *secularism* and nation-building. It also marked a major break from the burden of the past. As the Ottoman society's worn image was gradually being transformed, elevation of women's rights with the sponsorship of the state took women's rights and status argument to a different level.

In order to explicate the nature of complications related with seeking the public's approval for future reforms under hostile circumstances one has to be closely familiar not only with the specific characteristics of the Turkish republican ideals but also with the threat of mass rebellion and insurrections carried on tenaciously by the supporters of the *Shari'a law,* essentially the ultra-conservatives and the religious fanatics. Their hostility stemmed from Kemalist principles which had mandated the "liquidation of the 'theocratic remnants' of the Ottoman state and the establishment of a republican concept of citizenship."[32] On December 25, 1925, it was publicly announced that an extensive revolution was in place. "The new Republic of Turkey has no relationship to the old Ottoman state which is over and done with; it is merely a chapter in history books; we have cut all our ties with that portion of our history; actually you are witnessing the birth of the new Turkey."[33]

Mustafa Kemal's ultimate goal was to revive and elevate an exhausted nation, despite its limited resources and empty treasury, to the highest standards of civilization with vigor and prosperity. Nevertheless, as in his definition of "civilization", his *modus operandi* which outlined the parameters of the "new Republic was also 'the product of a Western' cultural orientation."[34] Henceforth, his policies concerning women's emancipation constantly provoked speculations and inquiries from his adversaries as to the origins of his reform ideology. They questioned whether such a forceful thrust for modernization was a consequence of changing times or a blueprint for a major conspiracy. Were reforms desired *by* women or rather imposed *upon* women? As Deniz Kandiyoti remarked, the changes introduced by the republican single-party politics were quite restrictive. On one hand they "opened up an arena for state-sponsored 'feminism', but at one and the same time circumscribed and defined its parameters" alongside those of other associations and cultural clubs.[35]

Despite relative confusion and uncertainties about the future of reforms, massive campaigns carried throughout the country convinced the majority of men and women to embrace the reforms. As numerous opportunities for self-enhancement began to emerge, women realized, possibly for the first time in the history of a long struggle for emancipation, that they could develop their skills mainly through education. Being hired by the public and private employment sectors as professional workers would help them advance their careers, improve their status and reach their goals both in personal and public domains.

As Kandiyoti observed, the prize did not come without a cost: "The authoritarian nature of the single-party state and its attempt to harness the 'new woman' to the creation and reproduction of a uniform citizenry aborted the possibility for autonomous women's movements."[36] Ironically, as pro-con arguments were being formulated around women's emancipation, only a few women openly participated in these debates. Those who attempted to voice their opinions endured criticism and public scorn. On the other hand, there were not many educated female activists who were willing to get involved and implement changes through emancipatory regulations. Only a few women were actually capable of forming alliances and contribute to the cause of emancipation during that era of transition. Rigid societal norms and men's influence upon women can be cited as chief reasons.

Nonetheless, as predicted, en route to Turkey's progress toward "true democracy and advanced levels of civilization" the future reforms were conceived as imminently auspicious developments indispensable for the stability of a republican democracy. Every Turkish citizen was expected to participate or support them. However, during the First National Assembly, as well as in 1924, there was profound resistance against voting by women, even among men who supported Mustafa Kemal throughout the struggle for national independence. Some were hard-liners who believed neither in women's rights nor in their enfranchisement. Because of their objection, the clause about the voting rights of "every Turkish citizen" was replaced with "every male Turk."

Setbacks and delay tactics could not halt the progress of women's advancement. Therefore, from the educated upper middle-class to lower income groups, almost everyone benefited immensely from women's emancipation. The reforms facilitated women's full participation in the social, economic and political life of the state in various roles. Factories demanded industrial workers and provided significant job opportunities where men and women were trained to develop various skills. Women were able to pursue training and educational goals not only at workplace but in newly established Turkish schools and universities, as well as in foreign countries through state-funded scholarships. Among hundreds of women who followed the "fashion of their souls" there were distinguished authors, poets, doctors, musicians, actresses, aviators, opera singers and one "Ms. Universe"—Keriman Halis—in 1932.

The Struggle for Emancipation: Halide Edip Adivar

The women's rights struggle in Turkey is marked with its progressive characteristics and noted as a "triumphant" movement ever realized in a Muslim and Middle Eastern society. One of the most ardent advocates of Turkish reforms was Halide Edip Adivar (1884-1964) whose life and career corresponded not only with the era of transition to modernization but with the harrowing years of the war for independence. Recognized as the leader of the women's emancipation movement in Turkey, Halide Edip Adivar was an internationally recognized author, a college professor, a war correspondent, an activist, and a public speaker.

Prior to the war she was actively engaged in the women's movement, establishing the Society for the Elevation of Women in 1908. She dedicated herself to the improvement of education for Turkish women and co-operation among women of the world. The suffragette movement which was still in development in Europe was readily embraced by the *Teali-i Nisvan Cemiyeti (Society for the Elevation of Women)*. Extremely fluent in English, Halide Edip was a well-recognized speaker among the British suffragettes. Her organization required English proficiency from its members, which facilitated the discussion of Turkish women's struggles in international meetings and proclaimed their agency in pursuit of emancipation throughout the world. Due to her pioneering efforts Turkish women's muted voice was being heard for the first time.

Following her graduation from American College for Girls in Uskudar, Istanbul, a private school for girls, she began her career as a young journalist contributing articles to a local newspaper in 1908. When her liberal views were met with resistance, she was forced to flee Istanbul and went into hiding first in Egypt, then in England. In 1910 she came in contact with a group of young intellectuals known as "Pan-Turanists." After joining their organization, she lectured on behalf of the group. Within this organization of men, Halide Edip was the only woman. The group called itself "Moral Turks" and argued that the origins of Turkish feminism actually lay in the rituals and practices of Shamanistic religion (ancestor worship), alongside the pre-Islamic Turkish culture in central Asia, which conferred sacred power on women.[37] In her lectures and editorials Halide Edip often espoused the view that it was not just Islam but the influence of long-standing Persian and Byzantine hegemonies upon Turkish culture that caused the gradual disintegration of women's once elevated status.

Nevertheless, it was her fiery address at Sultanahmet Square in Istanbul on May 23, 1919, which inspired and set the model for future generations of Turkish women. A young, educated, and emancipated Muslim woman was calling for a mass demonstration in protest of Izmir's occupation by the Greek forces. Her extraordinary zeal and predicament was the product of an awareness of the ever-present duality embedded in her identity. As a western-educated Muslim woman, her "Turkish-Muslim" identity was clearly reflected in her work. In the opening statement of her speech at Sultanahmet she remarked:

Muslims and Turks,

This is *the* darkest day and the darkest night in our lives….however there is no day in human life when the darkness is not banished by the daybreak …tomorrow is a new day; we hope it will bring us the brightest of days.[38]

Several years later, during an interview, with regard to "the most memorable" moment(s) in her life, she traced her evolution from a private citizen to a political activist as follows:

I believe that the Halide at Sultanahmet was not the ordinary Halide. I was convinced that sometimes the humblest and most anonymous individual could represent the high ideal of a great nation. The heart of the Halide of

that day was beating in response to all Turkish hearts, warning her of
approaching disaster... I was but a part of this sublime national madness.
Until we recovered Izmir in 1922 nothing else mattered for me in life at
all.[39]

In reality she spent most of her life responding to transitions around
her; she adjusted herself to sweeping transformations at the personal and
public level. When she first joined the resistance movement, she had
recently divorced her first husband who had brought a new wife to *their*
home through a second marriage. Halide Edip's refusal to succumb to
polygamy and challenge the social norms of her time was naturally
interpreted as an act of defiance stemming from "female pride." However
as a modern woman educated in a private college, she felt she was entitled
to seek her legal rights in marriage. With her two young sons—who were
still minors at that time—she chose to pursue an independent path. In later
years the characters in her novels would represent exceptionally resilient
women who aspired to become heroines with independent will and stern
determination. On the other hand her radical views would get her into
trouble with the new Turkish state in the long run.

In August 1919, Edip's controversial stance and support of the
American mandate (*manda* in Turkish), particularly during Turkish
struggle for independence, brought her unsolicited notoriety. She had set
off a major conflict with Mustafa Kemal, who used to be a close friend
and supporter of her ideas. The problem arose when a handful of
intellectuals, among whom Halide Edip held a central position, compiled a
letter addressed to Mustafa Kemal, suggesting that it was more realistic to
accept a "temporary American mandate" rather than perish in a deadly war
against the allied European nations. Surrender had never been an option
for Mustafa Kemal and he was prepared to take part in any battle in order
to halt the occupation. Halide should have known better. Still the petition
was sent to the American Congress signed by twenty-two individuals,
most of whom, including Halide Edip, were among Mustafa Kemal's long-
time friends. This incident, known as the "*manda* initation" (inviting
Americans to interfere, take control of Turkey which was then in its
weakest state) in Turkish history was organized to seek American
intervention. More precisely, it aimed to discontinue the War of
Independence which was expected to fail due to heavy casualties suffered
on the Turkish side. However both their plans for surrender and the *manda*
controversy sparked renewed enthusiasm among Turks to fight
colonialism by any means necessary.

As the *only* woman at the heart of the controversy who defended the
American mandate, Halide Edip quickly recovered from her ill-fated

demise when Istanbul was eventually occupied by the British on March 16, 1920. Upon observing the Parliament disbanded, she knew her life was in danger as the public spokeswoman of the new Republic. She fled to Ankara, which had become the new headquarters of Turkey's national resistance movement. From then on, a dedicated and most likely apologetic Halide Edip served on the Western front as a nurse, an interpreter, and a press secretary to Mustafa Kemal. Following the war, she got involved in relief efforts for women and their families who were widowed and dislocated by the tragedy of war. Due to her distinguished services she was promoted to the honorary rank of "corporal." Meanwhile she wrote and published extensively, both in Turkish and English, emphasizing Turkish women's achievements and future challenges.[40]

It is evident that, despite her idiosyncrasies, Halide Edip Adivar single-handedly brought forth an outstanding number of issues for deliberation into the public arena. Additionally, she was able to influence domestic politics of Turkish society in the 1920s on a wide range of issues such as the examination of women's multifaceted roles; the clash of modernism with tradition and challenges faced by women in a patriarchal society where men in general *expect* to be served by women. Surprisingly, in the twenty-first century these issues still remain unsettled within Turkish society. Moreover they constitute a major obstacle for women's political choices as prospects of public discourse are recently disengaged.

Interpreting the Millennium: Tansu Çiller

At first sight, Tansu Çiller seemed to have embraced one of the most distinguished assets of the Kemalist reforms—the right to represent and be represented—when she began to serve her nation as its first female prime minister. Her career, though a complex one, illustrates, the path chartered by secularism and its *transformative* power, which generated a new approach as a result of the turbulence centered on Turkey's socio-political environment in the twenty-first century.

As a matter of fact, Tansu Çiller's political life corresponds with one of the most chaotic eras in Turkey's political history as it was charged with incidents of political upheaval, lack of consensus among numerous political parties which represented different ideologies. The parties' inability to acquire the majority vote in order to establish a single-party government, led to successive coalition governments comprised of uncooperative party leaders and their mutually antagonistic supporters.

Mrs. Çiller formerly held a professional title as an economics professor educated in the United States. After her admission into the True Path Party

(Dogru Yol Partisi, DYP) she rapidly rose to power. Following the death of President Turgut Özal on April 17, 1993, Çiller was elected the Prime Minister in June 1993, replacing Mr. Süleyman Demirel, who became the President (*Cumhurbaskani* in Turkish). Several questions are yet to be answered about Çiller's rapid ascent to power. What could have prompted her unprecedented popularity among high-ranking party officials who were mostly male? Although she was a novice in circle of politics, she held several advantages which spoke directly to Turkish voters, specifically to women. Çiller was a young secular woman, dynamic, well-educated, extremely sociable and intelligent. Mother of two boys, she had also fulfilled the traditional role expected from a Turkish woman about mothering. Rather than taking her husband's last name in marriage, she had given her husband *her* own maiden name. She was fluent in English; she was extremely familiar with the West. As a professor of economics she could possibly navigate the course of the ailing Turkish economy with ease. Additionally, with her self-confident demeanor she seemed capable of enhancing Turkey's image in the West, and establishing close ties with the Europeans in order to facilitate Turkey's long-delayed acceptance into the EU. In short, Tansu Çiller was the "Turkish maverick"[41] who could serve as a role-model for women in Islamic countries, promoting the image of secular Turkey both as "Muslim and modern."

As a matter of fact, with her tailored mini-skirts, yuppie-ish designer suits, leather briefcases, modern make-up and chic hair-do Tansu Çiller became not only the embodiment of "success" but an icon, projecting a powerful public image for the "educated, emancipated and married Turkish woman" who could achieve ultimate success both at home and at work. In a relatively short time Mrs. Çiller managed to form a coalition government between the TPP and the Social Democratic Populist Party (Sosyal Demokrat Halk Partisi, SHP), whose representative body was composed of almost all-male members. Soon she was appointed the Prime Minister, remaining in power from June 25, 1993 until the elections of December 25, 1995. When her tenure ended, her rating among the female electorate—who made up almost half of the Turkish electorate, and who admired her as a role-model—was still at its highest. On the other hand, many female voters were forming an alliance with men in criticism of Tansu Çiller. These radical forces, which widely represented the general Turkish electorate from all classes, were soon going to play an inimical role in the political future of Turkey.

When the Welfare Party (Refah Partisi, RP) became the leading party, its chairperson Necmettin Erbakan—who was a U.S.-educated former college professor with a doctorate in engineering—established a coalition government with the DYP. The union of the RP with the DYP gave rise to the "Welfare-Path" coalition and the DYP chairperson Tansu Çiller was asked to participate in the newly formed government as the Minister of Foreign Affairs in addition to being the Deputy Prime Minister. Surely this union marked a turning point in Turkish political history when debates intensified on the rise of Islamic fundamentalism, causing further social and political disturbance. Prime Minister Erbakan represented, according to the secularists, a major separation from the Kemalist ideals and particularly from *laicism* with his veneration of religious worship, advocacy of public prayers and for instituting *mescits* (prayer rooms) in government buildings—a **first** in the Republic's eighty-seven year history. Meanwhile Mrs. Erbakan's *tesettur* clothing enraged not only the military generals but supporters of Ataturk's reforms. What secularists did not know then was that in less than a decade, *tesettur* was going to play a prominent role in Turkish politics. Mrs. Erbakan's "tesettur-act" represented merely an *overture* for the political melodrama that was about to debut while the rest of the actors were waiting in the wings for their turns on stage. Consequently, a new process began when the National Security Council issued a warning in its meeting on February 28, 1997 stating that the fundamentalism was on the rise. In addition to such precarious developments Prime Minister Necmettin Erbakan resigned on June 18, 1997 in order to transfer the prime ministry for a second time to Tansu Çiller, who was then his coalition-partner.

At this time Mrs. Çiller's attire was already reflecting radical changes and a break from her former image. Those who had been closely observing her rise to fame knew that she had started changing her image deliberately since her partnership with Erbakan began. She did not wear her usual designer suits any longer; instead she seemed to prefer midi-skirts which she completed with solid-color tunics, blouses. In addition to the length of her skirts, the jackets also grew taller which she usually covered with designer shawls reflecting her taste in color co-ordination. Gradually her blondish looks were transformed into a soft medium auburn until she literally became a brunette. Her silk scarves and shawls indicated a fundamental change as they complemented her new and conservative look during her popular public appearances. As Çiller was displaying a traditional style for the public, she was also espousing a renewed mind-set in her political dealings. She seemed to be a "conservatist-secular" yet less gregarious than she used to be.

With these policy shifts, and personal image transformations Tansu Çiller became the *first* publicly elected female official who succeeded in transfiguring modernism and re-interpreting secularism in her own terms.

Her model would be copied and replicated by the new-modernists and Islamist revivalists both at home and abroad as it facilitated the projection of "the *new-modern*, (highly educated and emancipated Turkish woman)" image. Meanwhile Çiller seemed to have gained further ambition to lead the country if and when the opportunity arose. Apparently she was looking forward to respond to the "needs" of a larger, more inclusive group rather than the secular Turks who had constituted the major thrust and support during her initial appointment as the prime minister. Indeed she was hoping to be able to form a second coalition government similar to the one she had formerly established in 1996 with Necmettin Erbakan, overthrowing her secular partner, Mesut Yilmaz. When Erbakan resigned from his position in 1997, she expressed interest in assuming power once again in order to chart the destiny of the Turkish people.

Contrary to her expectations, on June 19, 1997, President Demirel charged Mesut Yilmaz, who was then the chairman of the Motherland Party (Anavatan Partisi, ANAP) with the task of founding the new government. Yilmaz's appointment not only shattered Çiller's hopes of being re-elected for another term, but heralded an end to her political career which would permanently close in the aftermath of serious allegations of corruption.

Meanwhile, Turkish voters and the rest of the world looked on as one of the most unusually jam-packed coalition governments in history was being formed. Known as the "Main Left-D" (Anasol-D), the new government involved a partnership among three political parties, namely the Motherland Party (ANAP), the Democratic Left Party (DSP) and the True Path Party (DYP) established under the leadership of Mesut Yilmaz. The following seventeen months were going to prove equally vexing times in Turkish political history. As to Mrs. Çiller, she resigned from politics in 2002 after receiving a less than sufficient (10%) margin of votes. During her prime ministry she was unable to curb inflation which spiraled towards an economic melt-down. It was a tumultuous era for Turkey in many ways during which she proved ineffective in controlling the Kurdish separatists' continuous attacks on Turkish villages and the military personnel stationed near Turkey's southeastern border. Yet in Tansu Çiller Turks saw the transformation of a former secular female leader who gradually moved away from her long-established professional *center* and identity towards a newly-acquired, politically-geared conservative image as she opted to re-evaluate both her Muslim and secular identities, eventually choosing to settle for Islamic modernism which seemed to offer her political advancement—momentarily. Her surrender would have been more meaningful if only Çiller's Turkey and the late Benazir Bhutto's Pakistan had been similar constructs!

Looking back, the legacy of women's emancipation and activism in Turkey presents a diabolical view. Given the facts, clearly Halide Edip Adivar brought prominence to women's issues by supporting and advancing the status of Turkish woman in society. Although she was raised and educated in a fundamentally conservative society, she was unmistakably at the frontlines. At a personal level she claimed her own *agency*, and refused to be chastised by men. Additionally, she identified with the pioneers of the women's movement in the West and managed to carve a professional role both for herself and her sisters within the universal women's rights struggle, on behalf of the Turkish women. Meanwhile she fought, on a professional level, to attain equal rights in education, legal representation and voting *for* and *by* Turkish women.

Tansu Çiller, on the other hand, co-opted her secular image for a conservative look, almost relinquishing her former identity for political gains from feeble coalition partnerships. Her innuendos in setting the clock backwards by creating an identity-confusion for Turkish women during her tenure might be interpreted as betrayal of her own upbringing. More importantly, the office she occupied was a direct outcome of the republican reforms which sanctioned secularism. As opposed to Halide Edip's numerous scholarly publications, including editorials and speeches which revealed a well-grounded research about Turkish women's accomplishments throughout the history, Çiller did not produce a single publication to this effect. In her role as Turkey's first female prime minister (1993-1996), Mrs. Çiller could have been a significant source and an advocate for women's rights in order to improve women's health, education, abortion rights, legal and economic status within Turkey's patriarchal state system. In her leadership role as Turkey's top official her advocacy of women's issues was lacking. Currently she is listed among the Aspen Institute's Council of Women World Leaders, along with Madeline K. Albright and Angelina Merkel. Ironically the title of an interview conducted with her in June 1995 (published in the *Middle East Quarterly*) read: "Secularism is an indispensable principle for Turkey."[42]

Surprisingly, two notable women who shared so much in common— due to similar backgrounds in education and professional goals—could pursue such dissimilar paths and different agendas. Halide Edip Adivar's pioneering efforts clearly established the foundation to uphold the *agency* of secular, professional, independent-thinking, responsible, well-educated, compassionate and socially alert womanhood in Turkey.

Transforming Modernism

After almost a decade of provincialism, political corruption and a series of economic downturns combined with nationalistic crusades mandated by administrators who operated rather cautiously under the threat of military interventions, Turkey entered the twenty-first century with a different outlook. From a distance it appears to be a Muslim country with a thriving western appeal, where women project a new identity for themselves. The AK Party administration's determination to improve Turkey's approval rating by western credentials has paid off quickly in presenting a new image nestled in modernism. The country's new outlook is partly due to Turkish mobilization to join the European Union, which underlines economic reforms, instilling hopes of greater investment prospects and mutual profit both for Turks and foreign investors. For the first time in thirty odd years, inflation is reported to remain in single digits (6.2% in 2009, 10.4% in 2008); unemployment lurks around 7.9%; the real GDP growth forecasted for 2010 is 3.7%, a recovery from -6.5% estimated in 2009.[43] The Kurdish language, center of a long and unresolved debate, is allowed under a new law. The country's political and social landscape has been restructured and more changes are underway, since the EU demands Turkish military to distance itself from politics as the government aims to address further expansion and liberalization of human rights, as well as the freedom of speech. Yet controversies do exist, such as the 2006 court case which was set off by the Turkish author Orhan Pamuk—the winner of 2006 Nobel prize in literature—when he questioned Turkey's role in Armenian allegations of genocide.

Despite problems, since 1923 democratic discourses have conceded a favorable legacy of continuity in Turkey. The ripple effects of disruptions in democratic processes have rendered serious consequences such as prolonged military take-over, suppression of human rights and free speech, in addition to rising social and economic problems. Yet the democratic institutions have managed to survive, rendering hope about the unity of the Turkish state in the twenty-first century. Turkey remains the only Muslim country in the Middle-East which has maintained its allegiance to democracy and free elections over an extended period of time.

On the other hand, since 2002, a state-sponsored divergence from early commitment to Mustafa Kemal's ideals and a deeper immersion into Islamic indoctrination has been observed in Turkey. This trend is accompanied with concessions on freedom of expression and liberalization of free-speech, targeting the needs and desires of minority and ethnic groups who live in Turkey. Unquestionably, these developments mark a sharp break from previous practices. Unless one engages in a thorough investigation of historical circumstances, including the annals of the War of Independence (1919-1923), and the stages of Turkey's radical transformation from an Islamic-empire-state to democratic-republican-nationhood, it is hard to grasp the nature of the recent surge and range of global Islamic revivalism with its future aspirations for Turkey. Numerous factors and forces are at play; they relate to Turkey's recent past, and influence complex forces in play at present. Ultimately it is important to note that any analysis prioritize the dual heritage of eastern and western coordinates that circumscribe Turkey's socio-political sphere, which might call for an unprecedented depth and knowledge in perspective. However in all matters which are relevant to Turkish women's emancipation and quest for identity, it is actually the power of such *duality* which determines the coordinates and sets the precedent for the course of action in exploration of Turkey's intricate social fabric.

Notes

[1] Bozkurt Güven, *Türk Kimligi* (İstanbul: Remzi Kitabevi, 1995), 55-56.
[2] Jenny B. White, *Islamist Mobilization in Turkey: A Study in Vernacular Politics* (Seattle and London: University of Washington, 2002), x.
[3] White, 27.
[4] Graham E. Fuller, "Freedom and Security: Necessary Conditions for Moderation," *American Journal of Islamic Social Sciences*, 22:3 (Summer 2005): 21-28.
[5] Ibid., 23.
[6] Ibid., 24.
[7] Fuller, "The Erdogan Experiment in Turkey is the Future," *American Journal of Islamic Social Sciences*, 22:3 (Summer 2005): 60-68, 8.
[8] Ibid., 64.
[9] Taha Jabir al-Alwani, "The Reflections on the 'Moderate Muslims' Debate," *American Journal of Islamic Social Sciences* 22:3 (Summer 2005): 112-118.
[10] http://www.reuters.com/article/newsMaps/idUSTRE50H0R320090118. "Turkey's Long and Winding Road Towards EU", *Reuters*, January 18, 2009. Retrieved 6/21/ 2009.
[11] White, 29.
[12] For a comprehensive discussion of current terminology on "centeredness," "agency," and "location" in comparative cultural studies see Nilgün Anadolu-Okur, *Contemporary African American Theater: Afrocentricity in the Works of Larry Neal, Amiri Baraka and Charles Fuller* (New York and London: Garland Publishing Inc., 1997), 113-121.
[13] White, 35.
[14] Ibid.

[15] Deniz Kandiyoti defines *tesettur* as follows: "More than a style of clothing; it is part and parcel of a life-style that ideally encompasses a religio-cultural code of behavior prescribing the spatial segregation of men and women, appropriate spaces for the movement of male and female bodies in public places, and in the home, the proper relationship between men and women, authority of fathers and husbands over daughters and wives, and men over women, and proscribing the interaction of unrelated men and women". Kandiyoti also asserts that through *tesettur* dressing Islamist women "manage desire and display virtue". A long, loosely fitting, solid-colored coat and a matching scarf complete the appearance of a woman in *tesettur*. For further discussion, see Deniz Kandiyoti and Ayse Saktanber, eds. *Fragments of Culture: The Everyday of Modern Turkey* (London and New York: I.B. Tauris, 2002). 206. books.google.com/books?isbn=1860644279. Retrieved 6/15/ 2009.

[16] Secularism in the Turkish Constitution refers to *laicism*, separation of religion from the state.

[17] *Ataturk's Speeches and Lectures* (Ankara: 1959), Volume 2, 55.

[18] "Why Shariah?" *New York Times*. http://www.nytimes.com/2008/03/16/magazine/16Shariah. Retrieved 10/05/2008.

[19] Perihan Arif Sariguzel, "Azim ve Sebat" (Determination and Perseverance) in *Kadinlar Dünyasi* Vol. 34 (May 1911): 3-4.

[20] Feride Izzet Selim Gedikpasa, "Kadinlarimizda Luzum-i Tahsil," in *Kadinlar Dünyasi* Vol. 160 (December, 1911): 4-5.

[21] Anonymous, "Avrupa'da Osmanli Kizlarimizin Sadasi" (Voices of Our Ottoman Daughters in Europe) in *Kadinlar Dünyasi* Vol. 42 (May 1911): 1.

[22] Necdet Sakaoglu, "Egitim Tartismalari" in *Osmanlı'dan Cumhuriyet'e Türkiye Ansiklopedisi*. Vol.15 (İstanbul: İletisim Yayınlari, 1985), 5-6.

[23] Emel Dogramacı, *Türkiye'de Kadinin Dünü ve Bugünü* (Ankara: Türkiye İş Bankasi Yayınlari, 1989), 20.

[24] Suna Kili and A. Seref Gözübüyük, *Türk Anayasa Metinleri: Sened-i Ittifaktan Günümüze* (Ankara: Türkiye İs Bankasi Yayınları, 1985), 42-43.

[25] Fatma Aliye, in *Hanimlara Mahsus Gazete* (Istanbul:1895): 2-3.

[26] Tezer Taskiran, *Cumhuriyetin 50. Yilinda Türk Kadın Hakları* (Ankara, Başbakanlık Kültür Müsteşarlıgı: Cumhuriyetin 50. Yıldönümü Yayınlari, 1973), 30.

[27] Ibid.

[28] On July 19-20, 1848, in Seneca Falls, New York, a group of women met under the leadership of Lucretia Mott, Mary Ann McClintock and Elizabeth Cady Stanton. There were 300 attendees, among whom Frederick Douglass spoke in favor of women's suffrage to settle an inconclusive debate on the subject. In 1850 Lucy Stone, Abby Kelley Foster, William L. Garrison, Wendell Phillips and six other women organized the National Women's Rights Convention. Susan B. Anthony, Virginia Minor and Sojourner Truth also joined the effort. In 1896 the National Woman Suffrage Association (NWSA) was established by Susan B. Anthony and Elizabeth Cady Stanton, who argued against the passage of the Fifteenth Amendment unless it was changed to include a clause to guarantee the

right to vote for women. The Fifteenth Amendment of the US Constitution stated: "The right of citizens of the United States to vote shall not be denied or abridged by the United States or by any state on account of race, color, or previous condition of servitude." In January 1918, Woodrow Wilson acceded to the women who had been protesting at his public speeches and made a pro-suffrage speech. In 1919 the Congress passed the Nineteenth Amendment giving women the right to vote. During the Presidential election of 1920 women were able to exercise their right of suffrage for the first time in the United States. http://en.wikipedia.org/wiki/Women's_suffrage_in_the_United_States. Retrieved 6/21/ 2009.)

[29] Deniz Kandiyoti, "End of Empire: Islam, Nationalism and Women in Turkey," in *Women, Islam and the State* (Philadelphia: Temple University Press, 1991), 22-47; 41.

[30] Ibid.

[31] W.E.B. DuBois, "Damnation of Women", in *Darkwater: Voices From Within the Veil* (1920), (New York: Dover, 1999), 95.

[32] Ergün Aybars, *Türkiye Cumhuriyeti Tarihi* (İzmir: Ege Üniversitesi, 1984), 2.

[33] *Atatürk's Speeches and Lectures.* Volume 2: 76.

[34] Kandiyoti, 43.

[35] Ibid., 42.

[36] Ibid., 43.

[37] Ibid., 35.

[38] Aybars, 143.

[39] Halide Edip, *The Memoirs of Halide Edip,* (London: John Murray, 1926).

[40] Her most famous novel, *Ateşten Gömlek* (1922; *The Daughter of Smyrna*), depicts a young woman whose primary goal is to work for the liberation of her country. The following novels are centered upon social issues: *Zeyno'nun Oğlu* (1926; *"Zeyno's Son"*) and *Sinekli Bakkal* (1936, originally written in English, entitled *The Clown and His Daughter*, 1935). Her other works in English are as follows: *The Turkish Ordeal* (1928), *Conflict of East and West in Turkey* (1935, 1963), and *Turkey Faces West* (1930), in which she examines the ideological conflicts facing the young Turkish Republic. She published her memoirs in two volumes in 1926. From 1925 to 1938 she traveled extensively, lecturing in Paris, London, the United States, and India. Upon her return to Turkey in 1939, she began teaching English Literature at Istanbul University. She also served as the member of the Turkish Parliament from 1950 to 1954.

[41] A term borrowed from John McCain and Sarah Palin campaign during the 2008 Presidential elections in the United States. In the beginning of her political career, with her "non-conformist" style, Çiller was perceived as an independent and capable leader projecting a "maverick" image, who displayed a genuine interest in responding to ordinary citizens' needs.

[42] http://www.allaboutturkey.com/politikaci1.htm. Retrieved 6/20/2009.

[43] http://www.gfmag.com/gdp-data-country-reports/157-turkey-gdp-country-report.html. Retrieved 11/22/ 2009.

THE RIGHTS OF WOMEN IN SHARI'A AND IRAN'S LEGAL SYSTEM

REZA SOMEA

The rights of women constitute an obvious area of conflict between Shari'a and modern international human rights standards and laws. In Shari'a, the equality of rights before the law, regardless of gender, is not recognized, and men and women do not enjoy equal rights.[1]

Before examining women's rights in Shari'a, a distinction should be made between the approach of Shari'a sources towards the dignity and honor of women and Shari'a laws in this regard. The Qur'an declares the equality of all human beings with equal value in dignity and honor.[2] It states that the best person is the one who is the most pious.[3] Compared to the degraded status of women in the *Jahiliyya* (pre-Islamic traditions), where female infanticide was commonly practiced, "the changes in women's status are in the direction of enhancing their rights and elevating their status and dignity."[4] Against the prevailing conditions of the time, the Qur'an removed some abuses to which women were subjected, and guaranteed certain rights which Western women did not even have until the beginning of the twentieth century.[5] Islam recognized women's independent legal personality and allowed them to inherit and own property. Historically, this was quite advanced.[6]

From a legal point of view, however, Shari'a laws on the rights of women were codified through only the legal verses of the Qur'an, not through those verses which recognized the equality of men and women in dignity and honor. The laws pioneered by the Qur'an and considered appropriate then,[7] nevertheless have had a negative impact on women's rights today.[8] Early jurists resorted to Qur'anic legal verses to place some disabilities on women and to create a subordinate role for them. This resulted in male-oriented discriminatory laws and rules in almost every public and private domain of human life.[9] Below is a short review of women's Shari'a rights in the public and private spheres.

In personal status laws, while a man has the right to freely marry up to four wives under certain conditions,[10] a woman, for her first marriage, needs the permission of her legal guardian—her father or grandfather.[11]

In inheritance, the general rule accords women only half of what men are entitled to with the same relationship to the deceased person.[12]

In family matters, the man, as head of the family, has the authority and *qawama* (guardianship) over the woman.[13] She has the duty to obey him and to abstain from anything that might contradict his control and guardianship.[14] She also must obtain her husband's permission to leave the house,[15] travel,[16] or engage in any kind of work or profession. The man could withhold maintenance for her disobedience.[17]

Only a man may initiate divorce through a unilateral repudiation. Moreover he need not provide any reason to justify it. On the other hand, the woman must obtain either her husband's consent or a legal order on very specific grounds to get divorced.[18] The custody of the children also goes to the husband at age two for boys and at age seven for girls.[19]

Women's rights and positions in personal and family issues have resulted in further restriction in public life. In fact, the dominant definition of a woman as a daughter, wife, or mother of a male, intrinsic to localized laws of Shari'a, has long prohibited women from participating actively in social and public affairs. Moreover, women are disallowed to adjudicate as judges; they cannot take part in the leadership of Muslim societies.[20]

Regarding evidence, the woman's testimony is not accepted at all in serious criminal cases which involve the application of certain *hudud* and *qysas*[21] punishments. In other cases and civil subjects, the testimony of two women is equal to that of a man.[22] In other words, if it took the testimony of two males to prove a case, the testimony of four females or one male accompanying two female witnesses would be necessary to prove the same case.[23]

In *diya* (monetary compensation paid to surviving blood relatives of a victim), the general rule of Shari'a is that the *diya* of a woman is half that of a man. In other words, a male murderer would not be retaliated (*qysas*) for killing a woman unless her family pays him half a full *diya* (*diya* of a Muslim male) in advance.[24]

Muslim jurists and Shari'a advocates have always tried to justify Shari'a's gender-biased laws by comparing them to women's circumstances in pre-Islamic period (in case of personal issues); by referring to physical, mental, and emotional differences between men and women (in family matters); and by pointing to women's various social duties and obligations which result in different rights (in public affairs).[25] These reasons, the discussion of which is beyond the purpose of this essay, fail to justify the great differences between the rights of men and women in Shari'a. The great social, economic, and political changes that occurred in human societies in modern times necessitate an alternative to the traditional male-centered approach of the past and respect for the principle of equality of genders before the law.[26] Human rights are conferred on individuals because of their humanness, and not as a result of their duties and obligations to the family or social milieu recognized in Shari'a.

One may conclude that women's rights in Shari'a do not comply with, and violate, the principle of equality of rights for all human beings before the law. In fact, Shari'a considers women second-class citizens in Muslim societies. This inferior position affects women from early childhood and places before them many obstacles to proper socialization and active participation in public affairs.[27] Any proper legal system should, first, conceptualize a woman as an independent individual and a person with rights separate from her status in the family. It must also legally guarantee these rights and freedoms in private and public life.[28]

Before discussing human rights in Iran's legal and constitutional system, it would be helpful to examine briefly certain Islamic declarations on human rights in order to illustrate Islamic states' response collectively to the rights of women.

The Cairo Declaration restricts the rights of women to the limits of Shari'a. It does not stress the equality of genders in rights before the law and the equal protection by the law.[29] Article 1(a) of the Declaration, while referring to the equality of all human beings in human dignity and basic obligations and responsibilities, falls short of stressing the equality of rights and freedoms for all. Moreover, it only refers to the equality of all people before the law (Shari'a) "without distinction between the ruler and the ruled,"[30] not between men and women.[31] Article 6 of the Declaration reads:

(a) Woman is equal to man in human dignity, and has rights to enjoy as well as duties to perform; she has her own civil entity and financial independence, and the right to retain her name and lineage. (b) The husband is responsible for the support and welfare of the family.[32]

Obviously, the equality of genders in dignity does not guarantee the equality of rights and liberties.[33] In addition, Article 6 of the Cairo Declaration does not specify women's duties; its reference to the family, however, clarifies that the traditional definition of family in Shari'a would apply here as well. In fact, the article regards the man as the provider and maintainer,[34] which in Shari'a corresponds to the duty of obedience by women.[35]

The Cairo Declaration, in its various articles, refers to other rights of women, such as the right to free movement and choice of residency,[36] the right to work,[37] and the right to marry.[38] These imply Shari'a restrictions on women. In fact, the Declaration affords no right or liberty to women more than what is already included in traditional Shari'a. Although it employs the format and terminology of international human rights documents, it limits the scope of the principle of equality to Shari'a laws. The Islamic Declaration only refers to the "rights of married women"[39] within Shari'a limits, and provides no provision for the rights of unmarried women. This confirms Shari'a position, where the contours of "an adult woman's life are primarily shaped by her domestic obligations to her husband as his wife and as the mother of his children."[40] In contrast, the international human rights law focuses on the rights of individuals, irrespective of their marital status. Naturally some of the provisions deal with marriage, but marital status cannot primarily determine one's rights in international law.[41]

Rights of Women in Iran's Legal System

The discussion on women's rights and the equality of men and women in Iran's legal system presupposes theoretical standpoints on specific issues that need to be addressed. First, however, a short review of some articles on the equality of genders and the equal protection of rights before the law are necessary.

Article 3.14, mentioned in the "Generalities Section" of the Constitution, guarantees the equality of genders before the law and corresponds to modern human rights standards. It should not be understood or interpreted in isolation but in relation to other contradictory and prevailing articles, especially to Article 4 and those mentioned in "People's Rights Section" of the Constitution. Article 19 addresses the principle of equality for all people regardless of their color, race, and language. But it does not refer to gender, since the principle of equality would violate Shari'a.[42] Although Article 20 guarantees equal protection for men and women before the law, it immediately subordinates that principle subject to Shari'a standards.[43] Henceforth, the constitutional articles have been formulated in a way that accommodates Shari'a restrictions; any article must be interpreted according to these standards.

Muslim jurists and the proponents of Iran's legal system, however, believe that Shari'a laws do respect the principle of equality and guarantee equal protection under the law. The reason is that Shari'a theoretically acknowledges the rights of both men and women with regard to their social and family positions. In other words, it is the people's role and position in the family and society that determines their specific rights and duties.[44] In this system, men and women are equal in dignity and honor. This view is derived from a philosophical standpoint; but equal dignity does not always lead to equal rights. Therefore, men and women do not enjoy equal rights.[45] Muslim jurists believe that because of their physical, psychological, and emotional differences, men and women bear different responsibilities and duties in the family and society. This implies different rights.[46] In this system, duties come first. Rights are granted to allow people fulfill their duties in society; they enjoy rights as much as the society they live in can accommodate. For example, inequality in the rights of inheritance between men and women and the major role a man plays in the family are simply justified by the claim that the male gender has the duty to look after his family's needs.[47]

This system, therefore, does not regard a woman as an individual but as someone attached to a man, be it her father, her husband or her male relatives. It is the kind of relation to a man that determines a woman's rights and requires the performance of her duties concerned. This is why this system does not advocate discrimination against women through its general laws.[48]

The reality, nevertheless, is that this theoretical consideration of human rights ignores a major philosophical point: human rights are attributed to human beings individually and only because of their humanness, "as autonomous and separate persons, and not as components of family or community structure in a social context."[49] The modern theory of human rights considers rights prior to duties and responsibilities, regardless of family position or social status. It does not consider women's rights conditional upon their family or social relations with men; nor does it consider physical and emotional differences between the sexes. It addresses the duties of human beings only after recognizing their basic and fundamental rights and freedoms.[50]

One theoretical problem is that Shari'a laws and any system based on it cannot picture females out of their family or social contexts. They "fall short" of acknowledging and appreciating the philosophical foundations of modern human rights theory and standards, which ascribe human rights to individuals unconditionally.[51]

In Shari'a and in Iran's legal order, men and women are considered as two beings that complete each other even in the field of human rights. They enjoy balanced rights, not equal rights, to fulfill their duties together.[52] This understanding contains a theoretical flaw from the perspective of the modern theory of human rights. It identifies women as second-class citizens,[53] and deprives them of their internationally-recognized rights and liberties. I will briefly highlight women's rights in Iran's legal system, where unlike what the Preamble of the Constitution claims, women do not "enjoy their rights proportionately more"[54] than before. Nevertheless the detailed examination of these rights is beyond the scope of this essay.

Article 21 of the Constitution enjoins on the government "the creation of an environment favorable to the personal growth of women, and to the restoration of their material and spiritual rights"[55] according to Shari'a criteria. It also provides legal and social protection and welfare for mothers, widows, and old women.

Article 10 repeats the family theme stressed in the Preamble[56] and stipulates:

> The family being the fundamental unit of the Islamic society, all laws, regulations, and programs which pertain to it shall facilitate the establishment of the family. They shall safeguard the sanctity of the family and the stability of family relationships, based on Islamic laws and moral concepts.[57]

Taken in isolation, these articles may well provide social and legal protection for families and women, in particular. Overemphasis on family and motherhood, nevertheless, leads one to think that, failing to acknowledge women's individual rights, this system considers women only as mothers to bear children and wives to look after the family,[58] not as active members in social and political life, particularly with regard to inequality of rights between men and women in public and private law domains.[59]

Concerning civil law and personal status, the moderately-formulated Family Protection Act of 1967, amended in 1975, was nullified after the Revolution, and Shari'a laws were closely reflected in the Civil Code. This represented a major setback for women's rights.[60] A woman, in general, needs her father's permission to get married.[61] After marriage, the husband heads the family[62] and decides on the location of residency.[63] He may prohibit his wife from pursuing any profession he considers harmful to the interests of the family.[64] A woman also has to secure her husband's permission to travel abroad.[65] The Civil Code, however, recognizes her financial independence and her legal entity.[66]

Despite some amendments in the marriage contract, the husband could initiate divorce unilaterally, and repudiate his wife without just cause; while the wife must apply for divorce in specific cases and through the court.[67] Custody of the children also reverts to the father after age two for boys and seven for girls, automatically.[68] A woman generally inherits only half the share of a man with the same relation to the deceased person.[69] In addition, the husband can inherit from his deceased wife more than what his wife can inherit from him.[70]

In criminal matters, too, Iran's Criminal Code applies Shari'a laws entirely. The testimony of a woman, if accepted,[71] is worth only half of a man's.[72] In other words, the testimony of two women is equal to that of a single man. As already discussed, in the cases of *qysas* and *diya*, a woman is worth only half the value of a man.[73]

Family duties and responsibilities leave women little opportunity to participate in public or political life.[74] Due to some degree of evasiveness in the political sphere, however, Iranian women have become more active in social unions and the political arena. Legally, women are prohibited from participating in the leadership of the country, and the Constitution implicitly deprives women from running for presidential office.[75] Although women have recently been welcomed by the Judiciary Branch, they are barred from serving as judges and are still not accepted to adjudicate or preside over a court.[76] Women are deprived of employment in the army except in health-related professions which require women.[77]

These articles in the Constitution, Civil and Criminal Codes, and other laws clearly contradict modern standards of human rights for women, as codified in different international covenants and documents-including the 1948 Universal Declaration of Human Rights (articles 1 and 2 on the equality of rights, article 7 on equal protection before the law without gender discrimination, and article 16 on the equal rights of men and women in marriage and its dissolution) and the 1966 International Covenant on Civil and Political Rights (article 2 on the guarantee against discriminatory treatment, article 3 on equality, article 12 on the freedom to leave any country including one's own, and article 26 on equal protection). Iran is signatory to most of these international documents. The constitutional and legal provisions also contradict various articles of the Convention on the Elimination of All Forms of Discrimination Against Women[78] of which Iran is not a member.[79]

Although Iran's constitutional and legal provisions, in their present forms, are hard to reconcile with international human rights standards with regard to women's rights, this essay proposes that even a brief review of Shari'a laws—to find the proper method to apply Islamic standards— would indicate great changes in most of those provisions. A more profound study of Shari'a sources, equipped with a modern understanding, would probably suggest changing public and private laws of Shari'a beyond recognition. It may also result establishment of a different, yet Islamic, constitutional and legal system in the country.[80]

This essay argues that many Shari'a laws are unreliably based on the main sources. Most are derived from a few traditions or single narrations, or from the consensus (*ijma'*) of the early *ulama* centuries ago. The proper methodology of deriving Shari'a laws from the major sources, therefore, must refrain from unverified and non-authentic narrations and outdated consensus; instead it must move towards acquiring a direct reference to the principal sources, with modern circumstances in mind. More importantly, it must turn to the consensus of contemporary jurists and intellectuals who seek to reconcile Shari'a laws with the requirements of the modern life.[81]

It should also be noted that, besides the legality of women's rights and freedoms, there are historical and cultural factors which in practice restrict women's activities in Iran. Some of these are supported by legal provisions. The notion of *hijab*[82] is one among many examples. Although it seems to be a purely religious or personal matter, *hijab* has been used to deprive Muslim women of participating in social activities like sports.[83] The law in Iran compels women to comply with a rather narrow-minded interpretation of Shari'a dress requirements.[84] Consequently, women risk arrest, prosecution, and punishment, including flogging for not observing *hijab* regulations. Although the majority of Iranian Muslim women freely wear *hijab*, the use of force to ensure compliance seems to contradict the official claim that it is merely reinforcing national cultural norms, and that "the ultimate purposes of these regulations are to preserve society's order."[85]

Based on the theoretical deficiencies of Shari'a and human rights law in Iran's legal system, one may conclude that men and women, as Reisman points out, "symbolize different aspects of human life and have separate rights and obligations."[86] This system recognizes neither equality of rights, nor the equal protection of men and women before the law. On the other hand, the natural equality of all human beings implies equality of all before the law, and any discrimination on the basis of religion or sex runs against administration of justice and equality for all under the rule of law.[87] The discriminatory treatment against women results from Shari'a codes formulated in vague legal provisions which restrict women's rights and freedoms in public and private life. These restrictions are in clear contradiction with international human rights standards.[88] Addressing these critical issues, however, requires a consensus within the society itself. Another issue is whether Iranian public is ready for a transformation in favor of women's rights and equality? The troublesome incidents which occurred in the aftermath of the 2009 elections indicated just the opposite.

Notes

[1] See the following sources for broader understanding of women's issues in the Muslim world: Fatima Mernissi, *The Veil and the Male Elite: A Feminist Interpretation of Women's Rights in Islam*, trans. by Mary J. Lakeland (Reading, MA: Addison-Wesley, 1991), also published as *Women and Islam: An Historical and Theological Enquiry*, trans. by Mary J. Lakeland (Oxford: Blackwell, 1991), first published as *Le harem politique* (Paris: Albin Michel, 1987); *An Introduction to Islamic Law*; Wiebke Walther, *Women in Islam from Medieval to Modern Time* (1993) at 47-55; W. Walther, *Women in Islam*, trans. from German by C. S. V. Salt (Montclair, NJ: A. Schram, 1981), also published as *Les femmes en Islam*, trans. by Madeleine Maléfant (Paris: Sindbad, 1981); Yvonne Yazbeck Haddad & John L. Esposito, eds., *Islam, Gender, and Social Change* (Oxford: Oxford University Press, 1998); Riffat Hassan, "Equal Rights Before Allah? Women-Man Equality in the Islamic Tradition" (1988) 7 *Harvard Divinity Bulletin*, no. 2; Barbara Stowasser, *Women in the Qur'an: Traditions and Interpretations* (New York: Oxford University Press, 1994); A. Ahmed An-Na'im, "The Rights of Women and International Law in the Muslim Context" (1987). For a different view on this, see Samih Atef al-Zein, *Islam and Human Ideology*, trans. by M. H. Omran (London: Kegan Paul International, 1996) 286-99.

[2] Qur'an, 4: 1 and 124, 49: 13, 33: 35. See also Hossein Mehrpour, *Huquq-e Bashar dar Asnad-e Beinalmelali wa Moze'a Jomhuri-e Islami-e Iran* [Human Rights in International Instruments and the Position of the Islamic Republic of Iran] (Tehran: Ettela'at, 1995), 218-23.

[3] Qur'an, 49: 13.

[4] *Islam and Human Rights, Tradition and Politics.*

[5] The Qur'an prohibited female infanticide, restricted the practice of polygamy, curbed abuses of divorce by husbands, and recognized women's financial independence. See Fazlur Rahman, "The Status of Women in the Qur'an" in Guity Nashat ed., *Women and Revolution in Iran* (Boulder, CO: Westview Press, 1983) at 38; For a summary of those changes, see also J. N. D. Anderson, *Law Reforms in the Muslim World* (London: Athlone, 1976); Tahir Mahmmod, *Personal Law in Islamic Countries* (New Delhi: Academy of Law and Religions, 1987); Abula'la Mawdudi, *Purdah and the Status of Women in Islam* (Lahore: Islamic Publications, 1981).

[6] See al-Saadawi, "Women and Islam" in Azizah al-Hibri, ed., *Women and Islam* (Oxford: Pergamon Press, 1982) 194-202; Naila Minai, *Women in Islam: Tradition and Transition in the Middle East* (New York: Seaview, 1981) 1-24; Jane Smith, "Women, Religion, and Social Change in Early Islam" in Yvonne Y. Haddad & Ellison Findley, eds., *Women, Religion, and Social Change,* (Albany: State University of New York Press, 1985) 19-35; Barbara Stowasser, "The Status of Women in Early Islam" in Freda Hussain, ed., *Muslim Women* (New York: St. Martin's Press, 1984) 11-43; Mernissi, *Women and Islam: An Historical and Theological Enquiry*; M. Wahibiddin Khan, *Women in Islamic Shariah*, trans. by

Farida Khanam (New Delhi: Islamic Centre, 1995); A. Rahman Doi, *Women in the Shari'a* (London: Ta-Ha, 1989); A. R. Doi, *Women in the Qur'an and Hadith* (London: Ta-ha, 1993).
[7] Rahman, "Status of Women in the Qur'an".
[8] Margot Badran and Nilüfer Göle, *The Forbidden Modern: Civilization and Veiling* (Ann Arbor: University of Michigan Press, 1996); Riffat Hassan, "Feminist Theology: The Challenges for Muslim Women" (1996) 9 *Critique: J. for Critical Studies of the Middle East*, 53-65; Camillia Fawzi, El-Solh, & Judy Mabro, eds., *Muslim Women's Choices: Religious Belief and Social Reality* (Oxford: Berg, 1994); An-Na'im, "The Rights of Women and International Law in the Muslim Context"; Tabandeh, *A Muslim Commentary on the Universal Declaration of Human Rights*; Yves Linant de Bellefonds, *Traité de droit musulman comparé, le mariage et la dissolution du mariage*, vol. 2 (Paris: Mouton, 1965); Jamal Nasir, *The Islamic Law of Personal Status* (London: Graham & Trotman, 1986).
[9] See Ghassan Ascha, *Du statut inférieur de la femme en Islam* (Paris: L'Harmatton, 1987); Anderson, *Law Reform in the Muslim World*; Khawar Mumtaz & Farida Shaheed, *Women in Pakistan, Two Steps Forward, One Step Back* (London: Zed, 1987), 77-122; Anita Weiss, "Implications of the Islamization Program for Women," in A. Weiss, ed., *Islamic Reassertion in Pakistan* (Syracuse: Syracuse University Press, 1986) 97-114; A. Ahmed An-Na'im, "A Modern Approach to Human Rights in Islam: Foundations and Implications for Africa," in Claude Welch Jr. & Ronald Meltzer, eds., *Human Rights and Development in Africa* (Albany: State University of New York Press, 1984) 82; Glenn, *Legal Traditions of the World*; J. J. Nasir, *The Status of Women Under Islamic Law and Under Modern Islamic Legislation*, 2nd ed. (London: Graham & Trotman, 1994); and D. Pearl & W. Menski, *Muslim Family Law*, 3rd ed. (London: Sweet & Maxwell, 1998).
[10] Qur'an, 4: 2-3. Although it is claimed that polygamy was partly allowed for the benefit of widows and orphans in Muslim societies, it violates the equality of genders before the law. See *Towards an Islamic Reformism*.
[11] *An Introduction to Islamic Law*; "The Rights of Women and International Law in the Muslim Context" and *Du statut inferieur de la femme en Islam*.
[12] Qur'an, 4:11and 176. See also S. Tahir Mahmood, *Personal Law in Islamic Countries: History, text and Comparative Analysis* (New Delhi: Academy of Law and Religion, 1987); Stowasser, "The Status of Women in Early Islam"; Freda Hussain, *Muslim Women;* Noel Coulson, *Succession in the Muslim Family* (Cambridge: Cambridge University Press, 1971).
[13] Qur'an, 4:34. The discussion of the kinds and extents of *Qawama* in different readings of Qur'an is not included; it is rather beyond the scope of this essay. "Human Rights in the Muslim World" in *Towards an Islamic Reformism*
[14] Mehrpoor, *Human Rights in International Instruments*.
[15] In some interpretations, the permission to leave the house is only for urgent issues, which is an orthodox understanding of the principle of *hijab* (veil) that, according to the majority of jurists, requires women to cover their hair and body

except face and hands. See Qur'an, 24: 31 and 33: 33, 53, and 59. See *Toward an Islamic Reformation*; Mawdudi, *Purdah and the Status of Women in Islam.*

[16] Iranian women willing to travel abroad, should by law secure the permission of their husbands or legal guardians. This issue is discussed below.

[17] Bellefonds, *Traité de froit musulman compare*; Nasir, *The Islamic Law of Personal Status.* Also Fadela M'rabet, *La femme Algérienne suivi de les Algériennes* (Paris: Maspero, 1969) 143-65; "Human Rights in the Muslim World"; Dawoud Sudqi al-Alami, *The Marriage Contract in Islamic Law, in the Shari'ah and Personal Status Laws of Egypt and Morocco* (London: Graham & Trotman, 1992); and Malladi Subbamma, *Islam and Women*, trans. by M. V. Ramamurty (New Delhi: Sterling, 1988).

[18] Qur'an, 2:226-32; *An Introduction to Islamic Law.*

[19] Ascha, *Du statut inférieur de la femme en Islam*; Elizabeth W. Fernea, *Women and the Family in the Middle East: New Voices of Change* (Austin: University of Texas Press, 1985); Nikki Keddie & Beth Baron, eds., *Women in Middle Eastern History: Shifting Boundaries in Sex and Gender* (New Haven: Yale University Press, 1991); Amira el-Azhary Sonbol, ed., *Women and the Family and Divorce Law in Islamic History* (Syracuse: Syracuse University Press, 1996).

[20] Mehrpoor, *Human Rights in International Instruments*; Mohammad Hussein Tabataba'e, *Al-Mizan fi Tafsir al-Qur'an* [al-Mizan Interpretation of Qur'an] vol. 4 (Tehran: Bunyad-e Ilmi wa Fikri-e Allamah Tabataba'i, 1992). Also mentioned in Deniz Kandiyoti, *Women, Islam and the State*, (Philadelphia: Temple University Press, 1991); Homa Hoodfar, "The Veil in Their Minds and on Our Heads: The Persistence of Colonial Images of Muslim Women" (1995); Resources for Feminist Research 5-18; Barbara Stowasser, "Women's Issues in Modern Islamic Thought" in Judith E. Tucker, *Arab Women: Old Boundaries, New Frontiers* (Bloomington: Indiana University Press, 1993) 3-28.

[21] See Ibid.

[22] Qur'an, 2: 282.

[23] "Human Rights in the Muslim World"; Amina Wadud-Mohsin, *Qur'an and Women* (Kualalumpur: Penerbit Fajar, 1992); Khan, *Women in Islamic Shari'ah*; and Doi, *Women in the Shari'a.*

[24] Qur'an, 2: 179, 186; 5: 45; 6: 92, 94, and 135; Bassiouni, "Quesas Crimes"; and "Human Rights in the Muslim World".

[25] Fazlur Rahman, "The Status of Women in the Qur'an"; al-Hibri, *Women and Islam*; Nasir, *The Islamic Law of Personal Status*; Mawdudi, *The Islamic Law and Constitution.* Mawdudi remarked that "the limited and conditional freedom that women had been allowed by Islam in matters other than home science is being used [in the work of Muslim feminists] to encourage the Muslim women to abandon home life and its responsibilities like the European women and make their lives miserable by running after political, economic, social and other activities shoulder to shoulder with men." See *Purdah and the Status of Women in Islam.*

[26] In practice, most Muslim countries, keeping some elements of the Shari'a system of personal status, have included many reforms improving the rights of women. See Anderson, *Law Reforms in the Muslim World*; *Islam and Human*

Rights, Tradition and Politics; "Human Rights in the Muslim World"; *Shifting Boundaries in Sex and Gender*, Herbert L. Bodman & Nayereh Tohidi, eds., *Women in Muslim Societies: Diversity Within Unity* (Boulder, CO: Lynne Rienner, 1998); Shahin Gerami, *Women and Fundamentalism: Islam and Christianity* (New York: Garland, 1996); Freda Hussain, *Muslim Women* (London: Croom Helm, 1984); Sajda Nazlee, *Feminism and Muslim Women* (London: Ta-Ha, 1996); Barbara Stowasser, "Gender Issues and Contemporary Qur'an Interpretation" in *Islam, Gender, and Social Changes.*

[27] See "Human Rights in Muslim World"; Ascha, *Du ststut inférieur de la femme en Islam*; Vieille, "Iranian Women in Family Alliance and Sexual Politics" in Lois Beck & Nikki Keddie, eds., *Women in the Muslim World* (Cambridge: Harvard University Press, 1978) 451.

[28] Fedwa Malti-Douglas, *Women's Body, Women's World: Gender and Discourse in Arabo-Islamic Writing* (Princeton: Princeton University Press, 1992); Azadeh Kian, "L'émergence d'un discours féminin independant: un enjeu de pouvoir" (1997) 47 Les Cahiers de l'Orient 55-72; Yvonne Y. Haddad, "Islam and Gender: Dilemmas in the Changing Arab World" in *Islam, Gender, and Social Change.*

[29] *Islam and Human Rights, Tradition and Politics.*

[30] The Cairo Declaration, Art. 19(a).

[31] Contrary to Article 26 of the International Covenant on Civil and Political Rights which states, "All persons are equal before the law and are entitled without discrimination to the equal protection of the law, ...".

[32] The Cairo Declaration, Art. 6(a) and 6(b).

[33] In contrast, the UDHR stresses that: "[a]ll humans are born free and equal in dignity and rights ..." The UDHR, Chapter One art. 1.

[34] The 1990 Cairo Declaration, Art. 6(b).

[35] The al-Azhar Draft stresses that the government should provide the means according to which "the wife would obey her husband ..." See the 1979 al-Azhar Draft, Art. 19.

[36] The Cairo Declaration, Art. 12.

[37] *Ibid.*, Art. 13; the 1979 al-Azhar Draft, Art. 38.

[38] The Cairo Declaration, Art. 5(a).

[39] The 1981 Islamic Declaration, Art. 20.

[40] *Islam and Human Rights, Tradition and Politics.*

[41] *Ibid.*

[42] In contrast, see article 2 of the UDHR, which guarantees to all people, rights and freedoms without distinction of any kind, such as gender.

[43] It does not seem accurate to claim that Article 20, in its first clause which refers to equal protection before the law means secular law, and, therefore, guarantees the principle of equal rights protection, as opposed to Shari'a laws which determine the scope and extent of human rights and liberties in the Constitution. See *Islam and human Rights, Tradition and Politics*. Although the term *qanun* (law) has been taken from the Greek word of *kanon* (normally employed to refer to secular law), it refers, in Iran's legal system, to any law, including Shari'a laws, which is in force

whether it is a constitutional article or a bill passed by the Parliament. All the laws, of course, are subject to Shari'a qualifications.

[44] Abdollah Javadi-Amoli, *Zan dar A'ineh-ye Jalal va Jamal* [Women in the Mirror of Glory and Beauty] (Tehran: Reja' Cultural Press, 1993); A. Javadi-Amoli, *Falsafeh-ye Hoquq-e Bashar* [The Philosophy of Human Rights] (Qum, Iran: Isra, 1996); Khan, *Women in Islamic Shari'ah*; Riffat Hassan, "Equal Before Allah? Women-Man Equality in the Islamic Tradition"; Bodman & Tohidi, *Women in Muslim Societies: Diversity Within Unity*.

[45] Doi, *Women in the Shari'ah*, Doi, *Women in the Qur'an and Hadith*; Mohammad-Taqi Mesbah Yazdi, *et al.*, *Status of Women in Islam* (Tehran: Islamic Propagation Organization, 1985); Mernissi, *Women and Islam: An Historical and Theological Enquiry*.

[46] Maududi, *Purdah and the Status of Women in Islam*; Mehrpoor, *Human Rights in International Instruments*; Murtada Mutahhari, *The Rights of Women in Islam* (Tehran: World Organization of Islamic Service, 1981); Farida Shaheed, *Controlled or Autonomous: Identity and the Experience of the Network Women Living Under Muslim Laws* (Grabels, France; Women Living Under Muslim Laws, 1994); Sonbol, *Women and the Family and Divorce Laws in Islamic History*.

[47] Barbara Stowasser, "Women's Issues in Modern Islamic Thought"; Tucker, *Arab Women: Old Boundaries, New Frontiers*; B. Stowasser, *Women in the Qur'an: Traditions and Interpretations*; B. Stowasser, "Gender Issues and Contemporary Qur'an Interpretation" in Haddad & Esposito, *Islam, Gender, and Social Change*.

[48] Amina Wadud-Muhsin, *Qur'an and Women* (Kuala Lumpur: Penerbit Fajar Bakti, 1992); Khan, *Women in Islamic Shari'ah*; Freda Hussain, *Muslim Women,*; Hoodfar, "The Veil in Their Minds and on Our Heads"; Riffat Hassan, "Feminist Theology: The Challenges For Muslim Women" (1996) 9 J. for Critical Studies of the Middle East 53-65.

[49] *Islam and Human Rights, Tradition and Politics*; See also A. J. M. Milne, *Human Rights and Human Diversity: An Essay in the Philosophy of Human Rights* (New York: State University of New York Press, 1986); Jack Donnelly, *The Concept of Human Rights* (London: Croom Helm, 1985); and Peter Jones, *Rights* (New York: St. Martin's Press, 1994).

[50] Alan Gewirth, *Human Rights: Essays on Justification and Applications* (Chicago: University of Chicago Press, 1982); Jack Donnelly, *Universal Human Rights in Theory and Practice* (London: Cornell University Press, 1989); and Warren Lee Holleman, *Human Rights Movement, Western Values and Theological Perspectives* (New York: Praeger, 1987).

[51] Fernea, *Women and the Family in the Middle East: New Voices of Change*; Gerami, *Women and Fundamentalism: Islam and Christianity*; Kian, "L'émergence d'un discours féminin independant: un enjeu de pouvoir"; Malti-Douglas, *Women's Body, Women's World*.

[52] Javadi-Amoli, *The Philosophy of Human Rights*; Mesbah-Yazdi, *Status of Women in Islam*; Mawdudi, *Human Rights in Islam*; Khan, *Women in Islamic Shari'ah*; Nazlee, *Feminism and Muslim Women*.

---

[53] Ayatollah Mohammed-Taghi Mesbah-Yazdi at a Friday prayer service, in Tehran stated: "We do not have first class and second class human beings; but, we can have second class citizens." Further, he added that "It is incorrect to say that since all human beings are equal in their humanity, consequently we do not have second class citizens." Cited in *Iran, Daily Newspaper*, January 17, 1999. Although the ayatollah did not elaborate on who these second class citizens might be, the mere belief in this division supports the proposition that Shari'a and Iran's legal system recognize the notion of inequality of citizens before the law. Mesbah-Yazdi is also reported to have said that: "Believing in equal rights for all citizens is worse than worshipping cows. If this is right, then Jews and Zoroastorians can become president. ... The idea of tolerance is thousand times more dangerous than AIDS." See also Javadi-Amoli, *Women in the Mirror of Glory and Beauty* and Mehrpoor, *Human Rights in International Instruments*.
[54] The Constitution, the Preamble.
[55] *Ibid.* Article 21.
[56] The Preamble on women and the Constitution reads: "... with the restitution of the noble and respected duty of motherhood, to raise faithful persons, women will be in the vanguard and, in fact, the comrade of men in all aspects of active life..."
[57] *Ibid.* Article 10.
[58] Adele K. Ferdows, "The Status and Rights Women in Ithna Ashari Shi'i Islam" in Asghar Fathi, ed., *Women and the Family in Iran* (Leiden: E. J. Brill, 1985) 13-36; Haleh Esfandiari, "The Majlis and Women's Issues in the Islamic Republic of Iran" in Mahnaz Afkhami & Erika Friedl, eds., *In the Eye of the Storm: Women in Post-Revolutionary Iran* (Syracuse: Syracuse University Press, 1994) 61-79; H. Esfandiari, *Reconstructed Lives: Women and Iran's Islamic Revolution* (London: John Hopkins University Press, 1997); Shirin Mahdavi, "The Position of Women in Shi'a Iran: Views of the Ulama" in Fernea, *Women and the Family in the Middle East: New Voices of Change.*
[59] Guity Neshat, "Women in the Ideology of the Islamic Republic" in G. Neshat, ed., *Women and Revolution in Iran*; Ziba Mir-Hosseini, "Women and the Shari'a in the Islamic Republic of Iran: A Changing Relationship" paper presented at the Carsten Niebuhr Institute of Near Eastern Studies Conference "Women, Culture and Modernity" (Copenhagen, February 18-21, 1996); Nahid Yeganeh & Nikki R. Keddie, "Sexuality and Shi'a Sexual Protest in Iran" in Juan R. I. Cole & N. R. Keddie, eds., *Shi'ism and Social Protest* (New York: Yale University Press, 1982) 108-36; Fariba Adelkhah, *La révolution sous le voile* (Paris: Karthala, 1991).
[60] Nouchine Yavari-d'Hellencourt, "Discours islamique, actrices sociales et rapports sociaux de sexe" in N. Yavari-d'Hellencourt, ed., *Les femmes en Iran: pressions socials et stratégies identitaires* (Paris: Harmattan, 1998) 190-229; Azar Tabari, "Islam and the Struggle for Emancipation of Iranian Women" in A. Tabari & Nahid Yeganeh, eds., *In the Shadow of Islam* (London: Zed, 1982) 5-25; Sohila Shahshahani, "Religion, Politics and Society: A Historical Perspective on the Women's Movement in Iran" (1984) 1-2 Samya Shakti 100-20; Eliz Sanasarian, "Politics of Gender and Development in the Islamic Republic of Iran" (1992) 8 *Journal of Developing Societies* 56-68; and Tamilla F. Godsi, "Tying a Slipknot:

Temporary Marriage in Iran" (1994) 15 *Michigan Journal of International Law*, 645.

[61] The Civil Code of Iran, Article 1043. It should be noted that she is considered an adult and mature at the age of 9, and can get married under certain conditions. In November 2000, the Guardian Council labeled a recent bill by the Parliament "un-Islamic" necessitating court's approval for boys under 18 or girls under 15 to get married. Islamic Republic News Agency (IRNA), November 11, 2000.

[62] *Ibid.* Article 1105.

[63] *Ibid.* Article 1114.

[64] *Ibid.* Article 1117. This is on the fault basis that since the husband provides the family's needs, he heads the family and she has the duty to obey him; meet his emotional and sexual needs, and refrain from any action or profession that may contradict these duties.

[65] The Passport Act, Article 18(3). In January 2001, the Guardian Council rejected a parliamentary bill allowing young women to travel abroad alone for academic purposes. The Parliament then had to amend the bill in order to meet Shari'a qualifications. Iranian Students New Agency (ISNA), January 22, 2001.

[66] The Civil Code, Article 1118.

[67] *Ibid.* Articles 1133, 1129, and 1130.

[68] *Ibid.* Articles 1169 and 1180.

[69] *Ibid.* Articles 907 and 920.

[70] *Ibid.* Article 946. For further information on women's rights on personal status, see Fatemeh E. Moghadam, "Commoditization of Sexuality and Female Labor Participation in Islam: Implication for Iran" in *In the Eye of the Storm*; Ziba Mir-Hosseini, *Marriage on Trial: A Study of Islamic Family Law: Iran and Morocco Compared* (London: I. B. Tauris, 1993); Z. Mir-Hosseini, "Divorce, Veiling and Feminism in Post-Khomeini Iran" in Haleh Afshar, ed., *Women and Politics in the Third World* (London: Routledge, 1996) 142-70; Firouzeh Khalatbari, "L'inégalité des sexes sur le marché du travail: une analyse des potentiels économiques de croissance" in *Les femmes en Iran*; Homa Hoodfar, "Devices and Desires: Population Policy and Gender Roles in the Islamic Republic" (1994) 190 Middle East Report 11-17; Shahla Haeri, *Law of Desire: Temporary Marriage in Iran* (London: I. B. Tauris, 1989); S. Haeri, "Temporary Marriage: An Islamic Discourse on Female Sexuality in Iran" in *In the Eye of the Storm*; S. Haeri, "Obedience Versus Autonomy: Women and Fundamentalism in Iran and Pakistan" in M. E. Marty & R. S. Appelby, *Fundamentalism and Society: Reclaiming Science, the Family, and Education* (Chicago: University of Chicago Press, 1993) 181-213; Haleh Afshar, "Women, Marriage and the State in Iran" in H. Afshar, ed., *Women, State and Ideology: Studies From Africa and Asia* (London: Macmillan, 1987) 70-86; H. Afshar, "Women and Reproduction in Iran" in Nira Yural-Davis & Floya Anthias, eds., *Women-Nation-State* (London: Macmillan, 1989) 110-25; Ibrahim Amini, *Principles of Marriage: Family Ethics* (Qum, Iran: Ansariyan, n. d.); Homa Hoodfar, "Bargaining With Fundamentalism: Women and the Politics of Population Control in Iran" (1996) in *Reproductive Health Matters*, 30-40.

[71] In serious criminal cases which involve *Hudud* and *Qysas* punishments, the testimony of women is not recognized. The Criminal Code of Iran, Articles 76, 119, 170, 189(2), 99(1), and 237(1).

[72] *Ibid.* Articles 74, 75, and 172.

[73] *Ibid.* Articles 209, 258, 300, and 301. See also Patricia Higgins, "Women in the Islamic Republic of Iran: Legal, Social and Ideological Changes" (1995) 477-95.

[74] Kian, "La formation d'une identité sociale féminine post-revolutionaire: un enjeu de pouvoir"; A. Kian, "Gendered Occupation and Women's Status in Post-Revolutionary Iran" (1995) 31 *Middle Eastern Studies* 407-21; A. Kian, "Women and Politics in Post-Islamist Iran: the Gender Conscious Drive to Change" (1997) 24 *British Journal of Middle Eastern Studies* 75-96; and Valentine Moghadam, "Public Life and Women's Resistance" in Saeed Rahnema & Sohrab Behdad, *In Iran After the Revolution* (London: I. B. Tauris, 1995) 251-67.

[75] The Constitution, Article 115.

[76] The Act of the Selection of the Judges (1983), amended in 1995. Article 163 of the Constitution also stipulates that the conditions for the selection of judges are determined by Shari'a in which only men could serve as judges.

[77] The Islamic Republic Army Act, Article 32; The Employment Act of the Islamic Revolutionary Guards Corps, Article 20. For further information on women's rights in public and political spheres see Parvin Paidar, *Women and the Political Process in Twentieth-Century Iran* (Cambridge: Cambridge University Press, 1995); Nesto Ramazani, "Women in Iran: The Revolutionary Ebb and Flow" (1993) 47 Middle East J. 409-28; Eliz Sanasarian, *The Women's Rights Movement in Iran* (New York: Praeger, 1982); Nayereh Tohidi, "Gender and Islamic Fundamentalism: Feminist Politics in Iran" in Chandra Mohanty, Ann Russo, & Laurdes Torres, eds., *Third World Women and the Politics of Feminism* (Bloomington: Indiana University Press, 1991) 251-67; Haideh Moghissi, "Women in the Resistance Movement in Iran" in Haleh Afshar, ed., *Women in the Middle East: Perceptions, Realities and Struggles for Liberation* (London: Macmillan, 1993) 158-71; and Chahla Chafiq, *La femme et le retour de l'Islam: l'expérience iranienne* (Paris: Le Félin, 1991).

[78] Convention on the Elimination of All Forms of Discrimination Against Women (the CEDAW), Dec. 18, 1979, G.A. Res., 34/180, 34 UN GAOR Supp. (no. 46), at UN Doc. A/34/46 (1979), entered into force (became effective) in 1981.

[79] Many Muslim countries that signed or ratified the CEDAW have entered several reservations to various articles, such as those that provide for the equality of men and women in all matters- i.e., marriage and family relations, during the course of marriage, and upon its dissolution. See "Human Rights in the Muslim World". Ayatollah Nasser Makarem-Shirazi, a leading conservative cleric, has recently denounced Iran's ratification of a UN document that encourages sex education for girls and condemns violence against women. He said: "I say it very clearly that it is religiously forbidden to adhere to these documents." The document was adopted in the UN Conference in New York, in June 2000, which was held to review progress made since the 1995 Beijing Conference. See Agance France Presse, "Influential Cleric Opposes UN Document on Women" Tehran, June 24, 2000.

[80] Ziba Mir-Hosseini, "Stretching the Limits: A Feminist Reading of the Shari'a in Iran Today" in Mai Yamani, ed., *Feminism and Islam: Legal and Literary Perspectives* (London: Ithaca, 1996) 284-320; Z. Mir-Hosseini, *Islam and Gender, The Religious Debate in Contemporary Iran* (Princeton, NJ: Princeton University Press, 1999); Afsaneh Najmabadi, "Hazards of Modernity and Morality: Women, State and Ideology in Contemporary Iran" in Deniz Kandiyoti, *Women, Islam and the State*; A. Najmabadi, "Feminism in an Islamic Republic: Years of Hardship, Years of Growth" in *Islam, Gender, and Social Change*; Hisae Nakanishi, "Power, Ideology, and Women's Consciousness in Post-Revolutionary Iran" in *Women in Muslim Societies*.

[81] Parvin Paidar, "Feminism and Islam in Iran" in Deniz Kandiyoti, ed., *Gendering the Middle East: Emerging Perspectives* (London: I. B. Tauris, 1996) 51-68; Azar Tabari, "The Women's Movement in Iran: A Hopeful Prognosis" (1986) 12 Feminist Studies 342-60; Farah Azari, "The Post-Revolutionary Women's Movement in Iran" in F. Azari, ed., *Women of Iran: The Conflict With Fundamentalist Islam* (London: Ithaca, 1983) 190-225; Fariba Adelkhah, *Être moderne en Iran* (Paris: Karthala, 1998); Haleh Afshar, *Islam and Feminism: An Iranian Case Study* (London: Macmillan, 1998).

[82] The veil. According to Shari'a interpretation of the Qur'anic verses, the principle of *hijab* requires women to cover their bodies and hair. The face and hands are generally excluded. See also Adele K. Ferdows & Amir H. Ferdows, "Women in Shi'a Fiqh: Images Through the Hadith" in Nashat, *Women and Revolution in Iran*; and Farah Azari, "Islam's Appeal to Women in Iran: Illusions and Reality" in Azari, *Women of Iran: The Conflict With Fundamentalist Islam, ibid.* 1-71.

[83] *Human Rights Watch World Report* (1995), 271. Also Farzaneh Milani, *Veils and Words: The Emerging Voices of Iranian Women Writers* (Syracuse: Syracuse University Press, 1992); and Azar Tabari, "The Enigma of the Veiled Iranian Women" (1982) 103 MERIP 22-27.

[84] The authorities in public departments and schools even limit the choice of *hijab* to solid and darker colors.

[85] The statement by the government representative at the United Nations, see UN GAOR, H.R. Comm., 46th Sess., 1195th Mtg., no. 15, at UN Doc. CCPR/C/SR. 1195 (1992). See also Ann H. Betteridge, "To Veil or Not to Veil: A Matter of Protest or Policy" in Nashat, *Women and Revolution in Iran*; Zahra Kamalkhani, *Women's Islam: Religious Practice Among Women in Today's Iran* (London: Kegan Paul International, 1998); Haleh Afshar, "Why Fundamentalism? Iranian Women and Their Support for Islam" (Working paper no. 2, Department of Politics, University of York, 1994).

[86] Reisman, "Some Reflection on Human Rights and Clerical Claim to Political Power".

[87] Nwachukwuike S. S. Iwe, *The History and Contents of Human Rights, A Study of the History and Interpretation of Human Rights* (New York: Peter Lang, 1986).

[88] Mahdavi, "The Position of Women in Shi'a Iran"; Mir-Hosseini, *Marriage on Trial*; Mir-Hosseini, "Women and the Shari'a in the Islamic Republic of Iran"; Stowasser, *Women in the Qur'an: Traditions and Interpretations*; Nayereh Tohidi,

"Modernity, Islamization, and Women in Iran" in Valentine Moghadam, ed., *Gender and National Identity: Women and Politics in Muslim Societies* (London: Zed, 1994) 110-47; Camillia Fawzi, El-Solh and Judy Mabro, eds., *Muslim Women's Choices: Religious Belief and Social Reality* (Providence: Berg, 1994); and Haleh Afshar, "Khomeini's Teachings and Their Implications for Iranian Women" in *In the Shadow of Islam*.

ENTITIES AND IDENTITIES
IN THE MUSLIM WORLD

NOUR JALLAD

In the eyes of the West today, Islam and the Muslim world are perceived as being miles away, both in distance and views, culture, religion and social characteristics. What westerners seldom realize is that this view is not necessarily reciprocated by the Muslim world. Muslims, and in particular Muslim women, are caught between two utterly dissimilar worlds that are juxtaposed within their own. These women are faced with constantly having to reconcile their situation as women who were raised in a traditional Muslim environment with the context of living in a modern, unavoidably western world. In a way, one could argue that these women are—and have to be—simultaneously Muslim and western, one identity not excluding the other.

In general, one's identity is based on how one perceives oneself in the world. As human beings, we are constantly aware of ourselves, of our identity and of our relationship with the physical world around us. This awareness of who we are and where we are is strengthened by imagery, as well as by the physical characteristics of the space around us. For Muslim women in particular, the concept of identity, and its relationship with the physical space, is very important in everyday life. A Muslim woman's struggle with identity is closely related with the overlap—or collision—of the worlds she lives in. It is that overlap, in its many definitions, that we seek to analyze here, as a way to better understand women's position in the Muslim world as Muslim, modern and inevitably western.

Looking more closely at this overlap between the traditional Muslim world and the contemporary western world, it is helpful to first define the concept of overlap itself. Conceptually, to overlap is "to occupy the same area in part" or "to have something in common." This definition in itself implies that there are different conditions that result from the coming together of two separate—sometimes conflicting—entities (or identities): they can either co-exist separately in the same physical space, or share more than just a physical space—an identity. If we refer to these two entities here as A and B, then we can possibly conclude the following about the overlapping entities:

$$A+B = A$$
$$A+B = B$$
$$A+B = A+B$$
$$A+B = C$$

These relationships are helpful ways to look at the status of women in the Muslim world and to understand their connection with the physical space around them, based on the context they happen to be in.

The overlap between the two worlds that a Muslim woman faces can manifest itself conceptually as well as physically. So much of a Muslim woman's identity can be related to her physical appearance: her commitment to follow the Islamic dress code plays a major role in the collision between her identity and that of the outside world. As she steps out of her home wearing the veil, chador, hijab, or a headscarf, she is bombarded with the images of a world that is quite contrary to her own identity. The outer world is laden with western advertisement, media and pop culture which are infatuated with explicitness and the power of the "image". Although her veiling partially provides a type of boundary, shielding her from the influence of that "outside world", the global phenomenon of westernization has made it impossible for a Muslim woman not to interact or even take part in that world beyond her own.

This overlap or collision of Islam and the western world is furthermore manifested in the physical environment. Traditional Islamic architecture had been inward looking. The presence of the courtyard, with spaces and circulation formed around it, emphasized the importance of life in interior spaces while de-emphasizing the outer envelope of the structure. For instance, the use of screening devices, such as *musharabiyya*, a geometrically patterned screen, ensured a sense of privacy for the residents, while maintaining certain porosity. Women in particular who lived in private spaces known as the *harem,* or women's quarters, were separated from men and concealed behind such screens, which enabled them *to see out* without being exposed to the public.

Since the introduction of modernization, westernization, technological advancements, as well as the impact of the modernist movement and the inevitable rise of globalization, new trends have delivered a different type of architecture into the Muslim world, one that contrasts with the elements of traditional Islamic architecture and its familiar concepts. Yet the predominantly western fascination with transparency, openness and the idea of eliminating the "envelope" in order to bring the outside into an inner space has introduced a novelty into the Islamic world—the use of all-glass building facades recently prevalent across many Muslim countries. The urban landscape of cities in the Muslim world is no longer strictly defined by minarets and domes; instead they display a collage of translucent, ultra-high glass towers and traditional solid structures.

It is essential to note here that the results of this so-called overlap, as defined previously, are of various types: the boundaries between the traditional Muslim and western worlds are more or less defined depending on the context and the specific identity of the country itself.

Whereas in some Middle Eastern and Asian countries Muslim women seem to have been able to find a way to juggle two different identities and balance their impact, this is not necessarily the case across the entire Muslim world. The case where the results of the overlap between Muslim and western is a merging and weaving of the two worlds (the case where entity A + entity B = entity C) appears to be exceptional and somewhat unusual. It seems to occur in more liberal countries that are not prevalently Muslim or in countries that have been more open and collaborative with the west than with the rest of the Islamic world.

We will focus here rather on cases where the overlap emphasizes the divergence between the Muslim and western worlds, as this seems to be more common and one that is more useful in analysis and understanding of the status of women and their relationship to the outside world.

The case of gated communities, particularly those in Saudi Arabia, presents us a situation where the two entities in question appear to be separate, adjacent and co-existing. Gated communities are mostly residential communities surrounded by a wall or a fence. The development of gated communities became a full-fledged reality in the early 1980s in many parts of the Arab and Muslim world. In certain ways, these gated communities can be considered utopias, or they manifest utopian qualities that are essential for their creation and existence. In fact, gated communities are defined by a boundary that cannot be broken without undermining the community itself. By nature, these communities are inward looking; they are concerned with what happens in their interior and tend to ignore—if not negate—their surroundings. Circulation in and out of the community is restricted, the element of control being crucial to the well-being of life inside the community.[1] A selective process determines who can enter the community: as Foucault argues, utopias—and these particular utopias are not an exception—"always presuppose a system of opening and closing that both isolates them and makes them penetrable."[2] In the context of gated communities, this mechanism of *opening* and *closing* involves residents and employees of the community, maintaining a safe distance from *others* who are outsiders, and those who do not belong to the community. This filtering process enables the community to remain autonomous and minimizes its dependence on the outside world.

Gated communities in different countries are viewed as the outcome of variable factors depending on the country and the culture in which they are set . In many places, the creation of gated communities ensures a safer life within the larger context of the place. In other cases, gated communities are formed by a specific group, usually with a specific social or religious status, whose members seek to interact among themselves and voluntarily separate themselves from other groups. In other situations, gated communities may originate from a conscious effort or a need to adapt to a different culture or to survive within that culture.

The case of gated communities in the Muslim world is particularly important as these utopian communities mark a gap between the interior space of the community and the exterior world—a gap that is more significant than in most gated communities in other areas. Arab gated communities are generally the result of an effort to accommodate another culture within the Arab lifestyle. In Egypt, for instance, many gated communities developed around Cairo to accommodate a rising social class whose culture was moving further and further away from the traditional Muslim, Egyptian and Arab culture. This class of "nouveaux riches" is constituted by people who have recently acquired wealth. Therefore they are more prone to embrace elements of the western culture, the European lifestyle and its material culture. In this case, rather than striving for a sense of security, the residents of the gated community seek the comfort of controlling who can or cannot *enter* into their lives. In a way, these residents are buying not only their own privacy, but also their ability to operate outside of the sphere of the Egyptian society with its Muslim and Arab values. [3] This is particularly relevant for women, as they are able to escape rigid rules of the traditional Muslim world through these gated communities.

Gated communities in Lebanon are similar to those in Egypt, as they are created to accommodate a specific group that wants to move away from the rest of the society. Even though these gated communities were originally created during the Civil War (1975-1991) between Christians and Muslims, in the post-war era they developed into gated beach resorts and ski villages, targeting a specific group of clientele. During the war, these gated communities had offered a safe shelter for citizens who did not want to be involved in a religious conflict. In a certain way, these communities provided a world that was not limited to the followers of a particular religion. They also offered, for their residents, the luxury of a secure supply of electricity and water, which were lacking in most residential areas around the country.[4] As one author puts it, "in the nineties, the search for an environment to realize a "modern" (often imported) lifestyle became the main motivation"[5] for these communities. Currently these communities exist in abundance particularly around the capital city and in the mountains. They have become enclosed complexes that offer a different culture than the dominant culture of the country,–an alternative culture,–where western influence is more accentuated. For instance French, which is widely spoken in Lebanon as a second language, has become the primary language used in these gated communities, as a way to mimic and claim a certain French identity, as opposed to the Lebanese/Arab identity.

The case of gated communities in Saudi Arabia, also known as "compounds," is crucial as it creates the most substantial gap between the interior community and the exterior world. These compounds developed as a result of the exploitation of oil in the 1940s that led to a major influx of western professionals into Saudi Arabia. Companies took the initiative to build residential compounds for these employees as an incentive in order to attract professionals and their families who would establish themselves in the country. Additionally, the Saudi government promoted the construction of these residential compounds, with the ultimate goal of limiting western influences on the Saudi society.[6] In a way, this was an attempt to further shelter Saudi Muslim women from the influence of westerners. These compounds were able to provide westerners with a "familiar" environment that would replicate, to a certain extent, their environment at home. At the same time, these compounds could control the influence of the foreigners by limiting their activities to the boundaries of the compounds and thus diminishing any possible interaction with the Saudis.

These compounds in Saudi Arabia are of three different types. Whereas the types differ mainly in their amenities and services, they all share the concept of a gated community that would not spread its influence outside the fences that enclose it which constitute a structural barrier, or a physical boundary. The compounds for unskilled or semi-skilled workers contain mostly pre-fabricated units and only the necessary amenities. The compounds for single semi-professionals and technicians provide units grouped around a few amenities. The compounds for expatriate professionals and their families are the most developed and well-maintained. They include a wide variety of amenities and services, such as security guard systems, sports facilities, landscaped yards, and even commercial programs.

ARAMCO, the Arab American Oil Company, is known to have played a determined role in the development of these compounds across Saudi Arabia. As part of its employment contract, ARAMCO offers its employees living units within its residential compounds and states that "the company wants all employees and families to enjoy a comfortable house with pleasant surroundings." The employees can take advantage of "a large grocery store, a post office, barber shops, beauty shops, a hospital, dentist offices, restaurants, snack bars, dry cleaners, laundries, flower shops, car repair shops and much more."[7] Most importantly, foreigners are attracted to the quality of life and living environment in these compounds. As a matter of fact, these compounds manage to create an almost completely western environment that is relatively similar to those in American suburbs. Within this western atmosphere, residents, especially women, can escape the strict rules imposed by the Saudi government on the society. Saudi Arabia is a strictly Muslim country, regulated by Muslim law, Muslim lifestyle and Arab traditions. Saudis, especially women, have to submit to rigid social rules and prohibitions. However within the limits of the compound, foreigners do not have to submit to these rules and can enjoy more freedom. "The *mutawwa* [Saudi police] cannot come onto the compounds and hassle the residents, but when you leave the compound, the women have to put on their *abayas* and follow the other strict rules." [8] Their lives are completely separate and different from that of the country in which they reside; at the same time they have little interaction with the Saudi culture and the Saudi people.

It is clear that the implementation of a western company—American in this case—in the heart of a Muslim country would have brought many western influences into the country. This strategy contained and isolated the effects of westernization on the Saudi culture, which could have otherwise spread throughout the country and compromise its uniformity.

The issue of whether these compounds are utopias or dystopias remains questionable. In fact, the perception of the compound depends on whether it is viewed from within or from without the compound itself. From within, the compound can be seen as a utopia suggesting a peaceful mode to co-exist with a society without interfering or conflicting with it. From without, however, the existence of such a compound is a dystopia, as it allows the creation of an environment that violates the rules that are vital for the continued existence of the society and the citizens' well-being. If Saudis believe in those rules as absolute guidelines for a way of life, then the existence of these compounds suggests a re-evaluation and a questioning of not only their rules but their makers as well. To an extent, binary qualities of utopia and dystopia widen the gap between the compound and its surroundings.

Although these compounds were originally planned to be used by and for the westerners, the boundary between them and the Saudi society is gradually dissolving. As social interaction between Saudis and westerners further developed in the workplace, Saudis slowly gained access to the compounds. In this context, Muslim women were even more affected by the characteristics of the boundary—both physical and cultural—which were created by these gated communities. In a literal sense, Muslim women experience a change of identity as they enter and exit the compounds. This is reflected in the fact that they can unveil themselves inside the compound but will have to put the veil back on upon exiting. This idea of "shedding the veil" is also illustrated in the physical architecture of the compounds. As the actual veil is removed, the architectural elements and their physical characteristics become the woman's veil hiding her from her actual community, the society, which remains outside the boundaries of the compound.

On the other hand, the typology of the compound is not limited to the residential communities reserved for foreigners. In fact, the Saudi compounds for extended families constitute a large segment of the residential typologies. Until the 1950s, residential architecture took the shape of clusters of courtyard houses around a shared public space. With the discovery of oil fields, a transformation occurred that was manifested through the replacement of the traditional web of circulation by a grid system of streets. This use of the grid was seen as synonymous with modernism and westernization. The *villa* was then introduced as a main dwelling type. "The ARAMCO Home Ownership Plan, a loan program initiated in 1951, played a major role in spreading the concept of the dwelling as a detached building, and determining the subdivision of land."[9] The typology of the villas developed as a box-like structure inside a walled compound. These villas were used as single-family dwellings that were incorporated into the grid plan.[10] This modern typology did not take into account the context in which it was set: the houses were separated from their neighbors. "Privacy is one of the most important values in a Saudi home. Hence, the courtyard housing with no exposure to exterior was ideal in traditional layout."[11] In the new housing arrangements, the privacy factor was not respected: windows and balconies faced the exterior of the house, and the residents were forced to use various screen systems to remedy this problem.

In the early 1980s, however a new trend emerged. It intended to create compounds for extended families with the advantage of strengthening the ties among families while maintaining the independence of each nuclear family. In fact, each nuclear family had a house with a separate entrance, and all the houses shared a public space that was similar to the courtyard in traditional typologies. In a certain way, this new typology could be considered a hybrid between the traditional layout and the strictly grid-like modern layout.[12] These gated compounds of linked houses could provide the family groups with a feeling of privacy and identity. It could be argued that this phenomenon of extended family compounds is similar to that of compounds reserved for expatriate professionals. Theoretically, the extended family compounds were based on traditional typologies, which envisioned the courtyard as a shared public space. In reality, the development of such compounds is potentially significant as an indication of implicitly rejecting the rules set by the Saudi government. Even Saudis closed themselves off into fenced compounds where their interactions were restricted to family members. There is no doubt that these compounds are not as autonomous and self-sustained as the compounds designed for foreigners, but there is nevertheless a desire to withdraw from the rest of the Saudi society and its rigid life-style. One could interpret this phenomenon as a voluntary transition from a model which consist one gated community within a larger cultural environment to several gated communities that form the larger cultural environment establishing its own identity. Contemporary Saudi society seems to be broken up into smaller communities—whether they include communities of extended families or communities of expatriates.

It could therefore be argued that these gated communities in the Arab world can be considered even more utopian than those in other parts of the world. Gated communities in the United States or in South Africa are characterized by an enclosure that makes them secure, protected and equally segregated. The primary purpose of the Western gated communities is maintaining safety—not necessarily the creation or protection of an identity or culture, though these may constitute legitimate reasons as well.

Whereas the case of gated communities in Saudi Arabia might purport an extreme example, it is certainly an illustration of a widely prevalent condition where the two identities within the Muslim world remain to a certain extent separate and do not merge into one combined identity. This is the case that has previously been depicted as Entity A + Entity B = Entity A or Entity B. In summary, it can be argued that as a currently prevalent model in some Islamic countries, gated communities reveal much about the status of women in such countries, which is of being halfway between the two worlds that have very little in common.

On the other hand, it is obvious that one would tend to view the formation of a third entity, one that is a homogeneous weave of cultures (the condition of Entity A + Entity B = Entity C) as a precedent for a successful merging of the East and the West, the traditional and the modern, the local and the global. However one should keep in mind that the third entity (C), which is a consequence of the unification of the two very different worlds, is the one that is different than either one of the two entities, being neither exclusively *one* nor *the other*. Nevertheless, the formation of the third entity is quite complicated; it is also quite difficult to locate one. Yet, could this *ideal* condition potentially and simultaneously exist without undermining (compromising) the values of each separate entity? In this respect challenges abound, yet it is worth considering for an improvement in Muslim women's lives in the dawn of the twenty-first century.

Glossary

Hijab	form of a veil
Musharabiyya	geometrically patterned screen
Mutawwa	Saudi police
abayas	loose-fitting robe for women

Notes

[1] Edward J. Blakely and Mary Gail Snyder, *Fortress America: Gated Communities in the United States* (Brookings Institution Press: Washington, D.C. 1997).

[2] Michel Foucault, "Of Other Spaces", *Diacritics* (Spring 1986): 26.

[3] Amira Abdel Latif, "It is Easy to Find Pastries in Marina, but It is Difficult to Find a Loaf of Bread" [Online: web]. Retrieved 22 March 2005. URL: http://www.cx.unibe.ch/islam/mitarbeiterPubl/amira

[4] Georg Glasze and Abdallah Al-Khayyal, "Gated Housing Estates in the Arab World: Case Studies in Lebanon and Riyadh, Saudi Arabia." *Environment and Planning B: Planning and Design* 29 (2002): 327-334.

[5] Gated Communities. [Online: web]. Cited 22 March 2005. URL: http://parole.aporee.org/work/hier.php3?spec_id=11973&words_id=356

[6] Glasze and Al-Khayyal. 323-326.

[7] Saudi Aramco Oil Company. Housing. [Online: web]. Cited 22 March 2005. URL: http://www.saudiaramco.com/bvsm/JSP/content/channelDetail.jsp?SA.channelID=-1073750238

[8] Eric Hooton, Living in Saudi Arabia: Living and Working in the Saudi Kingdom. [Online: web]. Cited 22 March 2005. URL:

http://www.escapeartist.com/efam/56/Working_in_Saudi_Arabia.html

[9] İsmet Kilin□aslan, "Quality of Residential Environments in Dammam, Saudi Arabia", *International Journal for Housing Science and its Applications* 19 (1995): 157-162.

[10] Kaizer Talib, *Shelter in Saudi Arabia* (London: Academy Editions, 1984), 111-132.

[11] Kilincaslan, 166.

[12] Glasze and Al-Khayyal, 324.

CHANGING ROLES AND PERCEPTIONS
OF WOMEN IN TURKEY:
TOWARD A MORE CONSERVATIVE FUTURE

ÖVGÜ TÜZÜN

If all societies ... that seek to produce a new man through a process of 'deculturation' and 'reculturation' set such store on the seemingly most insignificant details of *dress*, *bearing*, physical and verbal *manners*, the reason is that, treating the body as memory, they entrust to it in abbreviated and practical, i.e. mnemonic, form the fundamental principles of the arbitrary content of the culture. The principles embodied in this way are placed beyond the grasp of consciousness.[1]

The widespread perception that wearing "the Islamic headscarf" has been a growing trend among young women in educational institutions and urban professions despite official restrictions was recently confirmed by a survey published by KONDA, a leading research institute in Turkey. According to survey results, the ratio of Turkish women who cover their hair has risen from 64.2 percent to 69.4 percent since 2006. Among covered women, the ratio of those who wear the Islamic headscarf (*türban*) has risen sharply from 3.5 percent to 16.3 percent.[2] The aim of the KONDA research was to find out how the use of the Islamic headscarf and the politicization of the "*türban* debate" were perceived by the adult population of Turkey. KONDA's research also aimed to assess women's changing habits and perceptions regarding religion, covering[3] and secularism, while identifying the scope and direction of the changes that have been taking place.[4]

Given the particular socio-political and cultural dynamics in Turkey, the controversy raised by KONDA's research (entitled "Religion, Secularism and *Türban*") is hardly surprising. Ever since the survey results were made public, there have been endless speculations and discussions concerning these issues in various public platforms throughout the country. Most of these discussions centered on the ever-popular debate about the compatibility of religion and secularism with special emphasis on the ways in which the so-called "moderate Islamic model" championed by the ruling JDP ("Justice and Development Party", "AK Parti") affected this rising trend of religiosity. While several commentators celebrated the modernization of Islam as indicated by the increasing visibility of "covered women" in public life, many others started to wonder whether the only secular and democratic Muslim country in the world is on its way to become "another Malaysia".

As the most discernible symbol of political Islam for the last three decades, the Islamic headscarf has widely been considered a threat to secularism and gender equality, which are held to be two of the most cherished values of republican modernity in Turkey. The first legal measure taken against the Islamic headscarf was put into force in 1982 when the Council of Higher Education banned the wearing of the headscarf in universities. However, the ban was softened in 1984 and 1987 under the rule of the centre-right Motherland Party, (MP, "Anavatan Partisi") for which the Islamists "constituted the single most powerful faction in the party organization."[5] This decision was annulled in 1989 when the Constitutional Court argued that religion is a matter of private conscience and should not be politicized. Since 1997, when the ban was strictly enforced, many headscarf wearing young women attempted to reconcile their religious beliefs with their desire to get educated by removing the headscarf outside the university gates and wearing a wig or a hat instead. Others went abroad to pursue their studies. The grievances of headscarf wearing students, and their families were reiterated regularly throughout the political campaigns of the right-wing and Islamist parties. Consequently the JDP had been under increasing pressure from its base to take action against the ban.

These debates gained a new momentum and intensity with the approval of the constitutional amendments lifting the ban on headscarves in Turkish universities. Article 10 concerning equality and Article 42 concerning the right to education were intertwined since they both addressed the educational rights of female students wearing turban. The wording in Article 42 is as follows: "Except as otherwise stated in the laws of the Republic, no one can be prevented from pursuing the right to university education. The limit to the ways in which this right is pursued is specified by law." Interestingly the approval of the amendments required a joint effort: they were initiated and supported by the Nationalist Action Party (NAP, "Milliyetci Hareket Partisi"), in cooperation with the AK Party, whose large base in the Parliament ensured their quick approval on February 9, 2008. Nonetheless, many members of the country's Higher Educational Board and a vast majority of university presidents defied the reform, arguing that before they could be enforced, new regulations should be introduced, stipulating exactly how the "turban reform" should be interpreted and implemented. Their lead was followed by the opposition party, the Republican People's Party (RPP, Cumhuriyet Halk Partisi), which appealed to the Constitutional Court to have the amendments annulled. On March 8, 2008 the High Court agreed to take up the case. A 50-page petition submitted to the court by the RPP claimed that the constitutional changes lifting the ban on turban violate the basic and overriding clause of the Constitution (Article II), that the secular nature of the Republic cannot be altered or even considered to be altered. On June 5, 2008 the Constitutional Court ruled that the Turkish Parliament (and the majority of its members) had violated the constitutionally enshrined principle of secularism when it passed amendments to lift the headscarf ban on university campuses. Additionally the court upheld the ban on the headscarf. However throughout the 2008 and even into the 2009 the headscarf discussions continued, increasing further polarization in Turkey between the secularists and the fundamentalists.

This essay maintains to examine the changing roles and perceptions of women in Turkey in the light of "headscarf discussions" in order to make some projections about the future of discussions. While the emphasis is placed on practices regarding Islam and "covering" in Turkey, the Turkish case is evaluated within the larger international context in order to portray the interactive nature of these debates and their impact on the everyday lives of Muslim women. How the current religious revivalism as a global phenomenon is nurtured by a host of particular theoretical positions, namely cultural relativism, identity politics, and postmodernism, is also among the topics addressed in this study.

Behind the Headscarf

Even before the amendments were introduced, tensions had already been running high in Turkey following the second electoral victory of JDP in the July 2007 general elections. Before the elections, the prospect of a JDP president had brought huge crowds onto the streets. When Abdullah Gül, second in command of the JDP, was finally elected as the President, Turkey was introduced to a first lady—for the first time in its 84 year history—who is wearing the Islamic headscarf. Besides its political implications, Gül's presidency almost signified, to many secularists, that "the last bastion might be falling". With the JDP's control of the presidency as well as the parliament, many expect the party to take bolder steps towards Islamisation. In fact, the amendments lifting the ban are widely interpreted as one of the first signs of a more accentuated Islamist shift in the JDP's policies. Until 2009, the JDP representatives insisted that "the headscarf issue" would be solved through societal consensus. This attitude was in tune with the conciliatory and moderate approach employed by the party in aiming to solve the problems of Islamic identity through a consensus with the secular establishment. However, during a visit to Spain in January 2008, Prime Minister Erdogan said that the headscarves could not be banned even if they were worn as political symbols and he took everyone by surprise. According to one journalist, Erdoğan's decision to "solve" the headscarf issue through constitutional changes without seeking consensus was signaling that the party was moving back to its ideological home.[6]

Unlike its predecessor the Welfare Party, which sustained a more radical stance, the JDP had "found a safe haven in de-emphasizing ideology and in engaging with Kemalism on its own terms by pursuing Turkey's 'above-politics' EU membership Project."[7] However, the JDP's attempt to lift the ban on headscarves in universities contributed to a succession of political events that suggest a visible change in the way the JDP is perceived by large segments of Turkish society. One very interesting consequence in this regard was the rift that occurred between the JDP and liberals who had thus far lent almost full support to the party and its policies.[8] Dismissing widespread fears that the JDP had a "hidden" Islamist agenda, the vast majority of liberal intellectuals argued that the party should be given the benefit of the doubt, since its members had publicly disavowed political Islam and announced their dedication to a reformist agenda. Good relations between the JDP and liberals prevailed throughout the first term of JDP rule since the party refrained from overtly Islamist moves and went ahead with political reforms which eventually paved the way for the EU decision to start accession talks with Turkey in 2004. Liberals were also highly appreciative of the DP's commitment to neo-liberal policies and efforts to integrate Turkey with global markets. It is possible to argue that the initial support of Turkish liberals was highly instrumental in the consolidation of the JDP's image, in Turkey as well as abroad, as a moderate/conservative/centrist right-wing party that is essentially pro-Western and democratic.

What skeptics called "the unholy union" between the JDP and liberals was fundamentally shaken following the alliance of the JDP with the Nationalist Action Party (NAP) in order to lift the ban on headscarves at universities. Well-recognized liberal intellectuals such as Şahin Alpay, Mehmet Altan, Cengiz Aktar and Fuat Keyman were openly critical of this move since the lifting of the headscarf ban was handled as a "single" issue rather than as part of a long expected "package of human rights reforms" that would also include EU requested amendments to the Turkish Penal Code's Article 301. Although some liberal intellectuals like İhsan Dağı and Şaban Çalış continued to lend the JDP their unconditional support, they were outnumbered by others who began to question whether the reforms spearheaded by the JDP were meant to broaden freedom of Muslim religious expression, rather than the freedom of expression for all. In other words, for the first time since it came to power, the JDP had to face the most serious allegations about its conduct: Does the government prefer to be selective about rendering democracy and equality?

More importantly the JDP's attempt to lift the ban on headscarves was countered by the Constitutional Court's unanimous decision to file a lawsuit against the JDP on March 31, 2008. The case was brought by the chief prosecutor and contained a 162-page indictment against the Justice and Development Party for being the focal point of anti-secular activities. Chief Prosecutor Abdurrahman Yalcinkaya argued that the JDP was using democracy as a vehicle for imposing Shari'a law and asked for a five-year ban from political life on 71 JDP members including the Prime Minister Recep Tayyip Erdoğan. However on July 30, 2008 the court voted not to close the party, rejecting most of the prosecutors' demands.

Among other things, the amendments that were to lift the ban on headscarves were cited in the indictment as part of the process towards the Islamisation of public space. In this sense, the prosecutor's indictment illustrates how headscarves are related to social concerns, especially to the mounting influence of Islamism in Turkey. During the late 1990s and early 2000s, many people attributed the rise of conservatism and Islamism to the escalating public presence of headscarves. In doing so, they drew on deep-seated philosophical and political assumptions about what Turkish society ought to be and expressed equally deep-seated fears about what it had become.

Meanwhile, in a series of cases, the European Court had supported actions taken by the Turkish state that had been challenged in the name of religious freedom, including, most famously, the closing down of the Welfare political party.[9] In 2005, when the European Court of Human Rights ruled in favor of Turkey's ban of headscarves in the country's universities, supporters of the ban in Turkey euphorically claimed that the ruling was "binding", and it marked the end of the headscarf controversy. However, Prime Minister Recep Tayyip Erdoğan has hit back at such court decisions, saying that the competent authority on the headscarf controversy are the "ulemas," the Islamic religious authorities, rather than the civil courts.[10] His comments have further raised questions about his commitment to secularism and contributed to the escalation of polarized perceptions in the country.

Perception Matters: Is the Headscarf a Question of Individual Conscience or a Symbol of Political Islam?

Since the headscarf is an uneven signifier with manifold meanings, the headscarf controversy has triggered a "clash of perceptions". While the JDP and opponents of prohibition refer to the wearing of the Islamic headscarf as "a question of freedom of expression and the universal right to education", most secularists regard the headscarf as a serious threat to Turkey's secularism and fear that lifting of the ban would put social pressure on the rest of Turkish women who are not wearing the headscarf in predominantly Muslim Turkey. Secularists also fear that if the headscarf ban is lifted at universities, it will eventually be lifted also in schools and in public offices, where it is still in place. Consequently, the military, the judiciary and the groups that constitute Turkey's secular establishment, along with secular Turks, see any removal of the headscarf ban as a serious attack on the secular state. The fear is that once the secularists are put into a minority position, not only will secular women's rights cease to be respected, but they will be intimidated and oppressed by the rising tide of conservative gender roles and by fundamentalist Islam. As Georg E. Gruen suggests,

> The secularists are not so worried about the affluent and well-educated Islamic feminists at the universities in Istanbul or Ankara as they are about the "reactionary example" they are setting for the masses.[11]

In this sense, it is possible to argue that the "battle" over the headscarf is not really about a piece of cloth or how people dress in public spaces and educational institutions. Rather, it is symptomatic of a much larger problem, one that seems to be about the contending claims made on the secular regime of Turkey.

Women are inevitably caught up in the "political-cultural battle ground" of Muslim societies[12] and Turkey is no exception. In this context, the "headscarf controversy" cannot be fully understood unless it is analyzed within the specific socio-political and historical context of Turkey. At the root of this controversy lies the historical debate about the role of Islam in Turkish society and politics. Although the origin of Turkey's secularization dates back to nineteenth-century reform programs during the Ottoman Empire, particularly the modernization effort during the Tanzimat period (1839-1876), it was Mustafa Kemal Atatürk's radical secular reforms that progressively implemented structural changes aimed at the separation of religion and politics.

It is important to note that the "status of women in society" has been central to the Republican Kemalist Project which radically altered the status of women through a set of legal and educational reforms that were implemented in the early years of the republic. For example, the Civil Code adopted in 1926 gave women unprecedented legal rights by replacing Islamic law (Shari'a), abolishing polygamy, and recognizing women's equal rights with men with regard to divorce, custody of children, and inheritance. The 1934 reforms granted women suffrage and the right to run for office. It was also during this time that European dress codes were introduced, with the implication that Ottoman dress style, especially the man's *fez* and the woman's *veil,* carried implications of "backwardness". Some intellectuals of the period also argued that the Ottoman "covering" of women was an alien practice with Persian, Arabic or Byzantine origin and it was a violation of the "true Turkish culture" of Central Asia according to which women did not cover.[13] Consequently, as early as the 1930s, Turkey stood as an anomaly among Muslim countries, with large numbers of women in hitherto male occupations, as judges, lawyers, academicians and doctors, who had few equivalents, if any, at that time, even in the West.[14]

With the transition to multi-party politics in the second half of the twentieth century, various agencies of the state gradually incorporated religious elements to sustain and bolster their legitimacy. Although religiously oriented voters have formed the backbone of the centre-right parties since the Democrat Party (DP) (1946-1960), it was first by the National Order Party (NOP, 1970-1971), and later by the National Salvation Party (NSP, 1972-1980) that representation of religious interests was explicitly articulated.[15] Throughout the 1970s, the discourse that came to be associated with the veteran Islamist politician Necmeddin Erbakan and the NSP became standard fare for mainstream Islamists.

The ability to face left and right at the same time enabled the NSP to form a coalition with the social democrats in 1975 and, when that failed, [it] joined the Nationalist Front coalition with the Justice Party, the party of "freemasons, Zionists, and cosmopolitans", and the Nationalist Action Party. These coalitions gave the NSP legitimacy, a foot inside the state, and patronage with which to support and cultivate their clients, the religious orders and their off-shoots.[16]

Throughout the highly politicized yet culturally diverse environment of Turkey in the 1970s, there was a revival of Islamic learning in the cities. At the same time, a growing number of young women in educational institutions and work places began to defy the official secular dress codes by covering their heads in public. When the NSP was closed in the aftermath of the 1980 coup, Islamist politicians formed the Welfare Party that gained increasing influence in the Turkish political arena in the 1980s and 1990s.

As Mahmood Monshipouri argues, the economic and political restructuring during the 1980s transformed Turkish society in numerous ways:

> Özal's patronage policy and Demirel's connection to the provincial bourgeoisie brought a new class of politicians to the forefront of Turkish politics. The bourgeoisie, who had been in power since 1983, were conspicuously devout, since they came from milieus influenced by traditional cultural and religious values.[17]

While the modernizing elites of the earlier decades took as their basic mission the secularization of Turkish politics and the transmission of Western values to that polity and society, the technocratic elites of the 1980s defined their goals less in terms of educating the people than of synthesizing Islamic values and pragmatic rationality.[18] The kind of social conservatism based on Islam that colors all parties on the right was given a further boost with the 1980 military coup, which can be seen as a turning point in the state's relation to Islam. The military regime that ruled the country between 1980 and 1983 made religious lessons mandatory and actively promoted the idea of a "Turkish-Islamic" synthesis as an antidote for left-wing and ethno-nationalist movements.[19] Thus, Turkey became an important regional actor in the US sponsored "green belt project" that was designed to promote Islamic resurgence as an antidote to leftist movements in the Greater Middle East region.

Islamisation tendencies which evolved during the 1980s eventually paved the way for the rising tide of social and political Islam in the 1990s. Having increased its vote from 8 percent in 1987 to 16 percent in 1991, the Islamist Welfare Party emerged as the leading party in the 1994 municipal elections. The Welfare municipalities curtailed municipal corruption, directed public services to the poor and initiated a period marked by tighter controls on bars and the consumption of alcohol along with a larger place for Islamic and traditional symbols in public.[20] Capitalizing on its achievements in local government, the Welfare Party later had the highest share of votes (21.4 percent) in the 1995 general elections and became coalition partners with Tansu Çiller's True Path Party (TPP). During this time the self-consciously Islamist Welfare Party became a nationwide mass political movement as women's Islamic activism in Turkey also gained momentum. At the same time, women's public attire and visibility acquired new importance. On the other hand, the policies pursued by the Erbakan-led government divided the country along the secularist-Islamist axis and was met with increasing secular opposition and protest.[21] Amid growing tensions due to rising Islamic mobilization, the military asked the WP-led government at the meeting of the National Security Council (NSC), held on 28 February 1997, to take measures against the rise of political Islam. When the Welfare Party-True Path Party coalition government showed reluctance to adopt measures suggested by the military, the military leaders began to mobilize public opinion by briefing journalists, businessmen, university presidents and high-level bureaucrats. Under such quasi-democratic pressure, the coalition government resigned.[22]

The events that led to the closing down of the Welfare Party also triggered the division of political Islam into the reformist and traditionalist factions. The Welfare Party's successor became the Virtue Party (VP), which had a hard time coping with the rising tide of internal dissent in addition to external pressure simultaneously. It was eventually closed down by the Constitutional Court. While the traditionalists re-grouped under the newly-formed Felicity Party (FP) in July 2001, the reformist wing went on to establish JDP in August 2001. Whereas the Islamist parties of the past represented a peripheral force compared to the position of the so-called secular parties, the JDP claimed the political territory of the centre-right by toning down the Islamist rhetoric and emphasizing the universally accepted concepts of democracy and human rights. Moreover, in their attempt to synthesize market modernism and Muslim identity, JDP members were successful in presenting their program as a renewal of the conservative liberal legacy dating back to the Democratic Party tradition in the 1950s. In this regard, popularity of this newly formed party can be attributed to its ability to unite Turkey's fractious political field and occupy the center. In the absence of any credible alternative, 34.2 percent of the electorate voted for the JDP which thereby had the sufficient majority to form a single-party government following the 2002 general elections. The JDP leaders were "perceived" differently because they "had absorbed aspects of the radical Islamist revolt of the 1980s, to which they added big business, the Pentagon and a keen understanding [of the] New World religiosity."[23] While the JDP successfully capitalized on the spirit of the times, the legacy of hard-line political Islam left the Virtue Party with little chance for success. In the same elections that brought the "reformists" to power, the Virtue Party suffered a humiliating defeat receiving only 2.4 percent of the votes.

In the light of these observations, one may suggest that the JDP is the product of an embryonic Turkish Islamist tradition that has grown more moderate as it has moved closer to the realities of politics and the requirements of pragmatism. Whether the JDP's new-found admiration for democracy and human rights is tactical or strategic yet remains to be seen. Although the JDP government, which has admittedly pushed Turkey toward the EU membership, has consistently denied having any Islamic agenda, it has taken a number of policy initiatives that have stoked secularist concerns. In addition to the partisan methods with which the latest "headscarf crisis" was managed, the JDP tried to facilitate the entry of Imam Hatip High School (prayer and preacher school) graduates into the universities and expand religious education. Prime Minister Erdoğan also tried to criminalize adultery before being forced to back down under intense domestic and EU pressure. Moreover, some party-run municipalities use state funds for publishing and distributing religious books and have also taken steps to ban or restrict alcohol consumption. More recently, the directorate of religious affairs (Diyanet), which used to have a reputation for promoting moderate interpretations of Islam, published an article that urges women "to cover up and behave modestly to avoid provoking male sexual desires."[24] Indeed, as Yavuz and Özcan argue, "Erdoğan has failed to bridge the gap between Turkey's religious heartland and secular Turks, and his policies have deepened the feeling among secularists of being under siege."[25]

International Dimensions

Despite the apparent polarization in the country, it would be misleading to suggest that lives of women in Turkey are entirely determined by either Islamic doctrine or Kemalist ideology. Although both Islamic practice and the Kemalist heritage have marked the roles and perceptions of women in significant ways, the influence of global socioeconomic and political relations should not be underestimated. In this sense, it is important to contextualize domestic developments in Turkey within the larger international context and try to ascertain the ways in which perceptions and practices in Turkey are influenced by global debates about the headscarf and vice versa.

In many parts of the world, headscarves came to represent certain threats at specific moments and this is due to several historical processes and events. Especially in Europe, where the Muslim population has significantly increased in the second half of the twentieth century, the headscarf has come to signify not only political Islam, but also the oppression of women. When, in 2004, France outlawed the wearing of headscarves in public schools, for example, the decision was taken in the name of secularism and gender equality. The decision also promoted the understanding that "the Islamic headscarf is inimical to the values of state neutrality, tolerance, and pluralism that underlie *laicite*."[26] The events that came to be known as the *affaires de foulard* began on October 3, 1989 when Muslim girls who refused to remove their headscarves were expelled from their middle school in the town of Creil. Following extensive press coverage and several demonstrations organized by Muslim groups, Socialist Minister of Education Lionel Jospin issued a circular and left it to the school authorities to decide whether headscarves were admissible or not on a case by case basis. The ruling appeared to calm things down until 1994 when the question of headscarves was again raised by a right-wing deputy (Eugene Cheniere) who offered a bill that would ban all "ostentatious signs" of religious affiliation in schools. Although the bill was initially accepted, it was later overturned by several courts and eventually by the Conseil d'état which reaffirmed its 1989 ruling. As in 1989 and 1994, the "headscarf controversy" was once again the center of public attention in 2003 when the famous Stasi Commission was formed. At the recommendation of this commission, a law prohibiting the wearing of ostentatious signs of religious affiliation in public schools was eventually enforced in October 2004.[27]

In 1998, the Islamic headscarf raised similar fears in Germany when German courts debated whether school authorities in Stuttgart could deny a civil service position as an elementary school teacher to Fereshta Ludin, an Afghani woman, because she refused to take off her headscarf while teaching. The Federal Constitutional Court eventually ruled in Ms. Ludin's favor in 2003, despite significant criticism. The decision was justified on the grounds that the state of Baden-Wurttemberg did not specifically ban headscarves. The absence of a "legal ban" was speedily remedied the following year. Elsewhere, in the United States, in 2001 when Sultaana Freeman, a US-born convert to Islam, posed for a Florida state driver's license agency, wearing a headscarf and a veil, exposing merely her eyes, she was assessed through the lenses of heightened concerns about national security in the post 9/11 era. As Robert A. Kahn argues, headscarf disputes in Germany and in the US were compounded by the "private fears" of these countries, and shaped by national historical experience and traditions.[28]

As shown by the aforementioned developments, the headscarf has universally assumed a symbolic character and in the West it is commonly associated with various "threats" such as the rise of political Islam and Islamic militancy, the repression of women and fears of totalitarianism. Thus, behind these religious signs, many in the West see backsliding regarding the status and condition of women. Moreover, beyond the religious foundation undergirding the Islamic headscarf as a form of modesty, headscarves are widely perceived as markers of Muslim identity. The headscarf, as an identity marker, also has political implications and serves as a sign of political activism. In this light, it is possible to suggest that the "headscarf controversy" is more about the impact of the headscarf on the observer than it is about the intent of the woman wearing it. The headscarf may be worn as a sign of self-emancipation, religious conviction or as "a protection of chastity." However, in the eyes of those who do not wear it, the headscarf is far from simply being a matter of private conscience. In other words, it may be conceived as a "stigma symbol."

> The Islamic headscarf supplies information about the bearer, but it is also subject to public perception. It communicates the individual and collective motivations of those who adopt it as much as the perceptions of those who reject it.[29]

Thus, covering practices acquire their meaning and practice within the historically and socially situated conditions of their production. Yet one thing remains certain: the headscarf and other religious signs have taken on a political meaning and can no longer be considered as personal signs of religious affiliation.

Beyond the Headscarf Controversy: What Lies Ahead?

Some commentators have suggested that the current conflict in Turkey can be interpreted as a "battle for hegemony" between the secular elite who are losing their privileged status and the rising class of socially conservative pious Muslims.[30] As Öniş suggests:

> They have singled out the tensions between the authoritarian secularism of the Republican elite at the "centre" and the broad masses quite congenial to Islamic principles and values on the "periphery", and the attempts to resolve these tensions following the transition to multiparty democracy in the post-1950 era.[31]

While not denying the importance of the specific historical and domestic dimensions of the Turkish case, I agree with Ziya Öniş that the rise of political Islam in Turkey should also be examined in relation to the far-reaching transformations that are occurring at the global level both in the economic and the cultural sphere. Particularly important in this regard are the transformations brought about by globalization, the process of neo-liberal economic restructuring and the dissemination of postmodern ideas. The combination of these factors has facilitated, among other things, the resurgence of allegiance to out-dated worldviews, which manifests itself in the questioning of secular ideologies and paradigms. Meanwhile, this current process has also led to the transformation of many radical and/or fundamentalist groups in search for recognition and legitimacy in an environment marked by the hegemony of multicultural relativism. The transformation of the Turkish Islamist movement that culminated in the emergence of the so-called "moderate Islamist movement" and the subsequent rise of the JDP to power perfectly illustrate that there is plenty of room for politicized religion if its members denounce the radical Islamist posture and adopt the logic of the neo-liberal system in its stead.

On the other hand, one could also argue that the moderate Islamist/pro-market politics espoused by the JDP enables the integration of large segments of the Muslim population to global market operations. As Cihan Tuğal maintains, the JDP has played an integral role in transforming attitudes towards the marketization of the economy at a molecular level.

Although previous Islamist programs had already shifted away from social egalitarianism, this still mattered to the movement's supporters. That resistance to neo-liberalism has now been removed, and there is a broader acceptance of "market realities" among the popular sectors. One reason for the change is that, for the first time in Turkish history, practicing Muslims are spearheading the liberalization of the economy; it is their religious lifestyle that wins them mass consent.[32]

From this perspective, the JDP's discourse and policies have been indispensable in consolidating the neo-liberal project in Turkey by gradually transforming the outlook of millions of pious Muslims who had hitherto sustained an anti-American and anti-market view. This transformation in religious mindsets has also introduced new understandings and practices of covering and led to the creation of a "new market" based on the commercialization of religious practices and symbols. In this sense, new covering styles are inseparable from consumption, commodity, even pleasure patterns, and are stimulated by global and local trends of the market economy.[33] As popular/consumerist culture becomes more salient, various types of religiosities that are intertwined with the transformation of covered women and their understanding of privacy surface.

The dialectical relationship between secularism and Islamic revivalism will continue to impact the global socio-political environment in the years to come. There is also no doubt that the headscarf will continue to be a highly contested issue implicated in larger ideological struggles in Turkey as well as in those Western countries where Muslims reside. It is likely that Turkey will inevitably encounter myriad difficulties on the path to reaching a viable compromise between the increasing demands of its devout Muslim citizens and the basic tenets of its secular constitution. A practical equilibrium between these two may indeed be difficult to achieve. However one can only hope that such a discourse will create an environment conducive to political stability and societal peace over the longer term. Support for Islamists in Turkey, like in other Muslim countries in the world, is fueled by disparities in income, differences in world views and social alienation. In this sense, the rise of JDP to power and the popularity it currently enjoys have more to do with the past failures of the political parties than with the inherent strength or originality of the JDP's political agenda.

It is possible to argue that the JDP's program is not to work towards the ultimately impossible goal of overthrowing the secular regime, but rather to pursue "bottom-up" policies that would gradually Islamize the country.[34] Even so, excluding Turkish Islamists from the political process at a time when they enjoy extensive support and legitimacy in global public opinion is ultimately counterproductive and is bound to face resistance. An analogous point can be made in relation to the idea of presenting the "headscarf ban in universities" as a miracle cure that will prevent the further demise of secularism in Turkey. Forcing headscarf-wearing women to "adopt subversive strategies of parody"[35] and wear wigs and hats as they enter the university campuses, runs the risk of further alienating these women who feel "victimized" by the state.

This does not, however, mean that greater freedom for religious expression and accommodation of claims made by pious Muslims in public space will necessarily lead to the consolidation of democracy and human rights in a predominantly Muslim country. Contrary to what liberal and Islamist supporters of the headscarf argue, the "fears" of secularists are legitimate and cannot be simply dismissed as "paranoia." It is not unrealistic to assume that the end of the ban may introduce an initial step that will pave the way for the escalation of claims made by pious Muslims and the spread of the headscarf in places other than universities, such as in public schools, in the Parliament, and among public servants. It is also possible that the headscarf will not only acquire legitimacy but will be exploited to enforce conservative Islam upon others, especially on students who do not necessarily wear the headscarf in Anatolian universities. Outside the metropolitan centers such as in Istanbul, Izmir and Ankara, such "social pressure" already exists in various forms. Ideally, in a climate of resurgent religious conservatism and fundamentalism, any lifting of the ban must also be accompanied by appropriate safeguards for the rights of those who choose not to wear the headscarf. Herein lay the real challenge.

Finally, it is important to note that the ongoing political and social developments since the last quarter of the twentieth century point to the growth of multiple cultural identities that seek recognition in public space. In this context, Islamism as a mode of political agency has introduced new categories of identity into politics.

> Islamism is concomitant with the formation of new middle classes and is on the way to creating its own intellectual, political, and entrepreneurial elites, drawing on their increasing public visibility and commercial success. We can speak of a post-Islamist stage in which Islamism is losing its political and revolutionary fervor but steadily infiltrating social and cultural everyday life practices.[36]

This interactive process, shaped by secularist and ritualist interventions, generates "hybrid subjects who embody traces of many conflicting discourses and practices."[37] Unlike radical Islamists, then, the "moderate" Islamists of the twenty-first century do not reject the West single-handedly, but rather selectively adopt and adapt Western institutions and technologies without dispensing with their faith-based perspective. Thus, the secular and the religious are deeply implicated in one another in any given societal context.

The future of women in Turkey will be determined by the complex interplay of the aforementioned forces as much as by the ways in which women endorse and claim their agencies. Ultimately, whether covered or not, women's positions in society are determined by socio-economic conditions more than by the clothes they wear. Furthermore, as Nancy Hirschmann suggests, women can only act within parameters determined by social power structures and their ability to challenge them is nevertheless circumscribed by patriarchy. The crux of the matter about covering is thus underpinned by a paradox: women's ability to *choose* their practices is key to agency, yet the fact that women choose the headscarf or the veil does not *of itself* make it a free action, or even an act of protest.

> Thus, *the act of choosing* is necessary but not sufficient. What is also needed is the ability to *formulate choices*, and this requires the ability to have meaningful power in the construction of contexts.[38]

From this perspective, covering could be perceived as a sign of the closed circularity of women's political disempowerment and can only be remedied through the re-conceptualization of a progressive and egalitarian Islam that would contribute to Muslim women's emancipation.[39]

Finally, the rising conservative tide in Turkey, as elsewhere in the world, is far from being a unitary and monolithic movement, not only in that the agendas of those involved are diverse, but goals change over time. Most significantly, the "Islamic Revival" in Turkey is complicated by the global phenomenon of the "resurgence of religion." Thus, to the extent that the common geo-political and social crises of the post-Cold War world account for the many religious and ethno-nationalist movements in the world, the Islamist upsurge in Turkey should come as no surprise. The roles and perceptions of women are being reproduced and redefined in this process and it certainly appears that the important issues raised by the headscarf, such as those of freedom and agency, will continue to be deeply contested and re-articulated in the years to come.

Postscript

On July 30, 2008 the court turned down the attempt by state prosecutors to ban the JDP on the grounds that the party had become the focal point of anti-secular activities. Although a majority of six of the eleven judges had voted to shut down the party, the support of seven judges was required to pass such a measure. The court settled on the minority view of four judges to cut half of JDP's state funding. The verdict is widely interpreted as a serious warning to the party since ten of the constitutional court's judges argued that JDP was guilty of anti-secular activity. The judges disagreed merely on the nature of the verdict.

Notes

[1] Pierre Bourdieu, *Outline of a Theory of Practice* (Cambridge: Cambridge University Press, 1977). 94.

[2] *Başörtüsü* is the traditional, non-Islamic head covering which allows some hair to be seen, whereas the *türban*—or Islamic headscarf—is neatly pinned at the sides, leaving the face exposed. The turban associated with *tesettür* style covers the shoulders, neck and chest and symbolizes engagement with Islamism as both a lifestyle and political movement.

[3] Although the term "veiling" is extensively used, especially in Western media and scholarship, to refer to covering practices of Muslim women, the actual "veil" that covers the face is in fact very different from the Islamic and traditional types of headscarf. The mistake in terminology is admittedly problematic since the universalism it seems to endorse denies cultural specificities and variations. My usage of the words "covering" and "headscarf" instead of the more widely used "veiling" and "Islamic veil" is deliberate as I agree with Joan W. Scott that the substitution of veil for headscarf further complicates and obfuscates the meaning of an already complex signifier. It is also possible to suggest that the adoption of the ideologically loaded "veil" in headscarf-related debates is symptomatic of deeper Orientalist tendencies. In this sense, it is worthwhile to remember that unlike the headscarf which leaves the face exposed, veils that cover the face shroud girls in silence, rob them of their identity, limit their sight and allow for play of fantasies. For a detailed discussion of the fetishisation of the veil as the signifier of both Oriental women and of the Orient see Claire Dwyer, "'Ninja Women': The Representation of Muslim Women in the West." *Interwine* (1991-1992): 8-13.

[4] *Milliyet*, 3 December 2007.

[5] Sencer Ayata, "Patronage, Party, and State: The Politicization of Islam in Turkey" in *Middle East Journal* Vol. 50, No. 1 (Winter 1996): 40-56.

[6] Ece Temelkuran, "AKP 'evine' dönüyor: Açık büfeden ideolojiye." [The JDP is Going Back 'Home': From Open Buffet to Ideology], *Milliyet* 16 January 2008: 13.

[7] Menderes Çınar, "Turkey's Transformation Under the *AKP* Rule" in *The Muslim World* Vol. 96 (July 2006): 469-486.

[8] For more about the rift between JDP and liberals see Zafer Özcan, "AK Parti'yle Ittifak Sanal, Ayrışma Gerçek!" [The Alliance with JDP is Virtual, Separation is Real!] *Aksiyon* No: 689, 18 February 2008: 14-15.

[9] John R. Bowen, *Why the French Don't Like Headscarves?: Islam, the State, and Public Space* (Princeton: Princeton University Press, 2007), 139.

[10] Hilmi Toros, "Turkey: Headscarves Become a Headache" *IPS,* March 14, 2008. http://ipsnews.net/news.asp?idnews=41602. October 24, 2009.

[11] George E. Gruen, "Turks Debate the Role of Islam", in *American Foreign Policy Interests* Vol. 25 (2003): 286-298.

[12] Valentine M. Moghadam, "Introduction and Overview: Gender Dynamics of Nationalism, Revolution and Islamisation" in *Gender and National Identity:*

Women and Politics in Muslim Societies. ed. Valentine M. Mogador (London and Atlantic Highlands, N.J.: Zed, 1994), 18-39.

[13] Emelie A. Olson, "Muslim Identity and Secularism in Contemporary Turkey: 'The Headscarf Dispute'", in *Anthropological Quarterly* Vol. 58, No. 4 (October 1985): 161-171.

[14] Binnaz Toprak, "Islam and Democracy in Turkey." In *Religion and Politics in Turkey.* eds. Ali Çarkoğlu and Barry Rubin (New York: Routledge, 2006), 25-45.

[15] Ahmet Yıldız. "Politico-Religious Discourse of Political Islam in Turkey: The Parties of National Outlook", in *The Muslim World* Vol. 93 (April 2003): 187-209.

[16] Feroz Ahmad. "Politics and Islam in Modern Turkey" in *Middle Eastern Studies* 27:1 (1991): 3-21, p.17.

[17] Mahmood Monshipouri, *Islamism, Secularism, and Human Rights in the Middle East* (Boulder: Lynne Rienner, 1998), 111.

[18] Nilüfer Göle, "Toward an Autonomisation of Politics and Civil Society in Turkey" in *Politics in the Third Turkish Republic.* eds. Metin Heper and Ahmet Evin (Boulder: Westview Press, 1994), 213.

[19] For a historical review of Turkish-Islamic synthesis see Gökhan Çetinsaya.

[20] Cihan Tuğal, "Nato's Islamists." *New Left Review* 44 (Mar-Apr. 2007): 5-34. (p. 14). Also see Alev İnan Çınar, "Refah Party and the City Administration of Istanbul: Liberal Islam, Localism and Hybridity", *New Perspectives on Turkey* Vol. 16 (Spring 1997): 23-40.

[21] For a detailed analysis of the turbulent period that paved the way for the 28 February Process, see Binnaz Toprak, "Islam and Democracy in Turkey", pp. 30-36.

[22] Süleyman Sözen and Ian Shaw, "Turkey and the European Union: Modernizing a Traditional State?" in *Social Polity and Administration* Vol. 37, No. 2 (April 2003): 108-120.

[23] Tuğal, 34.

[24] The article stated that "Women have to be more careful, since they have stimulants. The women communicating with strange men should speak in a manner that will not arouse suspicion in one's heart and in such seriousness and dignity that they will not let the opposite party misunderstand them, that they should not show their ornaments and figure and that they should cover in a fine manner." The article also said that women and men should not be alone together unless they are married and questioned the role of females in mixed-gender workplaces. It blamed "social and moral" decline in the West for the legislation of abortion. Ironically, these statements come at a time when the directorate is sponsoring a study of the *hadiths,* sayings ascribed to Prophet Muhammad, with a view to striking out those judged inauthentic and misogynistic. See Robert Tait, "Secular Turks Attack Religious Council's Code For Women." *The Guardian,* 29 May 2008. http://www.guardian.co.uk/world/2008/may/29/turkey.islam.

[25] Hakan Yavuz and Nihat Ali Özcan, "Crisis in Turkey: The Conflict of Political Languages" in *Middle East Policy* Vol. 14, No. 3 (Fall 2007): 118-135. p. 125.

[26] Nusrat Choudhury, "From the Stasi Commission to the European Court of Human Rights: L'affaire Du Foulard and the Challenge of Protecting the Rights of

Muslim Girls", in *Columbia Journal of Gender and Law* Vol. 16, Issue 1 (2007): 199.

[27] Joan W. Scott "Symptomatic Politics: The Banning of Islamic Headscarves in French Public Schools" in *French Politics, Culture and Society* Vol. 23, Issue 3, 2005: pp. 106.

[28] For an in-depth discussion of the *affaires de foulard*, see Norma Claire Moruzzi, "A Problem with Headscarves: Contemporary Complexities of Political and Social Identity" in *Political Theory* Vol. 22, No. 4 (November 1994): pp. 653-672.

[29] Hakan Yavuz, "Cleansing Islam from the Public Sphere", in *Journal of International Affairs* Vol. 54, Issue 1 (2000): 21.

[30] For a thorough discussion of Ludin and Freeman cases and the ensuing debates see, Robert A. Kahn, "The Headscarf as Threat: A Comparison of German and U.S. Legal Discourses" in *Vanderbilt Journal of Transnational Law* Vol. 40, Issue 2.

[31] Ziya Öniş, "Islamic Resurgence in Turkey in Perspective" in *Third World Quarterly* Vol. 18, No. 4 (1997): 743-766. (p. 745).

[32] Tuğal, 22.

[33] Barış Kılıçbay and Mutlu Binark, "Consumer Culture, Islam and the Politics of Lifestyle: Fashion for Veiling in Contemporary Turkey" in *European Journal of Communication* Vol. 17, No. 4 (December 2002): 495-511. (p. 499)

[34] As Binnaz Toprak suggests there has been heightened press coverage of numerous attempts by municipal governments, public educational institutions and other government offices controlled by the Islamists to introduce changes that might indeed suggest the "Islamisation of public life," such as to include Islamic or "intelligent design" texts in primary and secondary school curricula, to permit the covering of young girls in certain extra-curricular activities even at the primary school level, to relocate restaurants that serve liquor to the outskirts of cities or refuse to give them licenses, to open "women only" public parks, to ban alcohol in municipal-owned recreational or art centers, etc. "The headscarf controversy" http://www.ssrc.org/blogs/immanent_frame/2008/04/16/the-headscarf-controversy. The government's unsuccessful attempt to criminalize adultery and Turkey's broadcasting watchdog RTUK's pressure on TV channels to ban cross-dressing and alcohol scenes have also been perceived as other manifestations of "creeping fundamentalism". For further discussion see "Turkey and Tolerance: Deviating from the Path." *The Economist* 12 January 2008 and "Turkey and Islam: Secularists' Lament." *The Economist* 29 September 2007.

[35] Nilüfer Göle, "The Voluntary Adoption of Stigma Symbols." *New School for Social Research* Vol. 70, Issue 3 (September 2003).

[36] Nilüfer Göle, "Snapshots of Islamic Modernities" in *Daedalus* 129.1 (2000): 91. This view is also supported by Hakan Yavuz who argues that most Muslims in Turkey are neither political militants nor religious purists. "Instead of trying to restore 'Islamic government' or impose 'Islamic law,' they have formed new voluntary associations in the media, in the schools, and in the business world. This has allowed religious identities and commitments to move into the public sphere of

civil society." See M. Hakan Yavuz. "The Case of Turkey." *Daedalus*_132.3 (2003).

[37] Cihan Tuğal, "The Appeal of Islamic Politics: Ritual and Dialogue in a Poor District of Turkey", in *The Sociological Quarterly* 47 (2006): 245-273. (p. 245).

[38] Nancy J. Hirschmann, "Western Feminism, Eastern Veiling, and the Question of Free Agency" in *Constellations* Vol. 5, No. 3 (1998): 345-368. (p. 361).

[39] Anouar Majid, "The Politics of Feminism in Islam." In *Signs* Vol. 23, No. 2 (Winter 1998): 321-361. (p. 322). For important contributions on this issue see Leila Ahmed, *Women and Gender*, and Fatima Mernissi, *The Veil and the Male Elite* (Reading, MA: Addison-Wesley, 1991).

Transforming Muslim Women's Rights Through International Human Rights Law and Islamic Law

Sarah Swick

Today, a clash between the West and the Muslim World seems like an inevitable reality. Rhetoric from both sides has turned violent and aggressive, leaving little room for communication and dialogue. Attacks by "Islamic terrorists" in Western cities and Western-led wars in Muslim countries have deepened the canyon of misconceptions, hatred, and distrust which exists between the two sides. Furthermore, a state of ignorance and intolerance in both societies has intensified the approaching conflict. Only in confronting the lack of understanding can we hope to build a bridge of trust between the West and Islam, and, thus, avoid a disastrous end.

One area that has historically been, and continues to be, plagued by misconceptions is the role and rights of women in Muslim society. When *Orientalists* first arrived in the Muslim world, they sent home stories of the veiled females who occupied the mystical, brothel-like *harem*. These "images of Arab women brought back to Europe by the *Orientalists* served to titillate the imagination of European men but were not founded in the real behavior or circumstances of Arab women."[1] Later, during the era of colonialism, the colonizers continued disseminating myths about Muslim women as a way of subverting Muslim culture and religion. In French Algeria, pornographic postcards of strategically veiled women were used as a means of attacking the prized honor of Arab men.[2] Today, "women and their roles [have] become a stick with which they can beat the East."[3]

"The image of Islam as the fount of unmitigated oppression of women, as the foundation of a gender system that categorically denies women equal rights and subjugates them to men, recurs in the movies, magazines, and books of [Western] popular culture as well as in much academic discourse."[4] Yet, contrary to the popular image, Islam had granted certain rights to women since the beginning. For instance in the 7th century AD, Muslim women were granted the right to own property, conduct their own business affairs, participate in the political process, receive inheritance, request a divorce, and marry of their own choosing. Western women continued to demand these rights throughout the 20th century.

Contrary to their once advanced status within the 7th century Arab society, at present many Muslim women do not enjoy such rights. Many reasons can be cited for the development of such a predicament. For instance Akbar Ahmed in his book titled *Islam Under Siege* draws a link between the ststus of women and the level of security and stability within the Muslim society. "When Muslim society is confident and in a state of balance, it treats women with fairness and respect. When Muslim society is threatened and feels vulnerable, it treats women with indifference and even harshness."[5] Ahmed partially blames the legacy of colonialism in certain Muslim countries for the deteriorating status of Muslim women. During colonialism, as a result of foreign rule and oppression, trust and honor was weakened among Muslims. Thus, Muslim men tried to protect their last shred of honor: their women. These men believed that the only way to protect their women was to seclude them. Women's isolation from public life led to the entrenchment of various patriarchal and un-Islamic traditions. It is during this period that women suffered the greatest loss of rights. Yet, "when the Europeans left in the middle of the 20th century, Muslim women once again emerged in public in varying degrees, but they were left to fight now-entrenched local traditions and male views and prejudices. Some of these have virtually nothing to do with Islam."[6] So, if the poor status of women has "nothing to do with Islam" and everything to do with local traditions, why engage in a discussion about women and Islam? For Muslim women the answer is simple: it is through a renewed Islamic perspective that Muslim women can be liberated.

Yet, introducing reforms to Islamic Law and values are not so simple, as they will be explored later in this essay. Further, in both the West and the Muslim World, the idea of implementing genuine Islamic Law is not only stigmatized but seen as dangerous and as a step backward. Some argue that International Human Rights Law has proved to be the only adequate liberating force for women. Nevertheless, some Muslim women perceive the Western idea of women's rights as "being tainted by the same kind of ethnocentric thinking that supported colonialism in the first place," and it is for this reason that International Human Rights Law lacks legitimacy throughout the Muslim world.[7]

Building an Understanding

However, rather than pinning Islamic Law and International Human Rights Law against each other, academics, activists and politicians should strive to use the two together to improve the daily lives of Muslim women. While there are many fundamental differences between the two legal systems, through increased understanding, one can hope to create a united front based on the advantages of each with the ultimate goal of bringing respect and dignity into the lives of Muslim women.

At first glance, it seems impossible that International Human Rights Law could be compatible with Islamic Law. The historical developments alone make it improbable that the two systems with over 1,400 years separating them could "work together without conflict." However, the differing methods used by each to construct justice can be utilized in synergy to ensure that women in Muslim societies are given the rights and dignity that they deserve. Their common aim to empower women and their individual techniques, ideologies and social understandings can actually form the basis for future partnership. Any reform of Muslim women's rights in the Muslim world must be situated within Islamic Law; yet, as will be shown, there are positive contributions that International Human Rights Law and its advocates can make to Islamic Law. The first step in this process is increasing the understanding between the two systems. A productive dialogue may then begin, which is necessary in deriving a strategy for using Islamic Law and International Human Rights Law simultaneously for the empowerment of Muslim women.

The 1,400 years between the revelation of the Qur'an (early 7th century A.D.) and the signing of the 1948 Universal Declaration of Human Rights and subsequent developments create a gap that seems hard to fill. Islamic Law is based primarily on divine revelation, represented by the Qur'an. The second important source of Islamic Law is the collection of sayings of the Prophet, or *hadiths*. In developing legal rulings, Islamic scholars use three different methods to interpret the two prime sources. *Al-Ijma*, (the consensus of opinions amongst the Prophet's Companions or amongst Islamic jurists) and *al-Qiyas* (analogical deductions) have been in constant use since the era after the Prophet's death. Al-Qiyas is the surviving member of a wide-ranging set of tools that constitute an additional legal source known as *Ijtihad*. Although this method of jurisprudence has been suspended in the Sunni schools for the past 1,000 years, many Islamic scholars are now calling for *Ijtihad* to be used again. *Ijtihad* is the effort by Islamic scholars to use reason and analysis based not only on other traditional sources but on such considerations as equity, public interest, and juristic preference, to give new legal findings to challenges Muslims are facing today. This is the most promising method in any effort to re-establish gender equity in Islamic Law.

Meanwhile, International Human Rights Law finds its origins primarily in natural law, which developed into a secular system of rights. Following the 1948 Universal Declaration of Human Rights, a separate field of Human Rights was established which specialized in women's issues. The most notable and influential document produced through this new venue was the 1979 Convention on the Elimination of All Forms of Discrimination Against Women (CEDAW).

In addition to differences in historical development and origins, Islamic Law and International Human Rights Law differ mainly in the primary subject area which each system seeks to protect. International Human Rights of Women focuses on the rights of women as individuals. As per International Human Rights Law, women have traditionally sought equality with men on the basis of non-discrimination. This view supports the idea that justice for women will be achieved when women have the same and equal role and opportunities that men have.

In contrast, in Islamic Law, the welfare of the community and family constitute the center of focus. Shari'a is a complete system with assigned roles and privileges for each member of the family or community. The system is based on obligations on the part of the individual towards the family, and the obligations of the family towards the individual. In the Qur'an, the equality of men and women seems to be an unambiguous fact. However, it is also clear that men and women do not have the same roles in a society or in a family, because men and women are different, each with their own strengths and weaknesses. While men and women have equally important and valued roles, these roles are complementary. The notion of "different but equal," which Islam promotes, has had some success for some time in penetrating International Human Rights Law. Nevertheless despite its seemingly "positive" outlook, the notion still posits discrimination.

Yet another difference between the two systems is whom each system defines as the primary obligation holders. International Human Rights Law acts primarily to pressure States to reform national legislation. This gives it a strong influence at the national and international political levels, yet little influence in the private sphere, where most of the violations against women occur. Meanwhile, Islamic Law defines the laws of a society in reference to that society's relationship to the Creator; futhermore Islam legislates even the most private of activities within the private sphere. However, because the idea of a nation-state is relatively recent, Islamic law is weak in placing obligations upon the State to improve the rights of women. Further, privacy considerations may limit the degree to which the State may intervene in domestic affairs.

Such differences in defining the primary subjects and obligation holders between International Human Rights Law and Islamic Law also point toward the reasons why it is advantageous for the two systems to work in mutual agreement. However, before further discussion about the strategy for bridging the two systems, it is important to gain a brief understanding of women's rights in International Human Rights Law and Islamic Law. For purposes of clarity, it is important to state that this essay focuses on traditional Islamic societies which strictly follow religious law.

Comparative Rights

When Westerners and even some Muslims mention Islamic Law, they seem to think of "Shari'a". Yet, neither a singular form of Islamic Law nor any dominant interpretation of it exists. Moreover due to major structural differences among Muslim nations, Islamic Law's interpretation differs extensively from one society to another.

> The lack of a universal policy among Muslim states who claim to follow religious law (Shari'a) in respect of women's rights is remarkable-in Iran women vote, and a woman—Dr. Ebtekar—has just taken up the post of vice president of the Republic, all of which is unthinkable in the traditionalist Saudi monarchy.[8]

Islam sets the outer limits of an acceptable scale of what is allowed, and a society decides where along that scale it feels most comfortable. The greatest impediment to the advancement of women's rights is that it is almost always the *men* in the society, not women, who decide how to interpret and implement Islamic Law.

For purposes of simplicity and consistency, the interpretation of Muslim women's rights used in this essay follows Jamal Badawi's book titled *Gender Equity in Islam*, which is neither apologetic for the different view Islam takes on equality nor is so rigid as to reject modern concepts of justice. After almost 1,000 years of *Ijtihad* being suspended, most Muslims today argue that "the Qur'an must be continually interpreted because dynamic manifestation of Qur'anic guidance is not only a form of interpretation but also the only way to actually attain the lived state of Islam."[9] Therefore, it is with the purpose of revitalizing Islam that reform of Islamic Law needs to take place in the Muslim World.

In International Human Rights Law, there are several different approaches towards women's rights, however the cornerstone of women's rights is enshrined in the Convention on the Elimination of All Forms of Discrimination Against Women (CEDAW), which is the second most ratified Human Rights treaty with 174 UN member States party to it. It set a new standard in defining non-discrimination, recognizing both formal equality, or equal opportunity; and de facto equality, or equal result.[10] It has included both first generation rights (civil and political) and second generation (economic and social). It also attempted to go beyond the public sphere and break through into the private realm, where most violations against women occur. Although it has not achieved all of its goals, CEDAW has helped curb discrimination against women and improved women's status.

Non-discrimination forms the core of CEDAW, which requires States to adopt legislative measures that prohibit gender discrimination by any person or organization. However, CEDAW also allows States to enact a temporary policy of positive discrimination as the Human Rights Committee General Comment 26 further clarified, "not every differentiation of treatment will constitute discrimination, if the criteria for such differentiation are reasonable and objective and if the aim is to achieve a purpose which is legitimate under the Covenant."[11] Islamic Law has a similar philosophy of permitting legitimate, positive discrimination if it results in justice and equity.

Political Rights

In terms of political rights of women, both CEDAW and Islamic Law promote the active participation of women in the political sphere. CEDAW establishes women's right to vote, hold office, participate in forming public policy and participate in civil society. Moreover, CEDAW requires States to ensure that women have "the opportunity to represent their governments at the international level" and the right of women to "acquire, change, or retain their nationality."[12] Despite claims by some Islamic extremists, the right of women to participate in political life was clearly established during the lifetime of the Prophet. In the Qur'an, God commanded the Prophet to accept the oath of allegiance from a woman, thus giving her the right to choose her leader.[13] Women were also given the right to help form social and legal policy. During the reign of the second *Caliph*, or leader, after the Prophet's death, at a "town hall" meeting when the *Caliph* tried to restrict the amount of money a woman could demand for her dowry, a woman stood up and told the Caliph that he did not have the right to make such a law. He realized his mistake and agreed with her, thus setting the precedence for women's participation in policy formation.[14] Furthermore, some conservative Muslims would argue that women should not hold political leadership positions. They cite a *hadith* in which the Prophet reportedly said, after hearing that the leader of Persia was a woman, "Never will such a nation succeed as makes a woman their ruler."[15] Badawi argues, "While this *hadith* has been commonly interpreted to exclude women from the headship of a state, other scholars do not agree with that interpretation... The Prophet's response to this news may have been a statement about the impending doom of that unjust empire, which did take place later, and not about the issue of gender as it relates to headship of the state itself."[16] Other scholars completely reject the reported *hadith* due to an unacceptable chain of narration in which the original narrator was a convicted perjurer.[17] In fact, Umm Salamah, a wife of the Prophet, was known to have "played a role equal to what we would refer to today as 'chief advisor' of the head of state."[18]

Education

While CEDAW declares that men and women have equal rights to education, under Islamic Law, education is not only a right, but also an obligation on both Muslim males and females.[19] Unfortunately, in some fundamentalist societies, Muslim men refuse to send their daughters to school which is a direct violation of Islamic Law. During the Prophet's time, he made it clear that the women in their community should have access to knowledge, and even took the task upon himself to help teach them.[20] In fact, one of the most revered scholars of Islam was A'isha, the Prophet's wife. Her knowledge was not limited to just religious affairs, as one of her pupils describes her, "I did not see a greater scholar than A'isha in the learning of the Qur'an, obligatory duties, lawful and unlawful matters, poetry and literature, Arab history and genealogy."[21] After the Prophet's death, when his Companions would dispute over jurisprudence, they would seek the advice of A'isha, recognizing her vast knowledge.[22] A'isha, along with many other women of her time, is an example of the important role knowledgeable women played in Islamic history. Through this example, it is clearly understood that Muslim society needs to educate their women. Islamic Law, like International Human Rights Law, insists on the significance of education and, therefore, and makes it an obligation on society and on the family to educate every woman.

Right to Work

CEDAW firmly insists that women should enjoy the freedom from discrimination at the workplace and the right to choose their own professions. "There is also an undertaking to provide equal remuneration, right to social security and a right to protection of health and to safety in working conditions."[23] Furthermore, States are obliged to prevent women from losing their jobs due to pregnancy and to give women the right to maternity leave with pay or benefits. While International Human Rights law has concentrated on the State and employers' obligation towards female workers, Islamic Law has concentrated on the balance and relationship between work and family.

Under the family structure laid down by Islam, a Muslim woman's primary job is that of a mother, guardian of the home, and educator of the next generation. Islam recognizes that being a mother is a full-time job, which can require a woman's complete attention; therefore men have the sole financial responsibility of maintaining the household. The wife has a right to whatever her husband earns because it is not expected for her to work outside the home. Yet, if she chooses to work outside the home, any money she earns is her own; her husband has no rights over her earnings. However, because of the financial arrangements and the woman's role as mother in the family, she must either seek permission from her husband or state in her marriage contract that she retains the right to work. A man is not required to ask for permission to work because it is an obligation on him to provide financially for the family. However, working women are not uncommon in Muslim society or history. The most prominent example of a working Muslim woman is Khadijah, the Prophet's first and most beloved wife who was a wealthy trader in Mecca and who remains a role model for all Muslim women. Although men and women do not have the "same" rights in terms of work, there is equity of rights between men and women.

Property and Financial Rights

Islamic Law and International Human Rights Law have similar property rights. CEDAW in Article 13, stipulates that governments must take appropriate measures to ensure that women have "the right to family benefits; the right to bank loans, mortgages and other forms of financial credit, and the right to participate in recreational activities, sports and all aspects of cultural life."[24] Article 15 gives women the "legal capacity to contract, to own and to administer property, and to move and to choose a residence and domicile," which were rights given in Islam 1,400 years ago.[25]

In addition to the right to keep her own earnings and the right to her husband's earnings, the Shari'a gave women the right to own property, whether attained before or during the marriage. "They may buy, sell or lease any or all their properties at will. For this reason, Muslim women may keep (and in fact they have traditionally kept) their maiden names after marriage, an indication of their independent property rights as legal entities."[26]

As well as the right to own property, the financial security of a Muslim woman is guaranteed throughout her lifetime, whether as a daughter, wife, mother or sister. Upon marriage, she is entitled to a dowry, the amount of which she names and of which she is the sole recipient. During the marriage, as stated earlier, the husband must provide full financial support for his wife. In cases of divorce, during the waiting period, or *Iddah*, the husband must also support her, and if she bears children, she is also entitled to child support. As she grows old, her sons must provide financially for her. This leads to the explanation of why women, under Islamic law, are entitled to only half of a male's inheritance.

Men are given twice the inheritance of a woman, because a man is always financially responsible for a woman and must ensure her comfort, whether it is his mother, sister, wife, or daughter, and in some cases all four at once. A man is obliged to share his wealth with the women in his family, while a woman may keep her wealth to herself (although she is always allowed to give a gift to her husband). Since it is an obligation on the male to share his inheritance, Islamic scholars argue that it would not be just and equitable to give a man the same share of inheritance as a woman, who has no financial responsibilities to anyone else, including herself. This idea of "same" rights resulting in inequalities in Muslim society is important in understanding the rights of women in marriage and divorce.

Marriage

In terms of marriage, CEDAW, in Article 16, gives men and women the "same" rights to enter into marriage (including freely choosing their spouse), the "same" rights and responsibilities during the marriage, and the "same" rights to dissolve the marriage. Many Muslim countries have issued reservations to Article 16 of CEDAW because Islam does not seek identical rights, realizing that women have different experiences than men and, therefore, need special protections to ensure equity.

Under Islamic Law, both the female and male must give their free consent before a marriage contract is valid. The Prophet was very clear in protecting the rights of women, when he said, "The widow and the divorced woman shall not be married until their order is obtained, and the virgin shall not be married until her consent is obtained."[27] However, under the Maliki school of thought, the father may veto the daughter's choice. This is meant to be a protection for the girl, as "it may sometimes happen that in her immaturity or over-zealousness, a girl may want to marry a man about whom she has distorted information or who does not possess good character or who lacks proper means of livelihood."[28] However, in the Hanafi school of thought[29], some scholars say, "the daughter is free to disregard the advice and to make her own decision, for, the father's role is, after all, merely advisory."[30]

Polygyny, the practice of a man having more than one wife, is another area where International Human Rights Law perceives an injustice in Islamic Law. Before the advent of Islam, men in Arabia married an unlimited number of wives and were free to treat them unequally, but with the arrival of the Prophet, polygyny was dramatically regulated and restricted. Women are not given the same right to have multiple spouses due to the simple fact, among various other reasons, that determining paternity of a child would be impossible. However, polygyny can also be placed in terms of a woman's right to financial and physical security. In times when there are disproportionate number of males to females, such as in war, every woman in society has the right to be married and taken care of, therefore in order to ensure this right, polygyny may be necessary. Yet, Islam gives a woman the right to stipulate in her marriage contract that her husband is not allowed to marry another wife.[31]

Divorce

In terms of divorce, while CEDAW gives each party the same rights, Islamic Law is more complicated. Islam allows both the husband and wife to initiate a divorce, however because it is so disliked by God, every opportunity to reconcile the problem must be exhausted first. There are several different ways of obtaining a divorce under Islamic law. "Forms of marriage dissolution include an enactment based upon mutual agreement, the husband's initiative, the wife's initiative (if part of her marital contract), the court's decision on a wife's initiative (for legitimate reasons) and the wife's initiative without a 'cause,' provided that she returns her marital gift to her husband."[32] Furthermore, before a divorce initiated by the husband is final, the couple must wait for three months and ten days.

During this time, the husband must continue to provide maintenance for his wife and treat her kindly. The purpose of this waiting period, or *Iddah*, is to give both parties time to reconsider and reconcile.

Child Custody

On the issue of child custody, CEDAW reaffirms that the right of the child should be paramount and establishes that both parents have the same rights, no matter what their marital status may be. Islam gives custody of young children to the mother, recognizing that a mother typically can better provide the necessary care and tenderness. However, the different Islamic schools of thought vary concerning the duration of custody and the chain of custody. For example, the Maliki school of thought gives the mother the custody of a boy until he reaches puberty and a girl until she marries. Yet, under all schools of thought, the mother upon re-marrying will generally lose custody of the children. This is meant as a protection for the children and a guarantee of paternal rights as Islam guarantees the rights and responsibilities of the father throughout the custody process. The majority of the schools of thought unite on the fact that at a certain age the choice of custody is given to the child. While these rules are the norm, Badawi reminds Muslims, "custody questions are to be settled in a manner that balances the interests of both parents and the well-being of the child." The rules of custody in Islam are guidelines, but realizing that each case may be different, Islam allows for variations or exceptions if it is in the best interest of the child, which is also stressed in article 16 of CEDAW.

Domestic Violence and Genital Mutilation

A formidable challenge for both systems in attaining equity between the husband and wife is domestic violence. A strong criticism directed against CEDAW is that it did not address violence against women. A woman's right to live with personal security was not officially recognized in International Human Rights Law until the 1993 Declaration on the Elimination of Violence Against Women. The Declaration clarifies that "violence" can be physical, sexual or psychological, and can occur at the family, community or state levels. However it specifically aims at eliminating domestic violence and female genital mutilation, among other forms of violence that many women face around the globe (Vienna Declaration 1993).

Under Islamic Law, it is forbidden for any person to do harm to another, specifically, for any man to beat or do harm to his wife. Some would defend the use of domestic violence in Islam by citing a verse in the Qur'an which is occasionally translated as "As to those women on whose part you see ill conduct, admonish them (first), (next) refuse to share their beds, (and last) beat them (lightly, if it is useful)..."[33] However, Badawi explains: "In extreme cases, and whenever greater harm, such as divorce is a likely option, it allows for a husband to administer a gentle pat to his wife that causes no physical harm to the body no leaves any sort of mark."[34] Moreover, this "pat" can only come after the husband has verbally professed his dislike for her actions and if she continues, he should not sleep with her for a period of time. Considering that men who beat their wives do so during a fit of rage or drunkenness (which is forbidden in Islam), it is highly unlikely that after waiting for a period of time, a gentle "pat" will be needed to resolve the dispute. Therefore, one can conclude that Islam never encourages or close its eyes to the issue of violence at home.[35]

Along with domestic violence, another misconception about Islam is that it requires female circumcision or genital mutilation. This is a practice that dates pre-Islamic times; moreover it is entrenched in local tradition rather than in religious teachings which is "highly disliked." First, in Islam a person is forbidden to do harm to his or her self and to others. Secondly, a woman who has been circumcised will not enjoy intimacy in marital relations. Therefore the Prophet specifically said that a woman should have the right to receive pleasure during marital relations. Therefore, one can conclude that, like International Human Rights Law, Islamic Law strongly discourages genital mutilation.[36]

Advantages and Disadvantages of Each System

One advantage of International Human Rights Law is that attaching women's issues to a human rights discourse provides women with a normative legal basis and requires States to be accountable for the plight of the female population. It also gives women the vocabulary and instruments to address the social and political structures which keep them in a disadvantaged position.[37] Placing women's issues within a human rights context also allows women "to claim specific entitlements from a specified obligation holder."[38] Furthermore, "international law now obligates states to use due diligence to prevent, investigate, and punish systemic and egregious human rights violations between private actors."[39] Eventually, internationalizing women's issues has allowed women from around the world to gather and establish networks, creating an international movement demanding increased protection and rights for women.

However, placing women's issues in the human rights context has its own drawbacks and disadvantages as well. As Charlesworth explains, "women's experiences and concerns are not easily translated into the narrow, individualistic language of rights..."[40] Furthermore, the rights discourse assumes that women are free and independent from a community setting, which is not true for most women.[41] "Rights discourse" tends to ignore the complex power structure which obstructs women from demanding their rights. In addition, the weak enforcement mechanisms of Human Rights, and CEDAW in particular, hinder any positive effect on a large scale. Moreover, the rights presented in international declarations are not always as clear as they appear, which leads to rights being highly susceptible to manipulation and weakening due to political compromise.[42] Human Rights, in general, are seen as a new form of colonialism in the developing world. Therefore, Human Rights Law lacks legitimacy in the everyday reality of such societies. Additionally, Human Rights also face a challenge from cultural relativism, which can be used as a justification for certain violations. This is a particular concern for women's rights as it pertains to Islamic Law. Therefore, both Western and Muslim women need to understand Islamic Law in order to be able to challenge the often misrepresented excuse of cultural relativism.

Yet, finding the right interpretation of Islamic Law can be like maneuvering through a minefield. Each step must be taken with utmost care and respect. Islam can be utilized both as a justification for the oppression of women or as a liberating force for women. Therefore, ascertaining a valid interpretation is vital for any Muslim society wishing to improve the status of its female citizens.

Another problem with using Islamic Law as the sole basis for women's rights is that not everyone, even in Muslim countries, are practicing Muslims who would like to follow the Shari'a. Islamic Law generates the perfect social and legal system amongst believers. If a man is God-fearing, then he will follow Islamic Law, knowing that he will later have to be accountable to God for every action he did and every word he uttered. But a non-believing Muslim is likely to skew Islam to serve his own purpose, which seems to be a contemporary "trend" in many Muslim communities. Furthermore, Islamic law does not hold legitimacy amongst non-religious or non-Muslim members of a society; therefore a State needs to develop a legal code, which will ensure the rights and justice for all women and ensure they will be respected by all members of that society.

Practicing Muslims advocate Islamic Law because it is more responsive to the actual, everyday needs of Muslim women than International Human Rights Law. It is more realistic in defining mutual roles of both men and women as it creates harmony amongst members of the family and the society as a whole. The advantage that Islam holds is that it does not need to work at penetrating the private sphere, as International Human Rights Law has constantly tried but failed to do so. Islamic Law actually defines the private sphere for believing men and women. For Muslims, disobeying Islamic Law not only holds the consequence of punishment in this world, but it also risks eternal punishment in the hereafter. This fear of God and God's judgment can give Islamic Law the authority needed to create a society where women are respected and given their due rights. However Islamic Law cannot achieve its above stated goals without the help of International Human Rights Law and its ardent activists.

A Strategy for Reform

Armed with a better understanding of both International Human Rights Law and Islamic Law, one can now focus on utilizing the two in synergy to empower Muslim women. In order for the reforms to meet the actual needs and desires of Muslim women, they need to be firmly based on certain aspects of the Islamic Law. Furthermore, if the reforms are to be accepted as legitimate by the Muslim population, changes ought not to contradict Islamic Law. Therefore, the next step in the reform process must be implementing an internal debate for which external actors may play an important supporting role.

The internal discourse, which must take place among different members of a society should primarily focus on re-examining how religious laws are interpreted and implemented rather than seeking to secularize these laws. Therefore, inclusion of representatives from across a large scale of religious piety is needed.

A horizontal dialogue among those who hold differing views in society must be fostered; however this requires the existence of freedom of expression and assembly in that particular society. Furthermore, a vertical, dynamic relationship between the government and the people needs to be established which requires the presence of a transparent, legitimate and responsive administration. In order to gain public interest and support for a grassroots reform movement, both formal and informal education programs must take the initiative in teaching the young and the old the need for a reform. This can happen only in an active civil society. These requirements highlight the role of external actors. For the reform process to be initiated, the State must be under international pressure to allow for freedom of expression and assembly along with its organizations supporting a strong civil society. By signing and ratifying various international human rights conventions and declarations, external pressure can be applied on a government to improve women's rights.

Moreover, once reform discussions have been initiated, women must constitute an integral part of the process. "One means of ensuring just and lasting reforms, particularly with respect to family law, is the inclusion of women in the legal-ethical deliberations about women's rights and status both in the family and in society."[43] This requires experienced and well-trained women who can navigate the minefield of Islamic interpretation and political negotiations. These women, however, will need assistance, guidance and expertise from external actors.

Furthermore, external funding and support is needed for various programs that would encourage people to become more involved in the reform process. For example, throughout the process, men and women must be educated about their innate rights. Human rights education from an Islamic perspective is vital in changing the attitude of the culture towards reform, but this requires funding and organization. Women's civil society organizations need to be established with the triple objective of educating, lobbying and rallying the people. In order to be effective such organizations need help in networking, fundraising and organizing. This is where Western feminists can play an active role by sharing their expertise, funds and networks with Muslim women.

However, while external actors can provide invaluable assistance to any reform movement, they increase the risk of undermining the project, particularly if they are observed to be "dictating" the reforms. This is a highly sensitive issue in the case of religious laws. The *Shah Bano* case in India is an example where an outsider (a Hindu judge) made a ruling based on Muslim religious law, and although most Muslim scholars endorsed the ruling, it was widely rejected by the Muslim community, simply because an "outsider" made it.[44] Therefore, it is important that external actors remain in the background and do not go beyond providing material support for the horizontal and vertical internal discourse happening inside a particular society. To supersede or pre-empt the existing principles within the society can cause more harm than good. Additionally any material support should be supplemental to a core support from within the society lest it be perceived as tainting the discourse on the principle of "who pays the piper calls the tune."

Such a knowledgeable strategy for women's rights reform requires several social and political prerequisites which may first seem improbable. However, as in the case of Morocco, it is possible to generate reforms which are based on Islamic Law, but are also in harmony with the principles of International Human Rights Law, resulting in strategic compatibility of the two concepts.

Family Code Reform in Morocco

In October 2003, King Mohammed VI of Morocco announced new reforms to the Moroccan Family Code or *Moudawana*, and he remarked: "I cannot prohibit that which God has authorized and I cannot allow that which God has prohibited."[45] The announced reform project subscribes to the framework of orthodox Islam as it seeks to reinforce the rights of women and children and guarantee the protection and stability of families.[46] Yet, at the same time, in the words of Zhor el Hor, who had served on the reforms committee, "the Family Code brings justice to women and goes in the directions of respect of Human Rights for the construction of a democratic State." He asserts that equality between men and women is not completely achieved, "however because of the promulgation of the law, the woman will have in her possession the tools to defend herself and to protect the children."[47] It is clear that the new reform is entrenched in Islamic Law; however the influence of International Human Rights Law and the movements which support it, cannot be ignored. The struggle for women's rights in the Muslim world is centered on the Family Code or Personal Status Law; it is also the basis of women's rights and status. In Morocco, reforming the *Moudawana* required a long and hard struggle which was won mainly because of the dialogue that existed amongst internal actors and support from external actors.

The 1957 *Moudawana*, which sought to protect men's dignity by guarding their women, was to a certain extent attributed to the legacy of colonialism. Since 1957, there have been several attempts to reform the Family Code. However, the traditional religious scholars (*ulema*) and political circumstances prevented the realization of any tangible reforms.

Yet, social and demographic shifts in Morocco during the 1980s helped increase the freedoms of expression and assembly eventually leading to the rapid growth of women's organizations. The expansion of women's organizations continued into the 1990s, which proved to be an important decade for the women's movement. These organizations took advantage of the changing climate in the international arena to initiate reforms. With the end of the Cold War, the issue of Human Rights finally gained the attention it deserved. Furthermore, there was a sharp increase in funding from international donors, such as USAID, who saw women as a priority. An increased emphasis on democratization on the international level led to the realization that women ought to play an important role in the political process.[48]

Moreover, developing events in the Middle East made local women's cause a political tool for a struggling king. King Hassan II's pro-American stance in the Gulf War led to a public rift between him and the majority of the population, who were pro-Iraqi. Furthermore, the 1991 UN cease-fire in the Sahara (a conflict which the King frequently used to rally the population behind him) left the King without a cause to regain public support. However, he quickly found the remedy in the popular women's rights movement.

In 1992, the Union of Feminine Action launched an initiative seeking to gain one million signatures supporting their reform petition. This strategy led to some reforms, most notably a law which requires a husband to inform his first wife before marrying a second wife. However, modernization stimulus in Morocco was quickly advancing the women's movement.

In 1993 there were national elections in which two women were finally elected to the Moroccan Parliament. Moreover, a sharp increase in the number of female judges pressured the judiciary to push for reforms, as well.

Also, in 1993, Morocco ratified the Convention on the Elimination of All Forms of Discrimination against Women. Although they listed several reservations (including article 16), Morocco showed, by ratifying the Convention, its new resolve to improve women's rights and status in society. It also put pressure on the Government to take a pro-active stance on women's rights, of which positive results were observed during the mid to late 1990s.

The 1996 constitutional reforms led Morocco to reinforce its democratization efforts. In 1999 King Mohammed VI ascended to the throne on his father's death. He was perceived as a representative of the "new Morocco." Even before ascending the throne, he publicly and actively supported the cause for women's rights and democratization process.[49] Nevertheless he has always been careful in balancing the demands of modernization with strains of growing "Islamization." Since taking power, several important initiatives and events have shaped his reign and tested that balanced harmony. He declared his dedication to improving Morocco's human rights record as well as women's rights in the Kingdom. He proved his dedication to the women's cause when he announced the creation of a committee to review potential reforms to the Family Code. In 2002 transparent parliamentary elections were held for the first time in Moroccan history. For women, however, the significance of the 2002 elections was not about transparency, but rather about the 35 women elected to the Parliament. In addition to the election of 30 women from a separate list solely reserved for women, five additional members, including one woman from a powerful district in Casablanca, were elected from the "regular" list.

The culmination of these efforts and the long struggle of women's organizations to change the Family Code resulted in the release of the new *Moudawana* in 2004, a document which required almost three years of intense negotiations by a committee appointed by the King.

The committee that the King had established included several members of the *ulema* along with three women. The women were accomplished and respected members of Moroccan society: a judge, a university president, and a doctor. For almost three years, the committee worked under complete secrecy, with only the King receiving updates.[50] While some might criticize the secrecy with which the committee worked, due to the heightened sensitivity of their mandate, it was necessary that external political or religious pressure did not compromise the final proposal. The King wisely insisted that the issue of women's rights should stay above the political fray in order to guarantee the future influence and validity of the Family Code reforms.

The new Family Code theoretically finds its legitimacy in its strong ties to Islamic Law. The aim of the reform was to correct injustices which originated from the old Family Code while taking into consideration International Human Rights Law, as long as it did not contradict the Islamic Law. The most evident change in the new *Moudawana* was the definition of marriage and the responsibilities of each spouse. Under the old law, the family was "under the direction of the husband." However, the new reform placed the family under the direction of both the husband and the wife. The old code listed the husband and wife's responsibilities separately. It assigned to the wife the duty of, among other things, being faithful and obedient to her husband. Meanwhile, the husband's responsibilities did not require either of those duties, but rather the responsibility to provide for the needs of his wife. Subsequently, in the new reforms, the responsibilities of the spouses are reciprocal. Article 51 states that both spouses must uphold justice in the relationship, remain faithful to each other, and respect each other.[51] This not only creates the equality required by International Human Rights Law, but also cultivates the spirit of the institution of marriage in Islam. Above all, marriage in Islam is based on tranquility and mercy[52], which requires, among other things, justice, faithfulness and respect.

In Morocco the reforms also aimed to improve another phase of inequality that had been present under the old code. Traditionally the minimum age of marriage for boys was eighteen, while for girls it was fifteen. The new code increased the women's minimum age to eighteen, equal to a man's. Because Islam allows for minors to marry, it is still possible for a boy and girl to marry below the age, but only with a judge's approval. Given the social pressures to get married at a tender age, this change is vital in preventing girls from dropping out of school in order to get married.[53] The requirement for a judge's approval would theoretically prevent young girls from being forced into marriage under family pressure. Such marriages specifically contradict the Islamic right of a woman to choose her husband with her own free will, a principle also laid out in CEDAW. Furthermore, Article 16 of CEDAW placed an obligation on States to prevent "child marriages". Under a judge's rule no one could force a young girl into a marriage that she is not ready for, or one that she does not want to.

The new reform intended to prevent forced marriages and uphold a woman's right to freely choose her husband by restricting the role of the *wali*, or guardian. Under the previous code, which strictly followed the Maliki School, a woman, no matter what her age may be, must have her *wali's* (usually her father's), approval to marry. However, under the Hanafi School, the *wali's* approval is not necessary for an "adult" woman.[54] The new code upholds the *wali's* role for a girl under the age of eighteen, however upon reaching her eighteenth birthday the woman may either contract her own marriage or choose to have her *wali* contract the marriage for her.[55] Therefore, the reform set the precedent for the woman's right under Islamic law to choose her own partner, but still accommodated the important role that her *wali* can play in this matter.

In terms of financial obligations, the old code was explicit in giving the wife the right to own property and to keep her wealth, while the husband had the responsibility to financially support her and their children. However, the committee realized that social norms have been changing and an increasing number of women are working outside the home. Hence, the new code allowed for a document to be signed, in parallel to the marriage contract, which assigned financial responsibilities to each party, during and after the marriage. This compromise gave men and women the option of dividing their assets equally. Without such a document, the husband is still responsible for the financial maintenance of the family and if he fails to do so, a woman may receive a divorce.[56] This change allowed a couple to opt for the internationally defined "equality" in financial matters or they may follow the Islamic rule of "equity." However, by making Islamic Law the default method, the financial rights of rural women who are unlikely to ask for a legal contract, were being protected.

Another inequality which was corrected by the new *Moudawana* was about the lack of a woman's tangible right to divorce. Previously, only the husband had the absolute right to seek a divorce, upholding an interpretation of Islamic law—a contradiction to the Qur'anic injunction that women have divorce rights similar to men—which gave the husband a unique right to repudiation, or the ability to divorce his wife *verbally*. While the new code did not challenge the man's right to repudiate, it called for a written document accompanied with a judge's approval. Furthermore, women would have increased rights in seeking a divorce. Under the previous code, a woman could only ask for a divorce if she could prove mistreatment, such as domestic violence or lack of support. In order to prove it she needed twelve witnesses. The new codes required only two witnesses to prove a woman's mistreatment. Upon proof, she can immediately be granted a divorce. But if she cannot provide evidence and still insists on her stance that she has indeed been mistreated, she may go through a longer process of arbitration first, before taking the case through the relevant legal process. Furthermore, the woman may always give back the amount of her dowry in order to obtain a divorce unilaterally. The new code also added the option for consensual divorce, in which both parties agree to the divorce.[57] Although the new procedures give both men and women the right to divorce, Islam insists that divorce should be the last option after all other possibilities have been exhausted. Therefore, making the approval of a judge a mandatory prerequisite to obtain a divorce provides the safeguards required by Islam and renders "equality" required by CEDAW.

Yet, another unjust interpretation which was planned to be corrected by the new *Moudawana* involved the terms for the waiting period after repudiation by the husband. The outdated interpretation of Islamic Law forced the woman back into the marriage if her husband so desired. However, under the Family Code reforms the husband could take his wife back only if she agrees to go back. Although the waiting period and its intention to give both sides time to think about the divorce remained, the woman was not to be forced into a marriage if she did not desire, which is compatible with both CEDAW and Islamic Law.

In both Islamic Law and International Human Rights Law, the interests of the child have always been paramount in matters of child custody. Although, Article 16 of CEDAW requires that both parents have the same rights in custody, it adds that the best interest of the child should always take precedence. Under the old Moroccan code, the mother was given custody, but upon re-marrying she would automatically lose her right to custody. Under the new code up until the age of seven, (regardless of her marital status), the mother is given custody. When the child reaches the age of seven, if the mother has re-married she will normally lose custody, although she will have the right to object the decision of a judge.[58] In the previous code, a boy at age twelve and a girl at age fifteen could chose which parent he or she wanted to live with. With the new *Moudawana* both children are given the choice at age fifteen.

The new code upheld the Islamic principle that the father must provide for the children after divorce. Previously, if the father repudiated the mother, the children could also be sent out of the family's home. However, with the new law the family's home would still belong to the children and the mother, since keeping the family home is in the best interest of the children, an important principle endorsed both in Islamic Law and International Human Rights Law.

These reforms indicated that it is possible for Islamic Law and International Human Rights Law to work in synergy in order provide a righteous set of laws for Muslim women. While they are two distinct systems, ideally a dialogue between the two should facilitate reforms. In Morocco such dialogue must further continue and reach a heightened level; the success of women's struggle entails the implementation and enforcement of the new *Moudawana* effectively.

The major challenge facing the new *Moudawana* lies in its application and enforcement across all ranks of the Moroccan society. As a matter of fact the implementation of the new code triggered a significant challenge and assigned central role to the judges. To help them in this new role, the King established a family court system whose judges were elected based on their willingness to uphold the principles of Islam and determination to defend the values of equality, modernity, democracy, justice and human rights. A process of inspection was initially instituted in order to guarantee the Family Courts efficiency and transparency. The judges' decisions were to be reviewed by a committee to ensure their honesty as well as testing the system's integrity.[59] However, women's organizations and international watch-dog groups were still needed to be involved in pressuring the government to maintain the reliability of these courts.

Furthermore, the Ministry of Justice planned to create a practical guide to assist people understand and interpret the new code. Considering that a large percentage of the Moroccan population is illiterate, majority of education was expected to be provided by women's organizations who would go to rural areas, explain the new code and provide advice and counseling for women.

Morocco like all Muslim countries, is facing an internal struggle between Islamization and Westernization. This struggle has the potential to erupt in violence and oppression, or it has the potential of creating an open and revitalized society based on the foundations of "tolerant" Islam. However a continued and renewed effort by both local groups and outside donors is needed to ensure sustained progress and development, leading to significant improvement for not only Moroccan women, but the entire Moroccan society.

The announcement of reforms in Morocco renewed hope and empowered not only Moroccan women, but all Muslim women around the world. Immediately following Moroccan reforms, the President of Algeria announced that he would establish a committee which would look into reforming the Algerian Family Code. Surely, the Algerian commission was looking at neighboring Morocco as a model to follow.[60] Since then issues of personal status law reform have been key concerns for women throughout the Muslim world, including those in Afghanistan and Iraq.*

In conclusion, despite difficulties Morocco potentially serves as a good example in which a Muslim nation can reap positive results when the two systems and their supporters work in synergy towards a common goal rather than as antagonists with mutually exclusive objectives. In the twenty-first century through a strategy of international dialogues and effects of globalism, Muslim women will finally be able to attain the rights they deserve through increased mutual understanding and partnership between the West and the Muslim world in general. These developments may take precedence and lead to a sustainable peace movement throughout the world.

* The Editor's Commentary: As this volume is being prepared for publication in December, 2009, the future of Moroccan *Moudawana* looks quite ominous. As the author predicted, despite considerable efforts, lack of education and public awareness caused the general public eventually become weary of the new family codes. Contrary to the initial plans of the King, courts and judges were not adequately trained; court decrees are open to interpretation or deemed "arbitrary" in divorce, custody cases and marriage contracts. Legal inconsistency, corruption and uncertainty generate public distrust in the court system. Currently the Moroccan public opinion seems to be divided into two disparate camps, with the conservative, the Islamist and the rural sects feeling substantially isolated and underrepresented. The reforms are perceived to be the advent of the secularist and modernist goals which are mainly supported by the Francophone and educated urban women. On the other hand, the problem does not lie in public's approval of the new Family Code but in the discrepancy between the law and its practice, as much as in the real-life application of the planned reforms in a country where population is more rural than urban, rather illiterate than literate. Essentially there are major distinctions between the rural and urban areas in Morocco. The women who live in cities lead different lives than women in villages do. Single mothers still do not have any rights; women in general earn less than men; inheritance by women is always a debated issue among men. In a recent article titled "Family Code Gets Nudge, But Women Seek a Push" the Moroccan *Moudawana* and circumstances which surround the lives of young—particularly the poor and uneducated—Moroccan women are discussed.

Thus the initial plans of combining the Islamic law with the International Human Rights in order to attain justice in support of women's rights are not entirely realized in Morocco. The reader is urged to refer to the below mentioned articles for a current evaluation of the *Moudawana*.

Sources

http://bisahha.blogspot.com/2009/08/moudawana-five-years-later.html, August 20, 2009. Retrieved September 16, 2009.

http://www.nytimes.com/2009/08/19/world/africa/19tangiers.html *New York Times.* August 20, 2009. Retrieved September 16, 2009.

Notes

[1] Suha Sabbagh, ed. "Introduction: The Debate on Arab Women," in *Arab Women: Between Defiance and Restraint* (New York: Olive Branch, 1996), xxii.

[2] Fadwa El Guindi, *Veil: Modesty, Privacy and Resistance* (United Kingdom: Berg, 1999), 24.

[3] See Sabbagh, "Introduction: The Debate on Arab Women," p. xxi.

[4] Sarah Graham-Brown, "Women and Politics in the Middle East', in *Arab Women: Between Defiance and Restraint,.* ed. Suha Sabbagh (New York: Olive Branch, 1996), p. 9.

[5] Ahmed, Akbar. *Islam Under Siege* (United Kingdom: Polity, 2003), 115-116.

[6] Ibid., 117.

[7] Lynn Walter, ed. "Introduction", in *Women's Rights: A Global View*, New York: Greenwood, 2001, xviii.

[8] Karen Ask and Marit Tjomsland. *Women and Islamization: Contemporary Dimensions of Discourse on Gender Relations* (United Kingdom: Berg, 1998), 2.

[9] Amina Wadud, "Alternative Qur'anic Interpretations and the Status of Muslim Women," in *Windows of Faith: Muslim Women Scholars-Activist in North Americas*, ed. Gisela Webb, (Syracuse, New York: Syracuse University, 2000), 11.

[10] Hillary Charlesworth and Christine Chinken, *The Boundaries of International Law: A Feminist Analysis* (Manchester: Manchester University, 2000), 217.

[11] Ibid., 215.

[12] Convention on the Elimination of All Forms of Discrimination Against Women.

[13] Qur'an 60:12

[14] Abdul Ghaffar Hasan, *The Rights and Duties of Women in Islam* (Riyadh: Darussalam, 1999), 14.

[15] Jamal Badawi, *Gender Equity in Islam* (Plainfield, Indiana: American Trust, 1999), 39.

[16] Ibid.

[17] Fatima Mernissi, trans. Mary Jo Lakeland, *The Veil and the Male Elite: A Feminist Interpretation of Women's Rights in Islam* (New York: Addison-Wesley, 1991), 49-61.

[18] Badawi, 41.

[19] Doi, 'Abdur Rahman, *Women in Shariah* (London: Ta-Ha Publishers, 1996), 138.

[20] Ibid.

[21] Ibid., 140.

[22] Ibid., 141.

[23] Javaid Rehman, *International Human Rights Law* (Dorchester: Pearson Education, 2003), 357.

[24] Convention on the Elimination of All Forms of Discrimination Against Women

[25] Rehman, 360.

[26] Badawi, 16.

[27] Doi, 35.

[28] Ibid., 25.

[29] Most Hanafi scholars have given the father of a 'virgin' the right to prevent an unsuitable marriage; however this is an area where *Ijtihad* is needed. Is the 'virgin' of the past equivalent to the 'minor' of modern society?

[30] Azizah Al-Hibri, "Introduction to Muslim Women's Rights' in *Windows of Faith: Muslim Women Scholars-Activist in North Americas*, ed. Gisela Webb, (Syracuse, New York: Syracuse University, 2000), 61.

[31] A woman may stipulate in her contract that if her husband marries a second wife, she, the first wife, will be granted a divorce with full financial rights.

[32] Badawi, 26.

[33] Qur'an 4:24

[34] Badawi, 25.

[35] For a more in-depth discussion, see Azizah Y. al-Hibri's "An Islamic Perspective on Domestic Violence" at http://www.karamah.org/docs/DomViolfinal.pdf

[36] See "Female Genital Mutilation: an Islamic Perspective" by Imad-ad-Dean Ahmad, published by the Minaret of Freedom Institute (www.minaret.org)

[37] Charlesworth and Chinken, *The Boundaries of International Law*, 210.

[38] Ibid., 212.

[39] Rebecca Cook, ed. "Women's International Human Rights Law: The Way Forward" in *Human Rights of Women: National and International Perspectives* (Philadelphia: University of Pennsylvania, 1994), 7.

[40] Hillary Charlesworth, "What are 'Women's International Human Rights?'" in *Human Rights of Women: National and International Perspectives* (Philadelphia: University of Pennsylvania, 1994), 61.

[41] Cook, "Women's International Human Rights Law: The Way Forward", 5.

[42] Walter, "Introduction," xxi.

[43] John Esposito and Natana DeLong-Bas, *Women in Muslim Family Law* (New York: Syracuse University, 2001), 162.

[44] Charlesworth and Chinken, *The Boundaries of International Law*, 224.

[45] Narjis Rerhaye, "Revolution de velours," *Le Matin*, 15 October 2003.

[46] Soumaya Naamane Guessous, "Une page nouvelle dans l'histoire du Maroc, un espoir fou dans le Coeur des femmes," *Ousra*, Nr. 29, November 2003, 12.

[47] Dounia Mseffer, "Autour d'un café avec Zhor El Hor," *Femmes du Maroc*, Nr. 97, January 2004, 48.

[48] Brand, Larry, *Women, the State, and Political Liberalization: Middle Eastern and North African Experiences* (New York: Columbia University, 1998), 65.

[49] Rerhaye.

[50] *Le Matin*, "Commission consultative chargee de la revision de la Moudawana: une action en deux temps," 15 October 2003.

[51] Fatne Sarehane, "De la Moudawan au code de la famille," *Femmes du Maroc* Nr. 95, November 2003, 51.

[52] Qur'an: 30:21

[53] Sarehane, 51.

[54] Under strict Hanafi fiqh, the distinction is between a virgin and a non-virgin or adult female. The assumption being that a virgin may be too naïve and impulsive,

needing her father's approval. The reform committee in Morocco made a distinction between a 'minor' female, under the age of 18, and an adult female. The intention of protecting a naïve and impulsive young woman is the same under both interpretations.

[55] Sarehane, "Code de la Famille: Vrai/Faux," *Femmes du Maroc*, Nr. 96, December 2003, 60.

[56] Ibid.

[57] Sarehane, "De la Moudawan au code de la famille," 58-60.

[58] Sarehane, 'Code de la Famille: Vrai/Faux,' 62.

[59] Mseffer, 48.

[60] "La Femme Marocaine au Coeur du Maghreb," Interview with Mireille Duteuil, *Citadine,* January 2004, 76.

PRAYERS FOR PEACE:
INTERVIEW WITH PLAYWRIGHT BINA SHARIF

MERA MOORE

After receiving an M.D. degree in Pakistan and a master's degree in public health from Johns Hopkins University, Bina Sharif began pursuing her dream of a career in the entertainment industry. She also continued her interest in visual arts through drawing and painting. Making New York City her home, she became a naturalized citizen of the United States. During the 1980s, she began performing professionally in theatre, television, and films; she also initiated her career as a playwright with Lower East Side theatre companies. Numerous plays and performance pieces by Sharif have premiered in New York, and she often directs and performs in her own works. She has toured one-person shows to theatres across the U.S., as well as making select appearances in Belgium, England, and Pakistan. This immigrant author's tragicomic plays, blending serious subject matter with irreverent comedy, have attracted diverse audiences. Whereas her plays serve the aims of political theatre, objecting to totalitarianism and seeking means for peaceful relations among human beings, the plays predominantly explore women in domestic settings and personal relationships. Even, or especially, when her characters express hostility, they reach across borders and boundaries towards mutual understanding.[1]

Following the suicide attacks of September 11, 2001, Sharif was doubly devastated as an American and as a Muslim. Her home town, New York City, had been brutally assaulted by nineteen men who claimed to be Muslims. Her initial artistic response was a series of paintings titled *Manhattan Days*. The inception of the war in Afghanistan led her to create the acclaimed mono-drama *Afghan Woman*, which features a single actor wearing a burqa, a play she calls "a prayer for peace." Soon after, by combining a trio of monologues excerpted from three of her plays— *Afghan Woman, Rats in the Tunnel*, and *My Ancestor's House*—she created the solo show *Women in Modernity*. Since that time, Sharif has written new plays and performance pieces addressing dilemmas faced by

Muslims in the West, including plays titled *Democracy in Islam, Muslim Glitter, Comedy of Terrors, Manhattan Spleen*, and *Republic of Iqra*.

When I first met her for an interview on November 3, 2001, Sharif told me that she had "gone through many things as a playwright, as a Muslim, as a South Asian." She perceives the struggles she faces as a human being through multiple identities. For a woman to claim herself first as an artist, a writer, is a political act. She embraces her Muslim upbringing and locates her Pakistani heritage within a broad cultural framework. Sharif's identification of herself as a South Asian speaks to her desire to forge alliances with other ethnic minorities. The following interview is an expansion on a 2002 conversation with Sharif, which previously appeared in the journal titled *Peace and Policy*.[2]

Moore: Playwright Amy Hill has criticized the way in which the entertainment industry in the United States rigidly enforces type casting. She says: "I would go up for Asian roles, and they would always say I didn't look Asian enough. . . . There must be some book somewhere that says this is what Asian looks like, and this is what black looks like."[3] You have said that you began writing in order to create interesting parts for yourself as an actor. Could you please elaborate?

Sharif: It's a very important question. I used to, when I was just an actress, I used to write poetry and prose. I used to get up early in the mornings, 7 o'clock five days a week, to sign up for and wait in line for auditions at the Actors' Equity office. After about a year, a casting director noticed me and took me aside. She said, "Listen, you know what, you are a wonderful actress. I've seen your reviews. You've been nominated for an award at the Goodman Theatre. But let me tell you the truth. You are Asian. You are Indian. We do not have any part for you in our scripts. I like you, and I want to let you know this." I wasn't thinking anything like racism. She was a very nice lady and had been very nice to me, and I could see that she thought that she was trying to help me. But I thought, "Does she mean that I will never act? Does she mean that I should give up acting?" I realized that I never saw a part for an Indian woman myself. Robert Patrick, a dear friend of mine, author of *Kennedy's Children*,[4] said, "You should write plays yourself." Once I started writing, I played any part I wanted to play, white woman, black woman, whatever part I wanted. I didn't even hide my accent. I'd still be sitting here waiting for an audition if I did not write my own plays. I wrote my first monologue, and then this whole thing began.

Moore: The one-person play is a frequently used vehicle in contemporary American theatre, especially by minority and women playwrights. Your *Afghan Woman* and your trio of monologues *Women in Modernity* are examples of solo-performance dramas. Can you talk about how the solo show gives you a certain type of freedom as a playwright?

Sharif: In their eyes, I was just one Indian woman. Once I began writing myself, I allowed myself the freedom. In the beginning, I didn't think of this idea giving me freedom. Out of necessity, I did the one-woman shows. Now I realize how much freedom it does give me as a playwright. My second play had thirteen characters, and my third play had five characters. Once the play closes, people are afraid to do it again because it has so many characters. I can make a one-woman show out of it and travel with it with all my props and costumes. Lots of my plays have monologues in them that I picked up for my show, like the homeless woman in *Rats in the Tunnel*. Now the monologue has become the greatest form of theatre.

Moore: Scholars and theatre artists have suggested that the one-person show in which the actor plays multiple roles, such as your play *Fire*, communicate the ways in which people put on social roles much like they put on items of clothing.[5] In *Fire*, the actor portrays both an Iraqi immigrant and a white American woman, which seems to emphasize that circumstances of social status and nationality constrict our common humanity. What do you see as the function of these multiple roles by a single performer?

Sharif: In *Fire*, the actor plays the Iraqi cleaning woman, the white woman from Idaho, the immigrant thrown out of the hospital, the immigrant thrown out of the bank, a TV journalist, and other parts. Consider different social roles like the waves of the same ocean. On different sections of the beach it seems different. There's a larger beach somewhere, or it's sandier, or the waves are bigger or smaller. People say, "Let's go to the 'other section.'" It's shadier, or less crowded, or cleaner. Every section assumes a different quality. If the actor is very good, you forget what the person looks like. Assuming different social roles—theatre is about making people aware of the conflicts in our lives, our wars, our habitats, the environment. In my plays, the emotions of every character create a play in itself. Every character brings different emotions. My characters are rooted in the personal, in the times in which they live, not just outside of what they look like. The audience knows where the person is from by what the character says and does. The sensibility of my work has depth of emotions.

Moore: And you want to use theatre to improve international communications?

Sharif: I examine the Western masses standing at one tiny section of a vast beach and refusing to see a different color of sand or the sea shells a few yards away. They don't want to explore a different answer. They have made opinions already, and it's good enough for them. But you know what? It's not good enough for me! Look around at the globalization, the looting of resources of other people. The Western world cannot expect everyone else to be smiling and say "thank you".

Moore: Your plays employ music and Muslim prayer. Several plays include the Islamic call to prayer, including *My Ancestor's House* and *Fire*. Do you see your cultural heritage as integral to your work?

Sharif: For me, what difference would it make for me? A Muslim woman from Pakistan here in the United States for twenty-five years, what good would it do if I write exactly the same kind of play as any American? How do you recognize any kind of thread of an identity? My identity is in tatters, but I keep the needle in my hand to protect the threads. One time, I saw a play by a few young Arab-American performers who included nothing Arabic. They wanted to do nothing with Arabic language or culture; they just wanted to be Americanized. Even when your identity is shattered, you have to be careful to try to protect the links of your heritage. I want to make the audience aware that there is another culture, a big world out there. Listen to this music. You may not understand it, but listen and realize how beautiful it is.

Moore: Could you comment upon what you see as themes of global miscommunication between the Islamic world and the West in some of your plays?

Sharif: I did not think that then, but when I read them now I see that it's there. It is about feeling lost, or not feeling free, or feeling lonely—or some kind of longing to embrace your culture, or your religion. Now, people are trying to learn about Islam. Before the September 11, almost no one talked about Islam. Even if they had miscommunication, that would be so encouraging! My play *Democracy in Islam* is important because

American audiences don't even have an idea what the Qur'an is about or what Islam is about. European people travel more. They are much more aware of the Arabic language and culture than most Americans.

Moore: Gandhi preached love for Muslims, especially at the end of his life when partition was imminent. He said that he studied and respected Islam. He argued that the way to peace was for others to embrace Muslims and love Muslims.[6]

Sharif: Yes, he wanted Hindus and Muslims to live like brothers. And perhaps that is the reason why he was shot. I wish that was not the case. It is very sad. That's how life is. Whatever is expected is not the case.

Moore: Some of your plays address economic marginalization of Americans, especially the sexual exploitation of poor American women. The white prostitute in *Fire* is an example of this. Similarly, your play *Sex Industry* relates to this theme. Would you comment on what drew you to this social concern?

Sharif: Immigrants look at things differently. When you first come to America, you buy the dream. You really believe in it. You are educated, you speak the language, and you never imagine the poverty. Then you look at the homeless. They talk about democracy and equality. How come the homeless are sitting out in the cold? I realized that it is deliberate. Somebody wants the homeless to be like this. This kind of marginalization in society is even more shocking. In the Third World, someone will help you, someone will give you food or some help. And on this other topic, the play titled *Sex Industry*, let me comment as follows: I'm in theatre, and there are lots of pretty actresses, and they tell you that they dance in clubs, strip clubs, topless clubs. White, black, Asian, they can make big bucks. They cannot earn that kind of money being a secretary or a waitress. I asked one of them the following question: "Is this *really* just dancing?" She told me that many rich married men put their cards in their garters. She wants to be a real actress, but she's a lap-dancer and there is no getting out of that because her trunk is full of money that she is hiding from the bank and the IRS. It's amazing in this country... if you want to lead a decent, honest life, you're going to be poor or not extremely wealthy. The white prostitute in *Fire* has more depth than the characters in *Sex Industry*. She does examine. She says, "I want to breathe." She sees that the Iraqi woman has ambition. The ambition of the cleaning lady is a wonderful thing for the prostitute. It gives her courage to leave the old man who hires her for b... jobs. In the Western world, the fundamentalist Muslim woman is considered "repressed" and "controlled". But the American lap-dancer is also controlled—by greed and by her pimp. We don't even know the definition of democracy. To me, democracy is a personal freedom of choice. Perhaps this Muslim woman is making her own personal choice to cover herself, to study the Qur'an. Perhaps she feels very free.

Moore: Your two-play collection entitled, *One Thousand Hours of Love* and *Sleeping with Horses*, addresses colonization, especially internalized colonization. In the first play, only two white men speak. The Indian woman they discuss is seen but not heard. The second play consists of an extended monologue by the woman. Could you tell us how the play works through issues related to the colonization of India by the British, or the East by the West, through the Indian woman's relationship with a British man?

Sharif: In the first part named *One Thousand Hours of Love*, she doesn't speak. The Western world always goes blabbermouth, because the media, TV, always give their points of view and do not allow others to speak. This British man is justifying his cruelty and exploitation. Once she took her clothes off, he lost his interest in her. He is blaming the victim like the conquerors do. The guy is pounding on her and justifying his own guilt over the colonization. She is in total shock. When the occupiers are there, they never give anybody a chance to speak...or, if allowed to speak, to make a complete point.

Moore: He only wants the longing for her?

Sharif: Exactly. He only wanted to chase her exotic look, her exotic image. Once he feels she wants him, he does not want her. The trick of the Empire, no matter who the Empire is,... it always gives the impression that the colonized people are inferior. Deep down, they respect only those 3 or 5 or 10 who refuse to be inferior, who struggle and maintain their dignity. Those people are punished by refusing them club membership. But they respect them. When you behave like a victim, even to the master, it's a little disgusting. I was reading James Baldwin, and he was talking about the history of blacks in Harlem.[7] He was talking about "Negroes"— that's the word they used in those days—as great actors. They were always perceived as "entertainers"....thus their survival depended on entertainment of the white folks. But great artists like Billie Holiday and many others still achieved stardom. Yet it was hard to sustain it because they were still being controlled by the media and the Hollywood, the Empire! The woman in *One Thousand Hours of Love* attracted the British man simply as an entertainment piece with her exoticness, but the moment she acknowledged her power (by taking her clothes off) he took her power away. The colonial dilemma—if the power is ever given, it's swiftly taken away.

Moore: What about the companion play, *Sleeping with Horses*?

Sharif: In the second part, the humiliated woman is dying but wants to die in dignity. She asks herself, "Why was I enamored?" She answers, "When my land was occupied, so was my soul." England lived inside India even after the British left. After the occupiers leave, the colonized people follow them and labor in menial jobs in those countries: Algerians in France, Indians in Britain. If you make love with someone as strong as a horse or as elegant as a horse, it's very seductive. The British in India were observed as very seductive in a certain manner. You are made to believe that you are not as good as them. Additionally, the colonized people have to fight for the rest of their lives in order to prove: "I am as strong as you." But if they were strong enough, they don't have to say that. Look at the literature and theatre about diasporas, about multiculturalism. It's about a cry from the heart, "I liberated myself from you." This means that I was once *not* liberated. My ancestors were once *not* liberated. Every minute of their lives, they have to struggle with themselves… just to survive.

Moore: What is the solution?

Sharif: Your dignity is the most important thing. Be yourself. You are not inferior. Your dignity is your pride, your fame, your skill, your enlightenment. In *Sleeping with Horses*, she has learned from her mistake. If she has daughters, she will teach them: maintain your dignity!

Moore: In his 1993 essay, "Intellectual Exile: Expatriates and Marginals," Edward Said talks about how the intellectual as exile embraces dissatisfaction, synthesizing a sense of unsettledness into imagination and investigation.[8]

Sharif: I love Said. I love his work. It's like what he says, the Indian woman in *Sleeping with Horses* is also unsettled, and she transforms the dilemma of colonization into love. The British man who has exploited her lives inside her. If someone lives inside your soul, how can you get rid of that person? She does have dignity because she likes herself; she likes her soul despite an isolated existence.

Moore: *Afghan Woman* was well received in New York City during its run at Theater for the New City. Audiences across the United States and in Pakistan have praised the excerpts which you have performed in. Can you tell us about the audiences' reactions in the U.S. and in Pakistan?

Sharif: In the U.S., people were more curious about that part of the world because of the September 11 and the war in Afghanistan. In Pakistan, they all wanted to talk about September 11, and what had happened. They were very sad about innocent people dying. They had only watched it on TV, yet I was like a witness because I was at home in New York City. Those people were not in New York City on that day. They were surprised about hearing how scary it has been for Muslims in this country since then. Muslims have been searched, have been arrested. American audiences could not believe that Muslims were sad. They thought and believed that Muslims were happy about the events of the September 11. Here people think everyone there is wearing *chador*, wearing *burqa*, reading Qur'an, carrying a sword. But there, everyone's dream is to come to America. They don't believe you when you tell them how difficult it is to be in someone else's country. They think you want to keep America for yourself!

Moore: What is the play *Afghan Woman*'s function in the search for global peace?

Sharif: It's a prayer for peace. Crying, pleading for peace. Even if she does not like Taliban, she's still saying that there could have been a better way. "Look at the history of Afghanistan", she says, "so much slaughter, so much war". I think it touches everybody because we forget that she is merely a singular voice. She becomes a collective voice though when she says: "Don't bomb children; don't bomb innocent people; don't do terror to remove terror. If you want to free me, you don't come and destroy the entire building. You don't kill my children and neighbors". It is as if she is saying: "you don't really want to free me".

Moore: Your play *Democracy in Islam* also seems to point in the direction of using theatre as a tool for improving international communication.

Might you discuss what you are attempting to do thematically and culturally in this play?

Sharif: Before the September 11, no one was really talking about Islam. Afterward, the words "fundamentalism", "terrorism", "Al Qaida", "Taliban" entered our daily conversations. "Democracy does not exist in the Islamic world at all" became a major assumption. The point of the play is to ask, "What is the meaning of democracy? Let us define democracy." Then we have to agree on a common definition, but we never will. Everybody's democracy is different. But let us assume, for the purpose of discussion, that there is no democracy in Islam. Why? Because the West does not want democracy. Then they could not open their markets; their globalization efforts would be useless. If they let them speak, some people will say, "We don't want McDonald's here, we don't want Nike sweatshops here." Many Muslim countries have puppet governments that are good to America but bad to their own people. Their leaders don't want them to say anything against America. How can democracy exist? I'm still exploring the question. Western experts of the Middle East and Islam have already decided that there is no democracy in Islamic countries. Western scholars never talk about how Prophet Mohammed brought Islam into the world to establish democracy. The religion is democratic, but the *practice* is not democratic. Whoever leads the country determines the shape of the government. Islam is much different than what most Muslim countries claim. If we talk about Islam, we cannot do so without imagining those 57 countries of different languages, cultural differences and social climates. I am a Pakistani. I am so absolutely different from Arabs. Islam is a religion; it's a faith. Democracy is a cultural thing. Prophet Mohammed's faith was based on democracy, but in different countries different socio-political circumstances prevail. Theater for the New City was so excited about some public readings from *Democracy in Islam* that they premiered the play. They heard that the reading at the East-West Center in Hawaii during the summer in 2002 went so well that they invited me to organize a reading for them. People loved it! Theater for the New City booked it right there and then, and it played from 5 December to the 29th. We had full houses nearly every night.

Moore: Your play *Muslim Glitter* features two women. How do these characters relate to one another?

Sharif: *Muslim Glitter* and *Comedy of Terrors* form a trilogy together with *Afghan Woman* because all three plays deal with the same subject matter: Islam, fundamentalism, the rise of terror about the word Islam in this country, and how and why one or everyone can be a suspect— especially an individual from a Muslim background. The two characters in *Muslim Glitter* are women. One is an American who is the kept mistress of a rich man on Park Avenue, and the other is her maid, Fatima, an Afghani immigrant who cleans the house.[9] The two become friends but later lose touch. After September 11, the American woman wants to change her life. She thinks about her friend, studies Islam, and converts to Islam. She becomes an actress who must travel for her work. One day, shortly after the arrest of the so-called "shoe bomber" Richard Reid, she is hassled by the security at an airport because she is wearing *hijab* and carrying tons of shoes in her bag. The shoes are her props for a performance. It's a very funny scene when she is explaining the shoes to the security guards. On the other hand, the play leaves Fatima's fate unclear, suggesting she may have gone back to Afghanistan and died in the war.

Moore: Might you comment on how your solo play, *Comedy of Terrors*, employs humor to address a serious topic?

Sharif: In *Comedy of Terrors*, there is only one woman who is an artist, a playwright, and a Muslim immigrant. She has a nightmare after reading Edgar Allen Poe's "The Raven."[10] She dreams that Federal Homeland Security authorities come in through the dark window to investigate her about her latest script. They go through everything in her house to find suspicious evidence that she is a terrorist. For instance, they find lots of Indian spices, which they suspect are some ominous powders. When she awakens, somehow her manuscripts are missing. This leaves it to the audience to figure out the Kafkaesque scenario. It's a satirical piece about fear of the authorities in the case of a completely innocent, funny, well-informed Muslim woman, an immigrant artist living in New York in today's atmosphere. It's one of my favorite pieces because it brings lots of humor to the surface.

Moore: Your 2006 play *Republic of Iqra* at Theater for the New City explicitly refers to events covered in the media. Some of your earlier works touch upon such topics, but this one seems to hinge on allusions to specific incidents in the news.

Sharif: *Republic of Iqra* was a full-length play which closed after a one-month run in early 2006 but came back from September to December in

2006 by popular demand. With ten characters, the play is a fiction based on current events dealing with the Iraq War, such as the investigation into the leak of the name of CIA agent Valery Plame, who is referred to in the play as "the Blonde," who never appears, Scooter Libby's indictment, the prosecutor Fitzgerald, and Ahmad Challabi of Iraq. I use different names in the play: Challabi is called Ghulabi, which means, in Arabic, "pink liar." This idea of truth and lies, reality and illusion, is central to the play. The play alternates between two Republics. The first is the "Republic of Iqra." Iqra is the first word in the Qur'an. It means to "read" or "recite" the truth. The other is called the "Republic of Make Believe," where everyone tells lies. The play is half serious—the war part—and half funny.

Moore: There is a standard question asked of playwrights. What is your opinion on the issue of drama as entertainment versus drama as social commentary?

Sharif: Theatre is neither social message nor entertainment—not one thing. Words like "Broadway" imply that entertainment is all. An artist working with the brain and vision must not think of any question like this, they should write organically when it comes to them, then edit later. Thinking "I want to make the audience happy" or "I want to communicate a message", you won't do your work. Dramatic art is different than standing up and giving a political speech.

Moore: Your plays seem to fit in the categorical framework of a tragicomedy. Some years back, scholar Bernard F. Dukore published a book on Harold Pinter's absurdist plays called *Where Laughter Stops*, arguing that in tragicomedy, spectators are led to expect to laugh, want to laugh, and do laugh, but then, upon realizing the horror of what they are laughing at, suddenly stop laughing.[11]

Sharif: Entertainment of the soul. When we see something very tragic, funny, shocking, we remember it for the rest of our lives. This reminds us of what we see in the world, what makes us think, laugh, be aware, want to go and talk with others about something, remember things some years later.

Moore: One reviewer called the play "static."[12] This remark reminds me of Pinter, whose plays have a lot of conversation.

Sharif: Yes, my plays have a lot of it.

Moore: When directing, Pinter was known to ask his actors "Do you feel that move is absolutely necessary?" He would advise them "Don't feel you have to move just because you've been there for a long time."[13] Pinter's plays, like those of Samuel Beckett and Edward Albee, seem to call for periods of static states in order to highlight occasional explosive movements.

Sharif: Beckett's pauses are considered "language." His silences are language. In *Happy Days*, a woman is buried up to her neck in a grave. In another of his plays, nothing moves except the lips.[14] My action is in my language and in my writing style, in action and in non-action. People are always interested in my language, and there is humor in everything. If a play touches your emotions, you forget if actors are sitting or standing or running around.

Moore: How would you classify your play *Republic of Iqra*?

Sharif: This is a "language" play. This play would be loved by people who love language and hate war. It's not about the Iraq war. It's about wars. It's about the obsession of humanity with war. This can never be yesterday's news. War is never yesterday's news.

Moore: What are some of your more recent works?

Sharif: *A Month in the Café*. An excerpt of this play was performed at the Lower East Side Festival at Theater for the New City in May 2007, featuring Crystal Field and Lola Pashlinski. The full production of this play was done at Theatre for the New City in November 2007. I also created a new one-person play that I performed myself, called *Say Hello to Arnie in Sacramento*. It was done at Theater for the New City as part of the Lower East Side Festival events in May 2008.

Moore: What are your plans for new plays?

Sharif: I'm writing two pieces, a serious one and a comedy. The serious play is called *Another Journey* and is a follow-up to *My Ancestor's House*, with the immigrant American sister returning home to Pakistan once more, dealing with unresolved issues of post-colonialism that affect the relationships of her family members with one another.

Moore: And the comedy?

Sharif: Theater for the New City has been wonderfully supportive of my writing. In the past, they have commissioned me to write many plays. This time, they want a comedy. The script I'm working on is very funny, relating to the run-up to the election of Barack Obama to become President of the United States. It's called *Here Comes the Change*.[15]

In conclusion, I would like to explain how the social dilemma presented in *Fire* is intrinsically connected to the journeys undertaken by most immigrant Muslim women. *Fire (Empty Your Closets If You Want No Fire)* is a tragicomedy which takes place in New York City during the 1991 Persian Gulf War. Mumtaz, originally from the small town of Balad in Iraq, immigrates to the United States hoping to become a doctor. Although she becomes a U.S. citizen, for several years she faces difficulties continuing her medical education, eking out a living by working at menial jobs. When Mumtaz works as the cleaning lady in a Park Avenue penthouse, she befriends an American woman who lives there as the mistress of a wealthy elderly man. Volunteering to serve as her manager, the woman convinces Mumtaz to become a stand-up performer in clubs and theatres around the city, and the duo begin to experience some success. Then Mumtaz receives news that an American missile has hit the mosque in her hometown of Balad, killing her mother, who was praying inside. Mumtaz goes mad, imagining she is back in Balad, keeping vigil beside her mother's body.

The play consists of flashbacks to the immigrant's life as she seeks comfort in her Muslim heritage. Grief destroys Mumtaz, but she takes a brave step forward regaining her sanity by returning to the Islamic faith which she was born into. Near dawn, she declares that it is time to pray for lost relatives and she finds peace and hope in her devastation with the help of her Muslim heritage. Confused and delusional, she says that she cannot remember who is living and who is dead, yet she still kneels on the prayer rug. She prays first for her mother and then for the entire humanity, as a song in Arabic plays in the background and the lights fade. *Fire* pays homage to women who are brave, persistent and self-confident in following their hearts' songs as they renew their faith in themselves.

Notes

[1] Information on Sharif's writings can be found in the following works: "Bina Sharif," by Rashna B. Singh, *Asian American Playwrights: A Bio-Bibliographical Sourcebook*, edited Miles Xian Liu (Westport, CT: Greenwood Press, 2002); "Bina Sharif," *Women Playwrights of Diversity: A Bio-Bibliographical Sourcebook*, edited by Jane T. Peterson and Suzanne Bennett (Westport, CT: Greenwood Press, 1997); John Clay, "The Artist Is the One Who Shouts: Interview with Bina Sharif," *Bhag: Online Magazine of Visual and Conceptual Exchange* (2002), http://www.bhag.net/intsharb/intsharb.html (Retrieved 1 June 2006); Mera Moore, "From Islamabad to New York City: Bina Sharif's Spiritual Politics," *Text and Presentation: Journal of the Comparative Drama Conference* (2002): 57-69; and the introduction to her play *Afghan Woman* in *Contemporary Plays by Women of Color*, edited by Kathy A. Perkins and Roberta Uno, 262-279 (New York: Routledge, 1996).

[2] My prior interview with Sharif appeared under the title: "Theatre as International Communication: Interview with Bina Sharif," *Peace and Policy: Journal of the Toda Institute for Global Peace* (2002): 44-48.

[3] Amy Hill in the introduction to her play *Tokyo Bound*, in *Asian American Drama: Nine Plays from the Multiethnic Landscape*, edited by Brian Nelson, 43 (New York: Applause, 1997).

[4] Robert Patrick, *Kennedy's Children* (New York: Samuel French, 1998).

[5] Examples include Judith Butler on the social construction of gender in art and literature, with her publications titled *Gender Trouble: Feminism and the Subversion of Identity* (New York: Routledge, 1990) and *Bodies That Matter: On the Discursive Limits of Sex*. (New York: Routledge, 1993.

[6] Works on this topic by Mahatma Gandhi include "Hindu-Muslim Unity [8 April 1919]" (*The Penguin Gandhi Reader*, 2nd ed., ed. Rudrangshu Mukherjee, 259-261 (New York: Penguin, 1995).

[7] Sharif refers to James Baldwin's *Nobody Knows My Name: More Notes of a Native Son* (New York: Dell, 1961).

[8] Edward Said, "Intellectual Exile: Expatriates and Marginals" [1993], in *The Edward Said Reader*, eds. Moustafa Bayoumi and Andrew Rubin, 368-381 (New York: Vintage, 2000).

[9] Similar characters appear in Sharif's earlier play titled *Fire (Empty Your Closets If You Want No Fire)*.

[10] The reference in Sharif's *Comedy of Terrors* to Edgar Allen Poe's 1845 poem titled "The Raven" provides a clue to the prevalence of macabre humor in this play.

[11] Bernard F. Dukore, *Where Laughter Stops: Pinter's Tragicomedy* (Columbia: University of Missouri Press, 1976).

[12] Neil Genzlinger, "A Mideast Conflagration All but Real," a review of *Republic of Iqra*, by Bina Sharif, *The New York Times* (27 Feb. 2006). Sharif's earlier play

titled *Dreamland* has also been reviewed in *The New York Times*, by Mel Gussow (1 Sept. 1988).

[13] Ronald Harwood praises Pinter's directorial choices when he directed Harwood's play *Taking Sides*, in *"Taking Sides* by Ronald Harwood, 15 May 1995, Minerva Studio Theatre," in *The Life and Work of Harold Pinter*, ed. Michael Billington, (London: Faber, 1996), 365-366.

[14] Here Sharif mentions Samuel Beckett's play *Happy Days* (New York: Grove, 1961). She also refers to *A Piece of Monologue*, in *Three Occasional Pieces* (New York: Faber, 1982).

[15] Sharif's play titled *Here Comes the Change* premiered at Theater for the New City on December 18, 2008.

FIRE:
(EMPTY YOUR CLOSETS IF YOU WANT NO FIRE)

BINA SHARIF

(The time: 1991. The place: New York City. One actor portrays both characters: an Iraqi naturalized citizen and a U.S.-born American citizen.

Lights down. Dimly lit backdrop with an abstract representation of skyline with mosques; upstage, immediately in front of backdrop, lies a body wrapped in white cotton, barely visible. Next to the body: a lit candle, flowers. Actor, upstage right, stands near a prayer rug. A chant from the Qur'an is heard, an Islamic prayer. Actor sits on the prayer rug.

The actor rises; lights come up on her, as she stands upstage.)

Any minute her heart will stop the beat.
Any minute my heart will be wounded.
I love her.
Soon we will bury her.
Once she was beautiful.
She loved the perfumes.
She wore silk and chiffon.
Soon she will be covered in white cotton from head to toe.
We do not bury our dead in a nicely carved oak wood coffin box.
We are Muslims.
We lay the bare body right down to the ground.
We are down to earth people.
We were not allowed to take care of ourselves.
Our religion will take care of us,
      we thought.
Our Qur'an will take care of us,
      we thought.

The poet said "less is more."
You need only a mat so you can say your prayer,
A lantern so you can have light,
And a cup so you can quench your thirst,
          and destiny will take care of the rest.
But the poet is dead,
          and my destiny has brought me to this corner.
Where less is less and more is more.
          (*Lights go down.*)

This corner is light and dark,
          but I am only dark,
          darkly lit . . . haunting . . . never amusing . . . never pleasing.
Why does darkness scare you?
Why do you welcome darkness into your lives when you are asleep?
Why not when you are awake?
Are you afraid to look at my darkness?
          (*Stands with her back to the audience, drops shawl, nude.*)
You are not looking.
You don't have to be ashamed.
That's me,
I am shame.
I have to bear the burden shame has accumulated in my body.

I am ashamed of my body so I have turned my face away.
I am ashamed of my belly so I have turned my face away.
I am ashamed of my breasts so I have turned my face away.
I am ashamed of my buttocks so I have turned my face away.
I am ashamed of my thighs so I have turned my face away.
I am ashamed of my face so I have turned my face away.

Who made me ashamed?

Me?
You?
Them?
They?
No . . . no . . . no . . . no.

Would you look at me if I were tall like a cypress tree?
Would you look at me if I were a donkey?

Would you look at me if I were a monkey?
Yes.
You would.
If I were a monkey I would be a source of amusement for you.

This way, I make you ashamed of me.

Who made you ashamed of me?
Me? You? Them? They? No . . . no . . . no . . . no . . .
Would you look if I turned around?
No you won't.
My face is more frightening than my body.
More frightening than my belly.
More frightening than my darkness.

Who made it so frightening?

Me? You? Them? They?
If you hurt me, I will shed red blood.
But here, blood is thinner than water, paler than water.
I quickly turn away from all mirrors.
Your eyes are so light, and you see so much darkness.

It's just another body.
(Puts shawl back on.)
Why are you so uncomfortable?
You are only here for a short while anyway.
You can leave if you don't want to look at me.
No one will stop you.
But I cannot leave.
I have to finish what I started . . . I'm in the middle of it.
You see, you are still freer than me.

And you have no shame.
Even if I left from here,
Where would I go?
Upstairs?
Into the street?
Around the corner?
Not my street. Not my corner. Not the road which takes me to my
mother's cottage

or to her mosque or to her grave.
These days, mosques are being destroyed by ghosts.
Ghosts are so powerful. They do what they say.
Lots of cars pass with lots of lights. They pass by without ever stopping.
Who rides in those cars?
Shameless people.
The less shame you have, the more cars you have.

But I don't have to be any place.
My corner is right here.
I just have to somehow move my mother's grave into my corner.
My mind has that power.
(Lights down.)

***

(Actor goes upstage right for costume change. Music: "Bad Girl" by Eartha Kitt. Actor comes downstage left in a spiky blonde wig, a short, tight, black silk mini-slip, fishnet stockings, high heels, necklace.)

Every time you can't answer, you call for Jesus. I thought you were a Muslim. Have you forgotten who your God is? If your God is Mohammed, and you call for Jesus, he is not going to show up. And Mohammed, knowing his Muslim pride, is not going to show up uninvited.

I really think that's why your life is the way it is. You have confused all the gods. And none of them will help you. They can't figure it out, what it is that you want.

When I first met you, you had clarity. Clarity of purpose. You were not sitting like me in a fabulous house on Park Avenue, house full of antiques, giving some old guy b…jobs. When you came in to clean his house, you were a real woman, with real composure, such dignity, such self-confidence. "Dignity to survive with pride, struggle and survive," you said to me. I admired you. I used to look forward to being with you, the foreigner. I depended on a foreigner for my happiness.

My old man has money. He gave me some money, but he was busy making more. I used to sit there all day long doing nothing but polish my nails and watch TV. I didn't have any need to make money. I also had no skills to make money. I just gave him b… jobs. I was so overwhelmed with that life of mine in that orphanage when I was growing up that I welcomed any chance of a decent life, and he gave me a decent life. I didn't love him, but I had a decent life.

As far as b… jobs are concerned, they were quite fashionable, and I figured, if I were married to a poor s.o.b, I still would have to do it because I always wanted to be fashionable. Rich or poor, I wanted to be fashionable. I wanted to be like my mother.

After she left us kids for her freedom and career in New York, all my life I looked for her. I stopped and looked at every fashionable woman and stared at her, in case she was my mother and would remember me, but I scared every one of them away.

The moment I came close to them, they walked faster and faster, and I knew that none of those fashionable women walking in the streets were my mother. Otherwise, they would recognize me and hug me and kiss me. Then, I realized my mother must have been one of those fashionable women who ride in chauffer-driven limousines with color TV and champagne, giving rich old men b… jobs.

I realize that in order to find my mother I had to be in that society, and then I met this old fellow of mine in the Plaza Hotel, where I used to check his hat and coat.

"A pretty girl like you doesn't have to check my coat," he told me one day. "What should a pretty girl like me check?" I said. "You can comfort me," he said. "How?" I said. "You can check my health," he said. "What's wrong with your health?" I said. "Nothing wrong," he said. "Just need some new energy, new blood."

And I had energy and he wanted me to transform my energy to his blood. "How would I do that?" I said. "I don't have a master's degree in rejuvenationally oriented career from Harvard." He laughed and said, "A pretty girl like you don't need no degree. You can make me happy without a degree from the Ivy League."

And I got all confused. I used to think that rich people are rich because they have degrees, and the only people who can make the rich people happy are the other rich people with degrees. But he made me feel relieved

. . . that I am capable of being with a rich man without being rich and without a degree.

And I was tired of hanging coats and filling out little forms for the fur coats.

Fur is the heaviest coat, you know, and no one in the Plaza ever wore anything lighter, not even in May. So he squeezed a hundred dollar bill and an address card in my hand and told me to take a cab to his house that night. "Don't you have a limousine?" I asked. "I do," he said, "but you can't be seen in it." Everyone has their reasons, so I didn't insist on why I can't be seen in it. I got all excited. Since he has a limo, he must know all the fashionable women, and I will be able to meet my mother one day, so after my job I went to his house. Oh god, what a house he had! A big house with a garden, lots of furniture—mahogany and oak. Lamps, crystal chandeliers, so many expensive rugs. I thought he was the cousin of the late Shah of Iran. And those paintings, Picasso, Renoir, Matisse, Chagall, the big ones. It certainly looked different than my parents' home.

I realized why my mother left.

I asked him, "How can I rejuvenate you?" He laughed, and said he liked my sense of humor. But first we must have champagne. All rich people have champagne . . . first.

I drank a lot of champagne. And then I was ready to do whatever he wanted me to do. But all he wanted was a b... job. He wanted to be rejuvenated through my mouth. That wasn't hard. Then I slept. And then I slept. And then I slept . . . there.

He said I can never be seen with him outside. But I can stay there as long as he needed to be rejuvenated. And I said, "Yes."

I stayed for a long time and did my nails, and then you started to come to clean. He didn't want his b... job lady to do the cleaning.

You had real class and distinction. You were a real woman. And the only human being who walked in there once a week. I had lost touch with the outside world. You were my only contact with life. I looked forward to being with you.

You had a smile then. Bright smile and glow of hopes and dreams. I asked you, "Why do you do cleaning? Why don't you give b... jobs so you can live comfortably?" And you said you have your degree. You don't have to give b... jobs. And I said, "You must be rich. You have your degree." And you said, "Not yet." And I said, "When will you be rich?" And you said, "After America recognizes my foreign degree. I am a foreigner, you know. I have to pass all the American medical exams, and they are not that easy. They are multiple-choice, you know. And I am not used to them." "I would take any exams," I said. "If I had a degree, I would pass all those damn exams. Why don't you pass them and get it over with?" You said, "It's hard work." And I said, "You are used to hard work—you clean. What can be harder than that?" And you said, "After cleaning, I can't do anything harder. My back hurts."

And after you finished cleaning I would make you a cup of tea. You would only drink tea. I guess that was okay. Your work didn't require champagne.

All that time, you never took those exams, did you? Well, I looked forward to that cup of tea of the week. Don't get me wrong. I had more than that in my life. The old man was nice to me. Gave me a home. Bought me beautiful clothes. Gave me lots of food. And asked for very little. He needed company. We are very lonely people, you know, we the rich ones.

I stayed there for a long time. Long, long time. Long enough to forget about my existence. I was very comfortable there. But I just couldn't breathe.

We will give you freedom, and you will help us breathe. I thought you had the understanding.

And one day I asked you if I could live with you, and you laughed. You laughed so hard I thought you would die of it. And you said, "I have no windows in my apartment." And I said, "Good. I need air."

And then I left the old man's house. I did leave him a note, thanking him for keeping me warm and indoors, but it was time for sun and air.

I came right to your apartment. And you took your exams and took your exams and took your exams. I guess you never passed them. After a while, you shut yourself in your room. And started staring at TV like I did in the old man's house. I didn't want you to become like me. So I said to you, "Forget about the f… exams. You have the personality of a winner. You should be in show business. You simply can't fail in that business. I will manage your career." That's the only career which is manageable without a degree.

You said, "Yes." Instantly.
And we haven't done badly, have we?

Show business is the biggest b… job of them all.
        (*Lights go down.*)

***

(Actor goes upstage left and changes into a loose, long red dress; takes off her stockings and wig; and sits on a low stool downstage right. She drinks water from a little bowl and takes off her high heels. She holds an imaginary remote control in her hand and uses it to change the channels on an imaginary TV downstage left. She watches TV.)

If God gave you a brain, you better use it because otherwise it's going to rot. My father educated me, and I'm making full use of my education by watching TV. When I watch TV, nobody can say I don't watch like no other ordinary human being. When I watch, I watch.

I told my parents, "Hey, listen, I gotta brand new career. TV career. I'm never coming back. You wanna go die, you go die."

They went ahead and they died.
They were simple people, and I guess this was their way of dealing with it. Simple people do things simply.

I think they both died at once.
At least one of them is dead. I am really sure of that.

One might be living someplace. I don't know because I get a letter every day from the living relative, but I can't think about that now. Now I have to concentrate on TV.

I get up really early and watch the exercise program. Eight and a Half Minute Video.

Then comes the sunrise university lectures: Spanish, French, philosophy.

There's so much education on TV . . . I really don't understand why people pay so much money to go to university when everything is available for free on TV.

Then comes the talk shows: Sally Jesse Raphael "Divorced Women Who Are Sorry They Are Divorced." "Women Who Are Racist," Tomorrow at 10.

> *(Switches channels.)*

Then comes the news. "Today's top story. The liberation has begun. In one week, we will have lots of oil. We don't know what to do with it yet, but we have invited lots of professors, experts from Columbia, Yale, Princeton, and we will very soon come to a conclusion. In fact, we have reached a conclusion this very second. We are going to swim in it."

Peter Jennings reporting. Live from Baghdad. Baghdad. Oh, that reminds me of a story my mother used to tell me when I was a little girl.

Long, long ago, in a far-off place, there existed a tiny country called Baghdad. In it there was a thief. He was called the "Thief of Baghdad." That thief stole lots of things and money from his people. And nobody did anything to stop him. Then he stole more, and nobody did anything. Then he stole lots of gold and money from his neighbors. That made some other very powerful thieves from across the ocean very angry. So the powerful thieves and the thief of Baghdad ended up having a battle where they killed everybody and got killed themselves. Everything got killed . . .

> *(Actor rises slowly, moves in a circle as if she has completely lost herself in sorrow.)*

. . . Camels, lambs, cauliflower, flies, dates, babies, goats, figs, nuts, lizards, snakes, horses, cows, and the whole city became a ruin. Everything was killed, and the cities turned into ruins, and the ruins were cursed. And God put a curse on the ruined land. And God said, "That no green grass will ever grow there and flowers will never bloom there and the strong howling winds will blow in the memory of the dead."

> *(During the last phrase, she creates the sound of the wind and swirls round in a circle faster and faster, then stops, saying to herself)*

Always the memory of the dead.

(She sits down on the stool, very quiet. Pause. Looks at TV.)
That's a bit depressing for me.
(Switches channels.)
Let me watch a soap opera.

Soap operas are great. Doctors on soap operas are smarter. When you get sick on soap opera, ambulance comes right away. You get to the emergency room right away. And get examined right away. Then you get diagnosed right away. Either you're under stress and you're cured and you're back on the next episode or else you have cancer and you die and you get replaced by another actor. But when I used to go to the hospital it was different.
(Stands downstage right.)

One time I waited in the emergency room for hours and I asked the registration nurse, "Excuse me, could you please tell me in how many more hours approximately will I be seen?" And the nurse said she can't tell me because it's against the rules and regulations of the hospital.

Another dark woman like me, a patient sitting behind me, said, "Come I'll tell you when you'll be seen." And I thought she was a bit crazy because if the registered nurse did not know how would she know? But I talked with her anyway.

And she asked me, "Has your blood pressure dropped to zero?"
"No, not yet."
"Has your temperature risen to 120 degrees Fahrenheit?"
I said, "No, not yet."
"Do you have a gunshot wound in your belly?"
I said, "No."
So she said, "then you won't be seen until tomorrow."
"Oh, you mean I have time to get some tea then?"
She said, "Sure."

So I went to get some tea and on the way back in I saw a woman wearing polyester, sitting outside the Emergency Room and really struggling to breathe. I ran to the registered nurse and I told her the woman outside is very, very sick. And the nurse said, "You are very sick." And I said, "yeah, but my illness is not diagnosed yet and by the time they find the diagnosis, the disease will be fully developed and then I will be ready to die, but the woman outside is going to die in exactly 1 minute and 39 seconds." And the registered nurse said, "if you don't shut up we'll throw you out so the dying lady can have some company. How dare you interfere with the rules and regulations of the hospital?" and I said "What rules and regulations? Rules and regulations my a.. ."

And then somebody came in and said the lady outside is dead.
And they all looked at me as if I were a witch.

In fact, the registered nurse asked me if I were a witch, and I told them, no, I am not a witch. And the registered nurse asked me how did I know the woman was going to die in exactly 1 minute and 39 seconds and I told them that I know, because I watch TV. This is how it happens in soap operas. I learned everything from TV. And I told the registered nurse, "You should throw your license in garbage and go home and watch TV so you can have some real knowledge."
And they threw me out.
        (*Returns to stool and sits down.*)
And I decided never to go back to hospital again. That's alright, because it's healthier to watch it on TV because everyone is being taken care of.
        (*Switches channels.*)
There are so many killings on Channel 7. Gunshots, pistol shots, kitchen knives, butcher knives, scissors, smoke, fire, rape, abortions, women being dragged in subway.
        (*Switches channels.*)
Oh, here is the President again. "Now you know who the peace-makers are. While he was preparing for war, I was preparing for peace. I am perfectly at peace with myself. So is Barbara. I slept very well last night. So did Barbara. And this morning I took my dog out for a walk as usual. My dog was also very peaceful."

Mr. President, when you do the carpet bombing to finish off everyone quickly over there, please save a few bombs for your own people. One for the homeless in Tompkins Square Park so their agony can be ended quickly too. One for the homeless at the Port Authority. One for Grand Central. One for Harlem. One for Bronx. Especially for Tompkins Square Park. A must. Because all of them have tuberculosis and that's one illness you can catch just by breathing the same air in case you didn't know and I live around the corner and I don't want to die of such a poverty-stricken illness. Give me some untreatable exotic illness any day.
        (*Switches channels.*)
Oh, Macy's is having a sale.

Cuisinart $99.99 only.
Cuisinart, Cuisinart. Oh, that's what my mother wants. She writes me a letter every day. "Do you mind very much if I ask you to send me some American items such as Cuisinart, electric carrot juicer, garlic press, aluminum foil, microwave oven. Do not worry about the money. I am enclosing an international money order. You will have no problem cashing it. All you have to do is deposit it in your bank account."

Bank account? They have no idea of my lifestyle. What bank account?
(*Actor puts on high heels, stands, moves downstage center and addresses the audience.*)

Every time I go to open a bank account, this is what happens:
"Do you have identification, Miss?"
"Sure," I say.
"Can I see it? What kind of ID do you have, Miss?"
"Wait a minute," I say, while I struggle to find it in my old worn out Lancome pocketbook.
"Can I see your ID, Miss, before we go any further?" he says.
What is he talking about? How far is he planning to go with my lousy bank account?
"Wait a minute," I say while I still struggle to get my ID. "Here," I show him my passport.
He stares at it for a while. Then he stares at me. Then at the passport, and then he shakes his head. "No."
"What do you mean 'no'?" I say.
"No," he says.
"No, what?" I say, shocked at his behavior.
"No, Miss, not good enough."
"Not good enough? What is not good enough? My American passport not good enough?"
"No, Miss, not good enough. No, not good enough. You want me to repeat it? Not good enough. Not good enough. Not good enough. I guess they repeat everything in your country," he says to me. "Do they repeat everything twice, Miss, in your country?"

What nerve.
He was putting an American citizen down. He was asking me about my country?
While I was showing my American passport, I was trying to be in control.

"Well, that's the only form of ID that I have and it's good enough. They let me in with this everywhere in the world. Why can't I open a lousy bank account with this?" I asked him politely. "Well, what kind of ID would you like?" I did not want to lose control over trivia. People tell me I do that a lot.

    (Politely.)

"Tell me, Mister, what else can I show you?"

"Driver's license."

"I do not drive."

"We want a driver's license, Miss."

"I told you I do not drive."

"We don't care if you do not drive. We need to see your driver's license if you want to open an account with us."

"But I told . . . "

"Miss, Miss, I am not going to repeat myself, though in your country . . . "

That was it for me. I lost control.

"What country do you think I come from? While I am showing you my American passport? How dare you ask me about my country, buster? How dare you tell me my American passport is not good enough? Well, it's good enough for me. It's mine. I am a real American citizen. Always pay my taxes. Live like a nice, quiet, decent, honest, law-fearing American. And you tell me my American passport is not good enough. For opening a shitty, f..., lousy account in your f..., lousy, shitty bank. With my last ten dollars. Do I care about your checking or saving or whatever account? And by the way, why the hell should I give you my last ten dollars? Why should I? If I give you my last ten dollars, I will not be able to have my coffee today. I will not be able to have my muffin today. I will not be able to buy *The New York Times* today. How do you expect me to know what's going on in the world? I need to know because my nephew is out there and I want to know how long he is going to piss in the holy sand.

And you ask me for a driver's license. Who has the money to own a car? Do you have a car? Oh, yes, you have a car, yes, you do. You stole the money from the bank and bought a big Chevrolet and your wife is driving it right now........... Does she have a driver's license? Did she show it to you? Oh, sure, she has a driver's license. I don't need to have a driver's license, okay? I don't need a f... driver's license, okay?"

By this time, they throw me out of the bank.

And I go to Boston to relax. While we are having a perfect cup of Darjeeling tea, my cousin starts. "Oh, you come from such a responsible family, you are so educated. You have thrown your education in the gutter. You use the four-letter word frequently. You eat pork. You have brought a lot of shame to the family name. I don't understand your lifestyle, but one thing I really don't understand is that you are an American and you don't even have a bank account."

I want to say to her "go f... yourself," but I can't because she goes to Harvard.
     (*Sits and watches TV again.*)
Well, she can keep Harvard. I have my TV, thank you very much. I am never going to visit her again. She gives me a headache. All I want to do is drink my beer, take some aspirin, and watch my murder mystery to relax.
     (*Switches channels, still sitting.*)
I love murder mysteries.

Especially when women murder men.

***

Guilty or innocent?
Ladies and gentlemen of the jury, I stand here before thousands of curious eyes. Faces full of frowns. Tight-lipped mouths. Waiting to condemn me.
Don't stare so.
Your marble brows serve no purpose day after day.
I admit my crime.
I killed him.
     (*Actor stands, foes downstage left. She will use the whole stage space in the next piece.*)
Pushed him to death at the subway station. I paid a dollar to enter. I thought of not paying because I expected to be caught, but I paid anyway. What would I have done with that dollar? Dollars had no value to me by that time.

Ladies and gentlemen, you know my story. There is not one person here who has not repeated it over a martini, across a linguini, in a health club. A dining room or a kitchen. And all these lovely ladies sitting here are for sure envious of me. They wish it was them instead of me who committed this crime. Because, ladies and gentlemen, all women want to kill some man. At some time of their lives.

The man who got away.
The man who hurt them.
The man who did not marry them.
The man who did not let them have children.
The man of their nightmarish dreams.
The man they loved . . . who loved someone else?

But ladies and gentlemen, I did not love this man. Nor did I hate him. I killed him because he murdered my mother.

But you are not satisfied.
You bring a new jury every week, and put me on a new trial every week. And then declare that I am a mad woman. And he was an innocent man. But truth of the matter is that I avenged my mother's death. I took justice in my own hands. Because the road to justice is a long one in your country.

Listen, if some strange man killed your innocent mother who lived across the ocean, for no reason—would you not kill him, if you had a very strong reason, especially if he lived just across your hallway?

He was not innocent at all. He murdered my mother without ever crossing the ocean.
    (*Moves upstage near backdrop.*)
When my mother was murdered in the Holy Mosque of Balad, he was found sitting and sipping cappuccino in New York City at Café de Robertis on 11th Street and First Avenue.

Only a devil can do that.

Ladies and gentlemen, this man, when he moved in my building, became my misfortune. My ultimate sorrow. He usually smiled at me. His smile always brought me sorrow.

Is this the man my mother raised me for, loved me for? Cherished me for? So he can destroy my existence in one second with a smile?
    (*Moves centerstage.*)

When he smiled at me, it was as if Allah was smiling at me. Mockery.
Yes. He was mocking me.
As if he believed himself to be a god.
As if he knew I would fail, fail, no matter how hard I tried I would fail,
like he always expected.
At nighttime, I heard him laugh a lot at me. His women friends joined him,
and they all laughed at me. They were all the same and the worst and the
cruelest.
I heard the clinking of the wine glasses and music creeping through the
hallway.
Vivaldi. And Wagner.
That was a bit strange. Because people who like Wagner do not like
Vivaldi. I only listened to Wagner. But then I got tired of the whole thing
and gave my radio away to someone in the street. I had too much noise in
my head. I could not concentrate on music.

But his music and laughter entered my apartment regularly. It was all
deliberate. He wanted to upset me. He had parties to upset me.

On Thanksgiving, I wished . . . he invited me in and introduced me to his
friends. "Hey, meet my nameless neighbor. Though I had a beautiful
name: Mumtaz Jahan Mahal, name of a queen. King Aurangzeb built Taj
Mahal for her. That was my name. But he did not know it. My own
holidays came and went. If he knew my name, he would have respected
me more. When you live in the West, you lose track of your own holidays.

I wonder if he knew what kind of work I did? If he ever held my hand, he
would know I scrubbed floors. But at least I scrubbed marble floors.
Marble is an elite thing to have in Balad. Almost no one can afford it. But
here I looked at it, and I polished marble every day. But he did not know
that. He would have respected me more if he knew that.
   (*Moves stage right, hugs the wall of the theatre.*)
Then his smile started to change. It became more sarcastic, ridiculing,
vicious, as if he was up to something horrible, dangerous.

And then one day he disappeared, gone. My money was gone, too. He
stole it. He knew I was saving, always saving, so I could buy myself a
plane ticket to go and visit my mother. But instead of me . . .

He went to Balad . . . to plan my mother's murder. I dreamed his ghost
was seen in the mosque where my mother used to say her prayers for her

daughter's well-being. Balad is known for its ghosts, but it never had a white ghost before. I never felt well after that.

And then I had to work harder, more marble toilets for me all over again. Finally, when I had saved enough, a day before my trip, the war started.
(Pause.)
And the bombs came
(Stops speaking for a moment.)
And the big bomb fell on the mosque where my mother was saying her prayers for her daughter's well-being. My mother closed her eyes . . .
(Pause. Actor moves upstage near the backdrop.)
She only opened her eyes when she heard the sound of airplanes. She thought I was in one of them.
(Cries out, speaks a few words in Arabic.)
It was the month of Ramadan.
Friday.
4:40 a.m.
The holiest of the holy time. The time of her prayer. She closed her eyes forever.

The cycle was complete.
The crime was committed.
He had traveled full circle.
My mother was murdered.
Her last breath had escaped her body.
No more waiting for her daughter's visit.

I knew I had to kill him.
How dare he breathe when my mother had no breath at all?
I had to kill him and send his ghost to Balad to uplift the evil he spread. So that my mother's spirit can rest.

Each time I heard him laugh, sneeze, snore, I wanted him dead. A death his mother would never forget.
(Moves downstage center.)
First, I thought of setting his apartment on fire and burning his home to the basic waste. Ashes. But I knew that he was not very far from my apartment and the fire will catch on. And obviously spread to my apartment. I mean, it's simple logic. And I studied logic because preparing for my exams I was a science major for a time in the night school of a major American university. One of the best. And the fire would spread fast

with my closets so full with my books and study notes. The fire would surely catch on and burn the entire building, maybe killing my innocent roommate, maybe destroying the innocent neighbors, maybe women and children. My religion forbids the killing of innocents.

So I discarded that idea. I would not die the same day. But revenge was strong on my mind. Blood for blood. So I followed him one day to the subway station. 34th Street and Park Avenue. He paid one dollar for his death. His death was cheap. And when the train came full speed, I pushed him. Just like that, though I am not that strong. I had the energy of two people.

And the greatest joy of it all was that, while his brains were being blown into a cloud of tiniest possible specks and scattered all over the filthy tracks of the subway, I was sipping cappuccino in Café de Robertis. Every bone in his body was crushed into tiny little burgundy, gold, and purple beads at once, making the walls of the subway shimmer into an abstract painting of most unusual colors. I was sipping cappuccino when his heart jumped out of his chest and was devoured by the hungry rats delighted by the feast provided by me. I was sipping. His liver was roasted charcoal black, a rare delicacy for the Labor Day Weekend. His torn toes were stored in museums of science and art for generations to look at. His eyeballs were torn out of their sockets and were put in formaldehyde and frozen forever. Eyeballs of a dead man are scary things to look at.

They stare at me at all times like all the people from the subway station came to stare at me where I was sitting at the café.

Police came and arrested me. I did not resist. But the owner of the café happens to like me, and he told the police the truth …that I never left the café the whole time.

But police insisted that I was noticed at the scene of the crime by hundreds of people. Not that I am well-known. But it was rush hour. And my hair, my hands, my height, my face were clearly seen by hundreds of people. My photograph was shown to them, and they all identified me.

They were quite right.

As I am growing older, little by little, I have started to look like my mother.

It was my mother who pushed him to his death. It was me who pushed him to his death. I live inside my mother. My mother lives inside me.
(Pause. Moves silently. Sits on stool and stares at TV.)
Innocent or guilty?
(Silence. Turns off TV.)
Oh, Jesus, scary stuff. I should not be watching TV so late anyway. 5:00 a.m. Time to say a prayer for my dead relative. Which one is dead now? Which one is living? Don't remember.

Grandpa Mohammed, dead.
Father Mohammed, dead.
Uncle Mohammed, dead.
Brother Mohammed, dead.
Cousin Mohammed, dead.
Grandma Fatima, dead.
Aunt Zaireb, dead.
Sister Suria, dead.
Sister Hujra, dead.
Cousin Khadija, dead.

Mother Zaineb.
(Pause.)
Dead.
(Pause.)
My mother is dead, too?

Then who sends me the letters?
(Gets up. Goes to prayer rug upstage right. Sits to pray.)

Soon her heart will stop the beat.
Soon my heart will be wounded. I love her.

Mother, I say a prayer for you, and you say a prayer for mankind. For the sands of time are running out. If you play with fire, you have to bear the consequences, for the winds can blow it either way.
(Song in Arabic as lights fade. End)

BIBLIOGRAPHY

Adivar, Halide Edip. *The Memoirs of Halide Edip*. London: John Murray, 1926.

Ahmed, Akbar. *Islam Under Siege*. United Kingdom: Polity, 2003.

Ahmad, Feroz. "Politics and Islam in Modern Turkey." *Middle Eastern Studies* 27 (1991): 3-21.

Ahmed, Leila. *Women and Gender in Islam: Historical Roots of a Modern Debate*. New Haven & London: Yale University Press, 1992.

Al-Alwani, Taha Jabir. "The Reflections on the 'Moderate Muslims' Debate" *American Journal of Islamic Social Sciences* 22:3 (Summer 2005): 112-118.

Aliye, Fatma. Editorial in *Hanımlara Mahsus Gazete*, 1895.

Anadolu-Okur, *Contemporary African American Theater: Afrocentricity in the Works of Larry Neal, Amiri Baraka and Charles Fuller*. New York & London: Taylor and Francis Group (Garland Publishing Inc.), 1997.

—. *Essays Interpreting the Writings of Novelist Orhan Pamuk, The Turkish Winner of the Nobel Prize in Literature*. Ed. New York & Wales: The Edwin Mellen Press, 2009.

Anonymous, "Avrupa'da Osmanlı Kızlarımızın Sadası," ("Voices of Our Ottoman Daughters in Europe") *Kadınlar Dünyası* 42 (May 1911).

An-Na'im, A. Ahmed. "A Modern Approach to Human Rights in Islam: Foundations and Implications for Africa." In *Human Rights and Development in Africa*. Edited by Claude Welch Jr., and Ronald Meltzer. Albany: State University of New York Press, 1984.

—. "The Rights of Women and International Law in the Muslim Context" *Whittier L. Rev.* 9 (1987): 491.

Ascha, Ghassan. *Du statut inférieur de la femme en Islam*. Paris: L'Harmatton, 1987.

Ask, Karen and Marit Tjomsland. *Women and Islamization: Contemporary Dimensions of Discourse on Gender Relations*. United Kingdom: Berg, 1998.

Atef al-Zein, Samih. *Islam and Human Ideology*. Translated by M. H. Omran. London: Kegan Paul International, 1996.

Aybars, Ergün. *Türkiye Cumhuriyeti Tarihi*. İzmir: Ege Üniversitesi Yayınları, 1984.

Ayata, Sencer. "Patronage, Party, and State: The Politicization of Islam in Turkey." *Middle East Journal* 50 (Winter 1996): 40-56.

Badawi, Jamal. *Gender Equity in Islam*. Plainfield, Indiana: American Trust, 1999.

Badran, Margot., and Göle Nilüfer. *The Forbidden Modern: Civilization and Veiling*. Ann Arbor: University of Michigan Press, 1996.

Baldwin, James. *Nobody Knows My Name: More Notes of a Native Son*. New York: Dell, 1961.

Beckett, Samuel. *Happy Days*. New York: Grove, 1961.

—. *A Piece of Monologue, Three Occasional Pieces*. New York: Faber, 1982.

Blakely, Robert J., and Mary Gail Snyder. *Fortress America: Gated Communities in the United States*. Washington, D.C.: Brookings Institution Press, 1997.

Bodman, Herbert L., and Nayereh Tohidi, eds. *Women in Muslim Societies: Diversity Within Unity*. Boulder, Co: Lynne Rienner, 1998.

Bourdieu, Pierre. *Outline of a Theory of Practice*. Cambridge: Cambridge University Press, 1977.

Bowen, John R. *Why the French Don't Like Headscarves? Islam, the State, and Public Space*. Princeton: Princeton University Press, 2007.

Butler, Judith. *Gender Trouble: Feminism and the Subversion of Identity*. New York: Routledge, 1990.

—. *Bodies That Matter: On the Discursive Limits of Sex*. New York: Routledge, 1993.

Charlesworth, Hillary., and Christine Chinken. *The Boundaries of International Law: A Feminist Analysis*. Manchester: Manchester University, 2000.

Cook, Rebecca, ed. "Women's International Human Rights Law: The Way Forward," in *Human Rights of Women: National and International Perspectives*. Philadelphia: University of Pennsylvania, 1994.

Dogramacı, Emel. *Türkiye'de Kadının Dünü ve Bugünü*. Ankara: Türkiye İş Bankasi Yayinlari, 1989. 20.

Doi, A. Rahman. *Women in the Qur'an and Hadith*. London: Ta-ha, 1993.

—. *Women in the Shari'a*. London: Ta-Ha, 1989.

DuBois, W.E.B. "Damnation of Women," in *Darkwater:Voices From Within the Veil*. New Ed. New York: Dover, 1999.

Dukore, Bernard F. *Where Laughter Stops: Pinter's Tragicomedy*. Columbia, MO: University of Missouri, 1976.

El Guindi, Fadwa. *Veil: Modesty, Privacy and Resistance*. United Kingdom: Berg, 1999.

Esposito, John and Natana DeLong-Bas, *Women in Muslim Family Law*. New York: Syracuse University, 2001.

Fawzi, Camillia, El-Solh, and Judy Mabro. *Muslim Women's Choices: Religious Belief and Social Reality*. Oxford: Berg, 1994.

Fedwa Malti-Douglas, Fedwa. *Women's Body, Women's World: Gender and Discourse in Arabo-Islamic Writing*. Princeton: Princeton University Press, 1992.

Fernea, Elizabeth W. *Women and the Family in the Middle East: New Voices of Change*. Austin: University of Texas Press, 1985.

Focault, Michel. "Of Other Spaces." *Diacritics* 26 (Spring 1986).

Hussain, Freda. *Muslim Women*. London: Croom Helm, 1984.

Fuller, Graham E. "Freedom and Security: Necessary Conditions for Moderation," and "The Erdogan Experiment in Turkey is the Future," in *American Journal of Islamic Social Sciences*, 22:3 (Summer 2005): 21-28.

Galvin, R. "Does Kant's Psychology of Morality Need Basic Revision?" in *Mind, New Series*. Vol. 100, No 2, (April 1991): 221-236.

"Gated Communities". [Online: web]. Cited 22 March 2005. URL: http://parole.aporee.org/work/hier.php3?spec_id=11973&words_id=356

Gedikpasa, Feride İzzet Selim. "Kadinlarimizda Lüzum-i Tahsil," in *Kadinlar Dünyası*, Vol. 160 (December, 1911): 4-5.

Gerami, Shahin. *Women and Fundamentalism: Islam and Christianity*. New York: Garland Publishing Inc., 1996.

Glasze, Georg, and Abdallah Al-Khayyal. "Gated Housing Estates in the Arab World: Case Studies in Lebanon and Riyadh, Saudi Arabia." Environment and Planning B: Planning and Design 29 (2002): 327-334.

Göle, Nilüfer. "Toward an Autonomisation of Politics and Civil Society in Turkey." *Politics in the Third Turkish Republic*. Edited by Metin Heper and Ahmet Evin, Boulder, CO: Westview Press, 1994.

Graham-Brown, Sarah, ed. "Women and Politics in the Middle East', in *Arab Women: Between Defiance and Restraint* by Suha Sabbagh. New York: Olive Branch, 1996.

Güven☐, Bozkurt. *Türk Kimligi*. İstanbul: Remzi Kitabevi, 1995.

Haddad, Yvonne Yazbeck and John L. Esposito, Eds. *Islam, Gender, and Social Change*. Oxford: Oxford University Press, 1998.

Hakan Yavuz, and Nihat Ali Özcan. "Crisis in Turkey: The Conflict of Political Languages." *Middle East Policy* 14, No. 3 (Fall 2007): 118-135.

Hasan, Abdul Ghaffar. *The Rights and Duties of Women in Islam*. Riyadh: Darussalam, 1999.

Hassan, Riffat. "Equal Rights Before Allah? Women-Man Equality in the Islamic Tradition." *Harvard Divinity Bulletin* 7, No. 2 (1988).

—. "Feminist Theology: The Challenges for Muslim Women." *Critique: Journal for Critical Studies of the Middle East* 9 (1996): 53-65.

Al- Hibri, Azizah. "Introduction to Muslim Women's Rights," in *Windows of Faith: Muslim Women Scholars-Activist in North Americas*. Ed. Gisela Webb. Syracuse, New York: Syracuse University, 2000.

Hill, Amy. "Introduction: Tokyo Bound." In *Asian American Drama: Nine Plays from the Multiethnic Landscape*. Edited by Brian Nelson, 43-70. New York: Applause, 1997.

Hoodfar, Homa. "The Veil in Their Minds and On Our Heads: The Persistence of Colonial Images of Muslim Women." *Resources for Feminist Research* 22 (1995): 5-18.

Hooton, Eric. "Living in Saudi Arabia: Living and Working in the Saudi Kingdom." [Online: web]. Cited 22 March 2005. URL: http://www.escapeartist.com/efam/56/Working_in_Saudi_Arabia.html

Javadi-Amoli, Abdollah. *Zan dar A'ineh-ye Jalal va Jamal*. Tehran: Reja' Cultural Press, 1993.

—. *Falsafeh-ye Hoquq-e Bashar*. Qum, Iran: Isra, 1996.

Kandiyoti, Deniz. Ed. "End of Empire: Islam, Nationalism and Women in Turkey," in *Women, Islam and the State*. Philadelphia: Temple University Press, 1991.

—. Kandiyoti, D., and Saktanber, A. eds. *Fragments of Culture : The Everyday of Modern Turkey* London: IB Tauris, 2002.

Keddie, Nikki., and Beth Baron. *Women in Middle Eastern History: Shifting Boundaries in Sex and Gender*. New Haven: Yale University Press, 1991.

Kili, Suna., and A. Seref Gözübüyük. *Türk Anayasa Metinleri: Sened-i Ittifaktan Günümüze*. Ankara: Türkiye İş Bankasi Yayınları, 1985. 42-43.

Khan, M. Wahibiddin. *Women in Islamic Shariah*. Trans. Farida Khanam. New Delhi: Islamic Centre, 1995.

Kian, Azadeh. "L'émergence d'un discours féminin independant: un enjeu de pouvoir." *Les Cahiers de l'Orient* 47 (1997).

Kilin□aslan, İsmet. "Quality of Residential Environments in Dammam, Saudi Arabia." *International Journal for Housing Science and its Applications* 19 (1995): 157-162.

Latif, Amira Abdel. "It is Easy to Find Pastries in Marina, but It is Difficult to Find a Loaf of Bread." [Online: web]. Cited 22 March 2005. URL: http://www.cx.unibe.ch/islam/mitarbeiterPubl/amira

Lois Beck, and Nikki Keddie. *Women in the Muslim World.* Cambridge: Harvard University Press, 1978.

M'rabet, Fadela. *La femme Algérienne suivi de les Algériennes.* Paris: Maspero, 1969.

Majid, Anouar. "The Politics of Feminism in Islam." *Signs* 23, no. 2 (Winter 1998): 321-361.

Mernissi, Fatima. *The Veil and the Male Elite: A Feminist Interpretation of Women's Rights in Islam.* Trans. Mary J. Lakeland. Reading, MA: Addison-Wesley, 1991.

Miles Xian Liu., ed. "Bina Sharif." In *Asian American Playwrights: A Bio-Bibliographical Sourcebook.* Westport, CT: Greenwood Press, 2002.

Minai, Naila. *Women in Islam: Tradition and Transition in the Middle East.* New York: Seaview, 1981.

Moore, Mera. "From Islamabad to New York City: Bina Sharif's Spiritual Politics." *Text and Presentation: Journal of the Comparative Drama Conference* (2002): 57-69.

—. "Theatre as International Communication: Interview with Bina Sharif." *Peace and Policy: Journal of the Toda Institute for Global Peace* (2002): 44-48.

Mümtaz, Khawar., and Farida Shaheed. *Women in Pakistan, Two Steps Forward, One Step Back.* London: Zed, 1987.

Nasir, J. J., *The Status of Women Under Islamic Law and Under Modern Islamic Legislation*, 2nd ed. London: Graham & Trotman, 1994.

Nasir, Jamal. *The Islamic Law of Personal Status.* London: Graham & Trotman, 1986.

Nazlee, Sajda. *Feminism and Muslim Women.* London: Ta-Ha, 1996.

Olson, Emile A. "Muslim Identity and Secularism in Contemporary Turkey: 'The Headscarf Dispute'." *Anthropological Quarterly* 58, No.4 (October 1985): 161-171.

Öniş, Ziya. "Islamic Resurgence in Turkey in Perspective." *Third World Quarterly* 18, No. 4 (1997): 743-766.

Pearl, D., and W. Menski. *Muslim Family Law*, 3rd ed. London: Sweet & Maxwell, 1998.

Patrick, Robert. *Kennedy's Children.* New York: Samuel French, 1998.

Peterson, Jane T. et.al, eds. "Bina Sharif." In *Women Playwrights of Diversity: A Bio-Bibliographical Sourcebook.* Westport, CT: Greenwood Press, 1997.

Qur'an, 4: 1 and 124, 49: 13, 33: 35.

Rehman, Javaid. *International Human Rights Law.* Dorchester: Pearson Education, 2003.

Renkliyıldırım, Önder. *The Speech: Mustafa Kemal Atatürk.* İstanbul: Metro Yayınları, 1985.

Robinow, Paul. *The Foucault Reader: An Introduction to Foucault's Thoughts.* UK: Penguin Books, 1984.

Sabbagh, Suha, ed. "Introduction: The Debate on Arab Women," in *Arab Women: Between Defiance and Restraint* by New York: Olive Branch, 1996.

El Saadawi, Nawal. 1980. "The Hidden Face of Eve: Women in the Arab World," in *Women and Islam.* Edited by Azizah Al-Hibri. Oxford: Pergamon Press, 1982.

Said, Edward. "Intellectual Exile: Expatriates and Marginals." (1993). In *The Edward Said Reader.* Edited by Moustafa Bayoumi and Andrew Rubin., 368-381. New York: Vintage, 2000.

Sakaoglu, Necdet. "Egitim Tartısmaları" in *Osmanlı'dan Cumhuriyet'e Türkiye Ansiklopedisi*, Vol.15, İstanbul: İletişim Yayınları, 1985. 5-6.

Sarigüzel, Perihan Arif. "Azim ve Sebat" (Determination and Perseverance) in *Kadınlar Dünyası* Vol. 34 (May 1911): 3-4.

Seth, J. "The Evolution of Morality," in *Mind, New Series,* Vol. 14, No 53 (January 1989): 27-49.

Sharif, Bina. *Afghan Woman* [excerpt]. In *Shattering the Stereotypes: Muslim Women Speak Out.* Ed. Nawal El Saadawi and Fawzia Afzal-Khan, 246-253. New York: Olive Branch Press, 2005.

—. *My Ancestor's House.* In *Contemporary Plays by Women of Color.* Eds. Kathy A. Perkins and Roberta Uno, 262-279. New York: Routledge, 1996.

Shilling, C and Philip A. Mellor. "Durkheim, Morality and Modernity: Collective Effervescence, Homo Duplex and the Sources of Moral Action," in *The British Journal of Sociology*, Vol. 49, No 2, (June 1998): 193-209.

Sözen, Süleyman., and Ian Shaw. "Turkey and the European Union: Modernizing a Traditional State?" *Social Polity and Administration* 37, No. 2 (April 2003): 108-120.

Saudi Aramco Oil Company. "Housing". [Online: web]. Cited 22 March 2005. URL: http://www.saudiaramco.com/bvsm/JSP/content/channelDetail.jsp?SA.channelID=-1073750238

Smith, Jane. "Women, Religion, and Social Change in Early Islam." *Women, Religion, and Social Change.* Edited by Yvonne Y. Haddad and Ellison Findley. Albany: State University of New York Press, 1985.

Sonbol, Amira el-Azhary, Ed. *Women and the Family and Divorce Law in Islamic History*. Syracuse: *Syracuse University Press*, 1996.

Stowasser, Barbara. "The Status of Women in Early Islam." *Muslim Women*. Ed. Freda Hussain. New York: St. Martin's Press, 1984.

—. "Women's Issues in Modern Islamic Thought." in Judith E. Tucker, *Arab Women: Old Boundaries, New Frontiers*. Ed. Judith E. Tucker. Bloomington: Indiana University Press, 1993.

—. *Women in the Qur'an: Traditions and Interpretations*. New York: Oxford University Press, 1994.

Subbamma, Malladi. *Islam and Women*. Translated by M. V. Ramamurty. New Delhi: Sterling, 1988.

Sudqi al-Alami, Dawoud. *The Marriage Contract in Islamic Law, in the Shari'ah and Personal Status Laws of Egypt and Morocco*. London: Graham & Trotman, 1992.

Talib, Kaizer. *Shelter in Saudi Arabia*. London: Academy Editions, 1984.

Taskiran, Tezer. *Cumhuriyetin 50. Yilinda Türk Kadın Hakları*. Ankara: Basbakanlik Kültür Müstesarligi, Cumhuriyetin 50.Yildönümü Yayinlari, 1973.

Toprak, Binnaz. "Islam and Democracy in Turkey." In *Religion and Politics in Turkey*. Edited by Ali Çarkoğlu and Barry Rubin. New York: Routledge, 2006.

Tuğal, Cihan. "Nato's Islamists." *New Left Review* 44 (Mar-Apr. 2007): 5-34.

Valentine M. Moghadam. "Introduction and Overview: Gender Dynamics of Nationalism, Revolution and Islamisation." In *Gender and National Identity: Women and Politics in Muslim Societies*. Edited by Valentine M. Mogador. London and Atlantic Highlands, N.J.: Zed, 1994.

Wadud-Mohsin, Amina. *Qur'an and Women*. Kualalumpur: Penerbit Fajar, 1992.

Walther, W. *Women in Islam*. Translated by C. S. V. Salt. Montclair, NJ: A. Schram, 1981.

Weiss, Anita. "Implications of the Islamization Program for Women." In *Islamic Reassertion in Pakistan*. Syracuse: Syracuse University Press, 1986.

White, Jenny B. *Islamist Mobilization in Turkey: A Study in Vernacular Politics*. Seattle and London: University of Washington, 2002.

Yıldız, Ahmet. "Politico-Religious Discourse of Political Islam in Turkey: The Parties of National Outlook." *The Muslim World* 93 (April 2003): 187-209.

CONTRIBUTORS

Maleeha Aslam is presently working as Research Fellow-Gender at the Sustainable Development Policy Institute, Islamabad (SDPI), Pakistan. She completed her M. Phil. and Ph.D. at University of Cambridge, United Kingdom, where she is a member of Wolfson College. She was a Cambridge Commonwealth Trust's Scholar from 2002 to 2005.

Reza Eslami-Somea is an assistant professor of Human Rights, at Faculty of Law, Shahid Beheshti University, in Tehran, Iran. Somea teaches and does research in the fields of civil and political rights, public liberties, rights of women, religious minorities and peace-building.

Nour Jallad is a native of Beirut, Lebanon. She received her BA in Architecture from the University of Pennsylvania and her M. Arch. from Harvard University. At Harvard, she was part of the Tsunami Design Initiative, where she traveled to Sri Lanka to design safe, affordable housing for Tsunami victims. Currently, she works for Gensler in New York City.

Mera Moore (T. Mera Moore-Lafferty) earned her Ph.D. from the University of Hawaii. Currently she teaches at the University of Pennsylvania courses such as critical writing, theatre arts, cinema studies, and Asian American Studies. Her research and publications include a variety of topics on immigration, ethnicity, and gender in literature, theatre, and cinema.

Bina Sharif is a New York based playwright, actress, director, poet, and performance artist. Her acclaimed play *Afghan Woman*, which premiered in New York, NY, has been performed throughout the U.S. as well as in England, Belgium, Canada, and Pakistan. Her play *My Ancestor's House* is published in *Contemporary Plays by Women of Color*. Ms. Sharif has taken her one-woman shows to college campuses throughout the United States.

Sarah Swick is the Program Assistant at the Minaret of Freedom Institute in Bethesda, Maryland. She received her MA in Human Rights from the London School of Economics and Political Science and is currently a

Ph.D. candidate in Anthropology at American University in Washington D.C.

H. Övgü Tüzün received her BA in English Language and Literature from İstanbul University, her MA and Ph.D. from University of Kent. She is currently an assistant professor at the Department of American Culture and Literature at Bahçeşehir University, in İstanbul, Turkey.

Assistant to the Editor: **Brent Olson** received his MFA in Writing from Columbia University. His poetry has appeared world-wide in journals such as *Presence* and *Ko*. Currently, he teaches at Immaculata University in Immaculata, Pennsylvania.

Editor Nilgün Anadolu-Okur, (Ph.D.) is an associate professor at Temple University in Philadelphia, Pennsylvania. She is the author of *Contemporary African American Theater, Afrocentricity in the Works of Larry Neal, Amiri Baraka, and Charles Fuller* and *Essays Interpreting the Writings of Novelist Orhan Pamuk*. She has published peer-reviewed articles on African American theater, literature, the Underground Railroad, abolitionism and universal women's rights. She is the recipient of two international Fulbright awards, and the co-founder of Civil War and Emancipation Studies (CWEST) at Temple University. She has been a Commonwealth Speaker for the Pennsylvania Humanities Council (PHC) and acted as the Director of Comparative/World Literatures with Northeast Modern Languages Association (NeMLA).

INDEX